Sir William Harris painted by his son-in-law Michael Brockway (1919-2007)

Photograph © 2018 Robert Eggar and used with permission

Sir William Henry Harris

KCVO, MA, DMus, FRCM, FRCO

Organist, Choir Trainer and Composer

by

John Henderson and Trevor Jarvis

The Royal School of Church Music

19 The Close, Salisbury, Wilts, SP1 2EB. England
Email: press@rscm.com Website: www.rscm.com
Registered charity 312828

First published 2018

ISBN-13:

978-0-85402-279-3

Cover Design by Heather Ponting-Bather
Type face: Gill Sans MT
Printed in Great Britain on acid–free paper by
Charlesworth Press, Wakefield

Introduction

For those whose acquaintance with the name William Harris is solely through the legacy of his church compositions, the subtitle of this book (Organist, Choir Trainer and Composer) may appear to have got the sequence of his achievements in the wrong order. Not so – this would seem to be the order that Harris favoured. More than one source observes that Harris thought of himself as an organist, teacher, and composer in that order. His self-deprecation in regard to his compositions led him to be highly critical of his own efforts – describing some of them as being fatally flawed, or not worthy of performance. In his presidential address to the Royal College of Organists in January 1948, Harris said: 'I have always wanted to be a cathedral organist' putting that aspiration at the top of the list. From our research into the life of Harris, we found that his greatest enthusiasm was for organ music, especially his beloved Bach, and he enjoyed a wide and considerable reputation for his performance and interpretation. This was followed closely by his love for music-making with choirs, describing it as the most rewarding part of an organist's job. A perfectionist by nature, it was his work as a composer which seems to have given him less satisfaction.

Harris's natural modesty and humility has, at times, made our research somewhat harder, especially in our pursuit of finding photographs of him for inclusion in the text. Not only was he reluctant to "blow his own trumpet" in any way regarding his compositions, or indeed his achievements, he would also appear to have been somewhat camera-shy.

This book does not purport to be a scholarly treatise, or a critical analysis of his compositional style. Our aim has been to look at the achievements and the legacy of a significant church musician of the twentieth century, through a study of his life, and the influences he encountered. Taking the landmark locations of his career in order (St Davids, London, Lichfield, Oxford and Windsor), we have attempted to give some historical background to each, and to add some biographical details of the friends and colleagues with whom he worked.

We hope that the aperitif of musical extracts provided in Appendix 2 will tempt performers to explore some of Harris's less well-known and unpublished music. Some of these, such as the choral introits and anthems, are quite short entrées, but others, such as the violin sonata, would make a substantial and rewarding main course.

Acknowledgements

The authors would like to express their thanks to the following publishers for allowing musical examples from the works in their catalogue: The Royal School of Church Music; Stainer & Bell; Music Sales Ltd/Novello and Oxford University Press.

We also thank the many people and libraries who have helped in our research, provided photographs, information and anecdotes and assisted in proof-reading. These include, Roy Massey, Andrew Carwood, Peter Phillips, Roger Judd, Malcolm Riley, Martin How, David Iliff, Jacqueline Banerjee, The Aberdeen Bach Choir, John Salmon, Stuart Eager, Peter Kirk (National Archive of Anglican Chants), Colin Brownlee (Archive of Recorded Church Music), Martin Holmes (The Bodleian Library), Kate McQuillian and Enid Davies (St George's Chapel Archives & Chapter Library), Allan Ledger (former chorister), The Dean and Canons of Windsor and the Royal College of Organists.

Many of the photographs have been sourced from the Internet. Where possible the source and permissions have been acknowledged, but in some cases the origin of the photographs was not stated and no reply was received to enquiries. We apologise if any copyright photographs have been used without due acknowledgement.

We especially thank Duncan and Robert Eggar, Harris's grandsons, who have loaned manuscripts and photographs and allowed us to pry into their family affairs. Without their cooperation this book would not have been possible. The comment has been made that articles and biographies of persons written with the help of relatives perhaps present a somewhat biased and rosy picture of that individual and not an impartial 'warts and all' perspective. That may be so, but we, the authors, whilst endeavouring to be objective in our presentation of the facts, have found little in the way of warts.

Abbreviations

BCP	Book of Common Prayer
CBSO	City of Birmingham Symphony Orchestra
CMS	Church Music Society
DOM	Director of Music
EGG	followed by a letter indicates a specific folder in the family archive.
GSM	Guildhall School of Music (GGSM – Graduate, LGSM – Licentiate, HonFGSM – Honorary Fellow)
HWD	Henry Walford Davies
IAO	Incorporated Association of Organists
KCVO	Knight Commander of the Victorian Order
ms./ mss.	Manuscript(s)
OUP	Oxford University Press
RAM	Royal Academy of Music (ARAM – Associate, LRAM – Licentiate, FRAM – Fellow, Hon RAM – Honorary Member).
n.a.	Not available
n.d.	No date available
RCM	Royal College of Music
RCO	Royal College of Organists (ARCO – Associate, FRCO – Fellow)
RSCM	Royal School of Church Music
RVW	Ralph Vaughan Williams
SECM	School of English Church Music (before it became the RSCM)
TCL	Trinity College of Music, London (GTCL – Graduate, ATCL – Associate, LTCL – Licentiate, FTCL – Fellow)
THOH	*The Hound of Heaven*
WHH	William Henry Harris

A Harris Time Line

1883	Born 28th March in Tulse Hill, London
1891	Composed his Op.1
1895	Attended Purcell bicentenary service in Westminster Abbey, with his father
1897	St Davids Cathedral – as Assistant (and pupil)
1898	Gained ARCO
1899	Gained FRCO
1899	Royal College of Music – as student (on organ scholarship)
1902	Finished at the RCM, assisted at a number of London churches
1903	Assistant at Wimbledon Parish Church (until 1906)
1904	Completed Oxford B Mus degree
1906	Assistant at Ewell PC (to 1911)
1908	Accompanist to the London Bach Choir (until 1921)
1910	Completed Oxford D Mus degree
1911	Lichfield Cathedral – as Assistant
1913	St Augustine's, Edgbaston (concurrent with Lichfield)
1913	Married Kathleen Doris Carter
1919	New College Oxford – as Organist
1921	RCM – as Professor of Harmony and Organ
1926	Conferral of Oxford BA and MA degrees
1926	Conductor of Oxford Bach Choir, also took charge of Balliol concerts
1929	Christ Church Cathedral – as Organist
1933	St George's Chapel, Windsor – as Organist
1946	President of Royal College of Organists (until 1948)
1954	Appointed KCVO
1954	President of the IAO (until 1956)
1955	Retired from RCM
1956	RSCM – as Director of Studies
1961	Retired from St George's and RSCM. Moved to Petersfield
1968	His wife died
1973	Died 6th September in Petersfield, Sussex

Contents

Foreword

by Dr Roy Massey MBE

Organist Emeritus of Hereford Cathedral

I feel very honoured to be asked to write a few words as a foreword to this excellent biography of Sir William Harris.

As an aspiring young church musician in the 1950's I knew of Sir William Harris as the eminent organist of St George's Chapel, Windsor Castle, whose other claim to fame was that he had taught the piano to Princess Elizabeth and her sister Margaret. I first visited Windsor as a teenager on a church outing and our party had attended Choral Evensong in St George's chapel and been much impressed by the lovely building and the wonderful choir. Presumably, I must also have been listening to Sir William playing for the service but, sadly, have no recollection of what was sung or what he played as the final voluntary. Perhaps, by then, at the end of the service our party had started to chat or risen to depart in typical Anglican fashion!

Eventually I became more aware of Sir William's work as I gradually discovered some of his music. I cannot recall when I first heard an anthem by him, but I remember encountering the Communion Service in F on my very first RSCM residential course for choristers at Rossall School. Out of the blue I'd received a telegram from Hubert Crook asking if I was free to serve as a Housemaster, and this became the first of many RSCM experiences. Crook was a wizard at training boys and the thrilling sound he produced from the assembled company of over three hundred youngsters singing that Communion service impressed me enormously and I went straight home and ordered copies for my own choir. It is a beautifully written setting, simple and unaffected but, in its way, a tiny masterpiece. Then, I discovered *O what their joy and their glory must be,* an anthem based on a stirring old melody to wonderful words by Peter Abelard translated by J M Neale. This was Harris in the grand manner, with a fine organ part and splendid writing for voices which led to a triumphant final verse. A wonderfully satisfying piece which my choir thoroughly enjoyed singing.

My next association with Sir William was on a more personal level as in 1960 I became a candidate for the post of Master of the Music at St Augustine's Edgbaston in Birmingham, a prosperous church that took its music seriously. Harris had been invited to adjudicate the appointment as he had been at St Augustine's himself from 1913 until 1919, during which time he ran concurrently the assistantship at Lichfield Cathedral.

I was on a short list of four and was asked to play to Sir William. I gave him the *Fantasia and Fugue in G-Minor* by Bach, *Introduction and Passacaglia in D-minor* by Reger. Also on the console was a piece of manuscript paper with a theme for extemporisation in Harris's handwriting. This I did, and brought my offering to a conclusion with an appropriate cadence. At this Sir William said 'Don't stop - please carry on.' So my meandering had to start again in the hope that it, too, might eventually reach a reasonably convincing ending. He spoke to me briefly after the audition and the Vicar gave me a ten minute interview in the churchyard and I went on my way. Two days later, I heard that I had been appointed and thus started five happy years in Edgbaston. During this time I began lifelong friendship with Fred Ledsam and his wife, who often invited me to supper.

After five years in Edgbaston, an unexpected invitation took me to Addington Palace as Warden for three years before another unexpected invitation enticed me back to Birmingham as cathedral organist in 1968. In my early days at the cathedral I mentioned one evening, at supper with the Ledsam's when Harris was present, that I was short of Responses for Men's Voices as we sang a Men's voice Evensong on Tuesday evenings. He said nothing, but to my delight, a few weeks later, a new set of Men's Voice Responses came through my letter box inscribed to me and the Lay Clerks of Birmingham Cathedral from WHH. Sadly, he didn't live to see my appointment to Hereford in 1974 but I treasure the memories of those pleasant evenings spent in his company and appreciate enormously the interest he took in me during my early professional years.

Sir William Harris was undoubtedly one of the greatest cathedral musicians of his generation and John Henderson and Trevor Jarvis cover both his life, professional appointments and his eclectic gifts as organist, choirtrainer, conductor, composer and teacher in affectionate detail. The inhabitants of organ lofts and choirstalls in cathedrals and college chapels have for centuries been a significant influence on the cultural life of this country. Fine musicians have served these places by directing performances at divine service or composing music to enrich their worship. They also have passed on their skills to the next generation. Harris was one of the finest of these and added lustre to a cathedral organist's calling, and I am delighted that this biography has been written. I hope it will help keep alive the memory of a modest, kindly and wonderfully gifted man, as I'm sure his masterpieces *Faire is the Heaven* and *Bring us, O Lord, at our last awakening* will perpetuate his genius as a composer for so long as there are 'Quires and places where they sing.'

Dr Roy Massey, MBE, DMus (Lambeth), ARCM, FRCO(CHM), FRCCO, ADCM, FRSCM, was born in 1934 in Birmingham. A pupil of David Willcocks, he studied at the University of Birmingham and was organist of St Augustine's in Edgbaston from 1960 until 1965. After serving as Warden of the RSCM at Addington Palace, he became organist of Birmingham Cathedral in 1968. He served with distinction as organist of Hereford Cathedral from 1974 until retirement in 2001.

Chapter 1: Early Life

William Henry Harris was born in Tulse Hill, London on 28th March 1883. He was the eldest of three children; his younger brother and sister were named Frederick (born 1885) and Ada (born 1888). His father, also named William Henry (1864-1958), was a post office official, and his mother was Alice Mary (nee) Clapp (1861-1946). The fact that his father, although not a trained musician was also an amateur organist acting as Honorary Organist at Brixton Prison, almost certainly influenced the young William. There was also an upright piano and a harmonium in the family home. He began piano lessons at an early age, and became a choir boy at St Saviour's Church in Brixton, as did his brother Frederick. He also played keyboard for the children's Bible class.

St Saviour's Church, Brixton Hill, Lambeth

Consecrated in September 1875, St Saviour's church seated 900 in a parish whose statistics in 1894 reveal that it had a partly paid surpliced choir who used *The Hymnal Companion to the Book of Common Prayer with accompanying tunes* and the *Cathedral Psalter*. The organ was by Brindley and Foster, installed when the church was new, but had been enlarged by Henry Jones in 1888 to 3 manuals, 25 speaking stops and 1560 pipes. William Harris would have been a choirboy there c. 1890.

The church was declared redundant in 1977 and leased to the New Testament Church of God. It was extended by them in 2000 and is still used for non-Anglican worship. There was also a Church Hall but this was demolished, together with the adjacent area, in 1968 and rebuilt by Lambeth Council as the Blenheim Gardens Estate.

St Saviour's in modern times.

Harris must have shown considerable promise because, by the age of eight, he became both a pupil and assistant organist to organist Dr Walmsley Little[1] at Holy Trinity Church, Tulse Hill, as well as being one of his leading choir soloists.

Recognising that they had a particularly talented youngster in their midst and on the initiative of Revd H Sinclair Brooke, curate of Holy Trinity, Brompton, a train of events was set in motion which were to play a pivotal part in Harris's musical training. Through various contacts, Brooke[2] was able to persuade the staff at St Davids Cathedral in Pembrokeshire to accept Harris, now aged 14, to study under the Cathedral organist, Herbert Morris, as an

---

[1] Henry Walmsley Little (occasionally written as Walmsley-Little) (1853-1913) was a pupil of George Macfarren and Charles Steggall and a graduate of Oxford University. He was at various times organist of Christ Church in Woburn Square, London, of St Matthew's, Denmark Hill, of St Giles-in-the-Fields from 1881 and of Holy Trinity, Tulse Hill from 1886 until his death. He was also a director of the Vincent Music Co, a flourishing publisher of choir and organ music, and an examiner and board member of the Trinity College of Music.

[2] H Sinclair Brooke (1865-1934) was a graduate of Trinity College, Cambridge. After his curacy at Holy Trinity, Brompton, he went on to become Vicar of Pembury 1898-1918 and also Captain of the Pembury Fire Brigade. He then moved to St Mark's, Tunbridge Wells, where he spent the last nine years of his life, combining the duties of the parish with many other activities. For some years he was Rural Dean of Etchingham and, on retiring from this post, was made a Canon of Chichester.

articled pupil. Why St Davids was chosen, situated as it is in the extreme south west corner of Wales, was because the newly appointed organist happened to be a friend of Sinclair Brooke. Considerable financial assistance was put in place through local support from various sources, including Dr A E Stevens and other friends in Tulse Hill, so that it became possible for Harris to go to St Davids. If it were not for this help, Harris's parents would not have been able to entertain the idea. It was through this corporate generosity that the fourteen year old boy was able to move to Wales in 1897.

Holy Trinity Church, Tulse Hill

The new parish of Holy Trinity was formed in 1856 from portions of the parishes of St Luke in West Norwood, St Matthew in Brixton and St Leonard's in Streatham. Seating 1150, the statistics of 1894 show that the surpliced choir was voluntary and unpaid. During Harris's time there was a 3-manual organ with 38 stops originally built on a West Gallery by Henry Jones for the consecration of the church in 1856, but subsequently rebuilt into the North Chancel in 1875 by Bevington. Just as Harris left Tulse Hill in 1897, a new Norman & Beard organ of 3-manuals and 36 stops was installed.

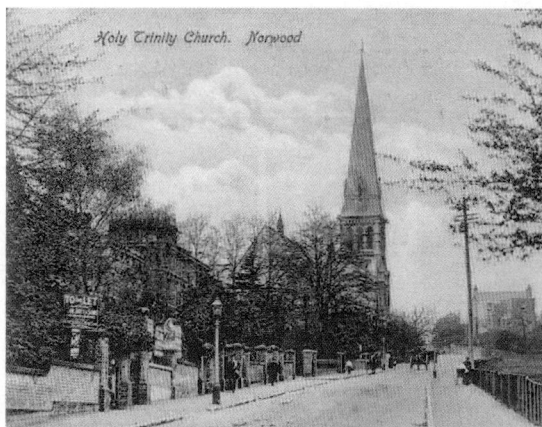

An early undated postcard of Holy Trinity

Harris's life-long affection for the organ music of J S Bach may well date from his first visit to Westminster Abbey as a child, in all probability with his father where, for the first time, he heard one of the organ works of Bach. He wrote:

'…I heard the *St Anne* Fugue played as a voluntary after Evensong. I have ever since associated that Fugue with Westminster Abbey. It seems almost to have the same shape, the same style of architecture, the same Gothic spaciousness.'[3]

Many years later, in his Presidential address to the Royal College of Organists in 1948, Harris recalled that, as a boy of twelve, his father had taken him to Westminster Abbey to attend the Purcell bicentenary service in 1895[4]. This must have been a different occasion to the above,

---

[3] Harris, William Henry, 'The Organ Works of Bach and Handel', *Music & Letters*, 1935, Vol. 16

[4] The 21st November 1895 service in Westminster Abbey must have been a truly memorable occasion. Although the Dean of Westminster gave an address, it was not so much a service as a major concert with music including Purcell's *Te Deum* and several anthems, sung by a choir of around 90 boys and 200 adults (both men and women) with orchestra. During the concluding voluntary, an *Elegy on themes by Henry Purcell* (themes from *I Was Glad* and 'The voice of the turtle' from *My Beloved Spake*), especially composed for the occasion by Edoard Silas, a procession moved to Purcell's grave. Wreaths (supplied by the Purcell Society, the Royal Academy of Music and the choir-boys of Westminster Abbey) were laid by Stainer, Bridge, Grove, Parry, Stanford, Cummings and Barclay Squire and the whole event was master-minded by Frederick Bridge, the Abbey organist.

either a prior, or more likely, a subsequent visit, given the particular nature of the music performed.

'The music of Purcell, the grey light and dark shadows of the Abbey, the concentrated attention of the big congregation made a deep and lasting impression.'[5]

Harris, in the same Presidential address, affirmed his early desire to pursue a career in church music. However, it is not clear whether this refers to a boyhood aspiration, or to a later period – possibly when he was a student at the RCM.

'Speaking for myself I can truly say I have always wanted to be a Cathedral organist, and that my love of Cathedral music was stimulated in early days when I lived in London and was able to make regular and almost weekly visits to Westminster Abbey and St Paul's Cathedral. There must be many who, like me, have attended Evensong at the Abbey, waited until the last triumphant notes of the concluding voluntary and dashed off to St Paul's in time for the Psalms or Magnificat, listened to yet another concluding voluntary and then walked on air down Ludgate Hill, unheedful of traffic, people or anything else, conscious only of the golden brightness of that final fugue.'[6]

This last sentence is revealing, in that Harris shows his ability to completely lose himself in music, to the exclusion of any outside distractions, traffic or otherwise. His daughter, Margaret, later made a similar observation, noting that he lived 'in the clouds and in a world of musical vision'.[7] This has been misunderstood by some as showing an occasional aloofness.

Another early memory, early because it mentions the first hearing of the Tallis Litany, but like the quote above, difficult to date, is mentioned by Harris in the same address:

'I remember, one lovely spring morning, entering in the west door of Winchester Cathedral just as the choir were beginning to sing Tallis's five-part Litany. I had never heard it before. I am not sure, but I think it was from that moment that I realised what church music at its best could be. That unusual succession of beautifully placed and strangely related common chords melting into one another made one feel in heaven at once.'[8]

This must have been before he started his association with the Temple Church when a student; as from 1903 onwards, if not earlier, it had become the custom at the Temple to sing either the Tallis five-part litany, or a shortened form of evensong on "Cantata Sundays" which Harris would certainly have heard. So, in all probability, the visit to Winchester was whilst he was still a boy. Here, Harris is clearly indicating his life-long affection for music of the Tudor period, as well as that of J S Bach.

Of Harris's non-musical interests, foremost was the theatre. His daughter Margaret Brockway recalled the following: 'Early family operatics, followed by regular visits to a succession of great productions on the London stage, including Henry Irving in "The Bells" at the Lyceum Theatre, all of which he remembered in some detail.'

Of this early period in Harris's life, the first flowerings of a musical talent can already be seen (almost certainly spotted and encouraged by his father, as well as by Sinclair Brooke) and evident in his first attempts at composition from the age of about eight or nine. These early compositions will be examined in Chapter 10. His move to St Davids Cathedral and the commencement of formal training mark the start of a life-long commitment to the making of music for the church.

---

[5] *The Musical Times* February 1948 & August 1948

[6] *ibid.*

[7] Erpelding, Matthew William, *The danger of the disappearance of things: William Henry Harris' The hound of heaven* (DMA Thesis), Iowa City, University of Iowa, 2014

[8] *ibid.*

Chapter 2: St Davids

St Davids Cathedral located at the most westerly point of South Wales was founded in 1115, with a choral foundation certainly stretching back to 1180, with the earliest reference to the existence of a choir dating from 1132. One wonders what level of competence was achieved in former years. A report taken from the Register and Statute Book of the Cathedral, and dated 24th March 1363, indicates that the musical standard of the choristers was not high. 'Now we observe [...] that the Choristers, few in number, and without proper vestments, attend the Choral Service

St Davids Cathedral seen from The Pebbles

irregularly and lukewarmly.' The number of choristers was augmented from four to six in 1501. It was also six at the time of the publication of Maria Hackett's survey of 1827. 'They are admitted between the ages of *five* [authors' italics] and ten, and are superannuated at about 16. They have lessons in music from the organist at his own residence.' It would seem that the boys were taught other subjects, namely Latin, Greek and the "principles of Religion" at the Cathedral Grammar School.

The year 1897 found Harris now installed as assistant to the cathedral organist, Herbert Charles Morris (1873-1940). Morris had been appointed the previous year in 1896[9] (after serving as assistant) with the somewhat unusual title of "Organist, Master of the Choristers *and Lay Vicar*". At the Royal College of Music, he had been a pupil of Sir Walter Parratt, as well as being pupil-assistant to Edwin H Lemare[10] at Holy Trinity, Sloane Street in London. At the age of 23 he must have been one of the youngest of Cathedral Organists. Morris had a reputation of being rather easy-going, and was soon quite content to let Harris take over at times, certainly when he 'preferred to sleep in during a weekday matins.'[11] This, surely, is a good indication of Harris's competency, that Morris considered him capable of such a role. Harris later referred to the wonderful experience of being left alone at these occasions, when he was entirely responsible for the music at a cathedral service.

Mʀ. H. C. MORRIS.

---

[9] Prior to his appointment in St Davids, Morris was assistant organist at Manchester Cathedral from 1894-1896. The photograph of him dates from his Manchester period and was published in the *National Portrait Gallery of British Musicians* ed. John Warriner in 1896.

[10] Lemare, generally regarded as the most talented (and most highly paid) concert organist of his day, was a church organist before he took to the concert platform. He was unusual in that he did not usually take on pupils – Morris was a notable exception. See also: Henderson, John. "Edwin H Lemare (1865-1934), *The Organ*, No. 347, Feb-Apr 2009, pp.24-30

[11] Wikipedia

At the time of Harris's appointment, the choir consisted of 14 Choristers (a considerable increase in numbers since Hackett's survey), four Lay Clerks and four Minor Canons. It is not known whether the newly-appointed Harris was involved in the formal teaching of music, in addition to the rehearsing of the boys, but it is quite probable that this was the case, given Morris's easy-going nature.

Certainly, the post of Assistant Organist was no sinecure. Matins was sung daily at 8.30am, with Evensong at 4pm, and on Sundays 11am and 3.30pm respectively, with all the attendant practices. The only day off from sung services was Wednesday.

Harris's own recollections of this period of his life show that it was the St Davids appointment that set him on a course that he was to pursue for the rest of his life.

> 'My first experience of Cathedral life was at St Davids where I first learnt to play the organ. The organist, Herbert Morris, had just gone there. He had studied with Parratt, had assisted Kendrick Pyne[12] of Manchester Cathedral and was himself a brilliant player. There was no choir school at St Davids and the boys were drawn from the village, the priest-vicars and a few lay-clerks forming the rest of the choir. In spite of slender resources there were two full choral services each day (except one) and it was there that I became familiar with the Cathedral system and the regular round of statutory daily services.'[13]

A survey entitled *The Present State of Cathedral Music*[14] shows that in 1934 Matins was still being sung daily, with the exception of Fridays, at 8.30am by the boys and Minor Canons.

Whilst he was at St Davids, Harris received tuition from Morris in organ and the requisite paperwork for the Royal College of Organists examinations. He also started preparing for a scholarship to the Royal College of Music. This period of study, along with the practical experience of daily rehearsing and accompanying services, marked the flourishing of a talent which had been spotted at Tulse Hill. For all of Morris's easy-going nature, he nevertheless was exacting in his expectation of Harris's studies. Straight off he was set to master Bach's "48", Harris having to practise before breakfast in order to fit it into a somewhat crowded day.

In addition, he attended the local school part time, in order that his general education was not neglected. This was the new St Davids County School, located in the old Town Hall[15], and opened, with only 25 pupils, in April 1895. The Pembrokeshire County Records Office shows that Harris was officially listed as being a pupil at the County School from the autumn of 1898 until the summer of 1899, but he may well have joined on his arrival in St Davids in 1897.

He had a good relationship with the newly-appointed Dean, David Howell[16], who advised him to study Latin, with a view to entering university. 'You must aim at a University Degree if you want to take a high place in your profession.'[17]

Morris also set him a prodigious number of exercises. The fact that Morris had been a pupil of Walter Parratt is, in all probability, significant. Parratt, well-known for his sense of restraint in both playing and choir training, would have certainly influenced the young Morris who, in turn, would have passed this on to his own pupil. All the hard work put in by both Harris and his tutor Morris certainly paid off as Harris was soon ready to take the Associate Diploma

12 James Kendrick Pyne (1852-1938) was pupil of S S Wesley and succeeded Sir Frederick Bridge as organist of Manchester Cathedral. Pyne also became a professor at the Royal Manchester College of Music and was organist to Manchester Town Hall where he gave many recitals.

13 Harris, William Henry, RCO January Presidential Address, *The Musical Times* February 1948

14 Church Music Society, 1934

15 A dedicated school building was not built until 1902.

16 The Very Revd David Howell (1831-1903) served as Dean from 1897 until his death.

17 Brockway, Margaret, Unpublished hand-written notes from Harris's daughter..

(ARCO), which he passed in July 1898, followed only six months later by the Fellowship Diploma (FRCO) in January 1899. He became the youngest candidate to receive a Fellowship distinction – at the age of 16. Added to this, in the same year, he was awarded an open scholarship to the RCM, to study the organ[18]. By all accounts, Harris was happy at St Davids, and never lost his affection for that corner of Wales, returning many times in later years for family holidays along the Pembrokeshire coast, spending time walking and sea-bathing. Another strong lifetime connection with Wales was that his future wife came from Carmarthen.

He also returned to St Davids to give the inaugural recital on the newly-rebuilt organ (by Hill, Norman & Beard) in August 1953.

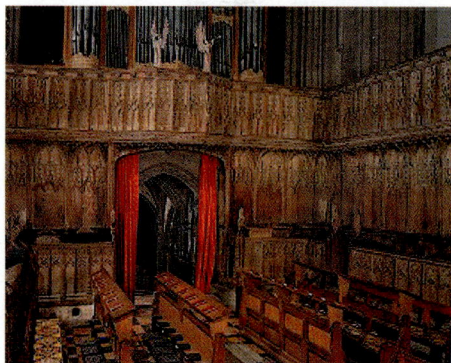

St Davids Cathedral: 15/16C choir stalls

An engraving for the periodical *The Musical Standard*[19] by J E Taylor[20] of the 1883 Willis organ (3-manuals, 31 speaking stops) of St Davids Cathedral. This drawing was published in September 1896, shortly before Harris arrived at St Davids.

---

[18] He took the scholarship examination in February 1899 whilst still at the County School in St Davids.

[19] *The Musical Standard* (1862-1933) was a weekly magazine which regularly printed drawings and specifications for organs. The RSCM library is fortunate to have a collection of these from 1889-1900.

[20] J E Taylor contributed many drawings to *The Musical Standard*. His identity is uncertain, but he may have been a partner in the London printing firm of R and J E Taylor.

Chapter 3: London

The Royal College of Music

Front Façade of the RCM[21]

The Royal College of Music opened its doors in 1883 with Sir George Grove appointed as its first Director, and the Prince of Wales (later King Edward VII) its President. There were about 50 students at the start, and the teaching staff included Grove himself, Parratt, Sullivan, Stanford and Parry, amongst others. Grove retired in 1894, just after the opening of the College's present building in Prince Consort Road, opposite the Royal Albert Hall. He was succeeded by Sir Hubert Parry as Director – a post he was to hold for 24 years until his death in 1918. Parry declared that the College was more than a place for merely teaching students. There was a need to broaden their musical horizon 'by spreading the appreciation of secular music, especially orchestral, chamber and operatic music, and training first-rate orchestral players.' Even for students engaged in organ playing as their first study, their musical training needed to extend beyond the narrow world of the organ loft.

In 1899, at the age of 16, Harris left St Davids, to move to London in order to begin study at the Royal College of Music, having been awarded an organ scholarship (the Lord Charles Bruce Scholarship). His organ tutor was Sir Walter Parratt, eulogized by Sir George Grove saying:

> 'Mr Parratt's gifts are very great. His playing needs no encomium, and in addition his memory is prodigious, and many stories of curious feats are told among his friends. His knowledge of literature is also great and his taste of the finest. He has been a considerable contributor to this Dictionary, and supplied the chapter on music to Mr. Humphry Ward's 'Reign of Queen Victoria' (Longmans, 1887). He is a very hard worker, and the delight of his colleagues, friends, and pupils. Nor must we omit to mention that he is an extraordinary chess-player.'[22]

---

[21] Photo by By Diliff, CC BY 3.0, https://commons.wikimedia.org/w/index.php?curid=1986218, used with permission.

[22] Sir George Grove (1820-1900) in *A Dictionary of Music and Musicians (AD 1450-1889) Vol IV*, London, Macmillan, 1900.

Sir Walter Parratt KCVO

When researching the careers of the most prominent organists and church musicians of the early 20C, the name of Walter Parratt seems to crop up with astounding regularity – he tutored, encouraged, and actively guided the careers of a great many pupils by suggesting them for school, church, cathedral and academic positions.

Walter Parratt (1841-1924), was a child prodigy who performed the complete *Well-Tempered Clavier* of J S Bach by heart, without notice, at the age of ten. He was appointed organist of Armitage Bridge Church near Huddersfield at the age of 11, but was almost immediately sent off to London to the choir school of St Peter's Chapel in Westminster. Here he was a pupil of George Cooper Jnr (1820–1876), assistant organist of St Paul's Cathedral. He returned to Huddersfield at the age of 14 as organist of St Paul's Church there.

Subsequently he served as organist to the Earl of Dudley, at Wigan Parish Church, then Magdalen College in Oxford and finally at St George's Chapel, Windsor, for 42 years.

Knighted in 1892, the following year he became Master of the Queen's Musick. In 1883 he became the first professor of organ to be appointed at the newly-founded Royal College of Music.

Above: Parratt at the St George's console.

Right: In Court Dress as Master of the King's Musick, 1902

According to Harold Darke, Harris developed his characteristic style of playing from his teacher. Interestingly, this was Harris's first indirect contact with St George's, Windsor, where Parratt was organist. There were numerous trips from the College in London to Windsor during this period, in order for Harris to receive an organ lesson from Parratt in the Chapel, and to practise on an organ which was in a somewhat different league to the instrument in the RCO.

'…it was my privilege and delight to visit him [Parratt] at Windsor, which I did as often as I could. Up there in the organ loft, one had a curious sense of detachment from ordinary affairs. It was like being on the bridge of a ship with Parratt in command. He had his hand on all the controls, and there was an air of enchantment about the whole thing, due partly no doubt to my own boyish enthusiasm, but more to his unique personality.'[23]

Parratt also gave "music classes" to the students at the RCM, the content of which we have a good example from Harris's own notes at the time - which also gives us a glimpse of the RCM syllabus covered in the early years of the twentieth century.

'He [Parratt] used to talk about the general theory of music, elementary acoustics, the harmonic series (a subject which fascinated him), modulation, transposition, the ecclesiastical modes, the compass of orchestral instruments and voices, and every sort of thing that interested him. Some of us students were encouraged to write little two-part polyphonic compositions which were used for dictation and transposition in class. Some of our productions were rather odd and seemed to amuse him! Sometimes he got right away from music and talked to us about the need for punctuality and the exercise of tact in our dealing with people who might reasonably be expected not always to see eye to eye with us; he stressed the importance of good manners. What is now called "musical appreciation" and "aural training" were part of our regular work; and Sir Walter was in these important matters our especial guardian and guide.'[24]

Harris soon came to the attention of Sir Hubert Parry[25] (Director of RCM) as a promising student. Looking back on Parry's life, Harris commented in 1926 that Parry had '...a soft corner in his heart for the "organ boys" of the College, and his admiration for the art of our master, Sir Walter Parratt, knew no bounds.'[26] Harris was the first student at the RCM to be invited to give a public performance on the organ that Parry had donated to the College. Parry had chosen Bach's St Anne for Harris to play, instructing him to take the fugue slowly and deliberately, 'not like so many young devils nowadays, who play Bach so fast that the old man [Bach] really hasn't a chance.'[27] .

Sir Hubert Parry

This account seems to be at odds with newspaper reports. The 14th June 1901 saw the opening of a new Concert Hall seating 900 at the RCM with a concert for which Parry composed his Ode to Music.[28] A few weeks later a further concert featured Harris playing Bach's Toccata and Fugue in D-minor on the new Walker organ given by Sir Hubert Parry. It seems likely that the St Anne performance refers to an inaugural organ recital given by Harris, at the request of Parry, probably on an earlier occasion. Harris later referred to Parry's comment regarding the undue speed at which some organists take Bach's music, in an article written in 1935.

'Nothing is so fatal to Bach's clearness of texture than the tremendous pace at which much of his music is taken nowadays [...] but it is useless to protest; the habit seems incurable.'[29] On another occasion Parry is quoted as saying to Harris; 'You played awfully well this morning – I

23 The Musical Times August 1947
24 Tovey, Donald F. and Parratt, Geoffrey, Walter Parratt: Master of the Music, London, Oxford University Press, 1941.
25 Charles Hubert Hastings Parry (1848-1918) was educated at Eton (receiving organ lessons from Sir George Elvey at St George's) and Exeter College, Oxford. He, together with C H Lloyd, conjointly formed the Oxford University Musical Club. In 1883 he was appointed Professor of Composition and Musical History at the newly-established RCM, and in 1894 became its Director.
26 Graves, Charles L, Hubert Parry: His life and works, London, Macmillan & Co, 1926, 2 Vols.
27 ibid.
28 One commentator noted that "The preponderance of girls in both orchestra and chorus was quite a novel feature, in sharp contrast to the usually sombre appearance of a band of musicians." (Bradford Observer, 14 June 1901)
29 Harris 1935 Op.cit.

could almost have thought it was Walter [Parratt].'[30] This was high praise indeed, as it shows at what level Harris was playing at this stage in his career, and also the extent to which he had been influenced by his teacher. Much later, on 5th Jan 1950 Harris gave an interview on the BBC Third Programme in the series *Teachers of Music* talking about Sir Walter Parratt. He spoke of his memories and illustrated it by playing examples to demonstrate points of style or preferences shown by Sir Walter.

He studied composition and counterpoint with Charles Wood, Walford Davies of the Temple Church, and briefly with Sir Charles Villiers Stanford. It would seem that although he did not have formal lessons with either Parry or Stanford, in all likelihood he was encouraged and certainly influenced by them. Harris recalled that, whilst practising, he would hear the familiar chuckle, and find Parry looking over his shoulder, amused by any difficulties he was experiencing.

'His [Parry's] enthusiasm, backed up by much emphatic and picturesque language, not to mention the prodigious thumps on the back which I can feel at this moment, could not fail to kindle in us a lively (and sometimes painful) interest in the "old man".'[31]

Harris goes on:

'His [Parry] favourite organ work was undoubtedly the *Toccata and Fugue in C* [BWV 564]. How he delighted in the big pedal solo of the *Toccata* – regarding the whole thing as a joke! On one occasion he showed me (mainly on my shoulder!) how to play that pedal solo so that it should not sound "stiff", or "like an exercise"'... Some years later after I left College, Sir Hubert asked me to play an organ solo at a College Union "At Home". I suggested playing some Buxtehude. "Why do that? He asked: "Buxtehude's interest nearly always collapses at some point or another. What's the matter with good old J S B? Play the big *Toccata and Fugue*, **with those pedals!** Of course he meant the C-major favourite which I played on that occasion. Unfortunately, the audience talked at the top of their voices and little music was heard. Sir Hubert was distressed that so noble a composition should have been talked down, and delivered himself on the subject in his next [RCM] terminal address.'

Those "prodigious thumps on the back" were Parry's usual greeting. H C Colles recalled the following:

'...that smack on the back which was his [Parry's] favourite token of recognition, and has made many of us still associate a sharp pain between the shoulder-blades with the glow of the Director's presence.'[32]

At the RCM there were, with Harris, a number of fellow students who supported each other. These included Ivor Gurney, George Dyson, Harold Darke, and Leopold Stokowski[33]. It had been the custom for both organ students and composers at the RCM to gain some additional experience by playing in an augmented percussion section of the college orchestra on

[30] Tovey/Parratt *Op.cit.*

[31] Graves *Op.cit.*

[32] *ibid.*

[33] Legendary American conductor Leopold Stokowski (1882-1977, and actually born in London), was almost an exact contemporary of WHH. His conducting career eclipsed the lesser-known fact that he was a skilled organist (ARCO 1899, FRCO 1900) and a church musician before taking up conducting. He sang in the choir of the St Marylebone Parish Church and assisted Walford Davies at The Temple Church in the same occasional way as did WHH. In 1900, he formed the choir of St Mary's Church in the Charing Cross Road and in 1902, he became organist of St James' Church in Piccadilly. Moving to the USA in 1905 as organist of St Bartholomew's Church in New York, he soon resigned this post in order to pursue his career as an orchestra conductor. Stokowski returned to Britain in 1972, eventually dying in his home at Nether Wallop in Hampshire. It is not known whether the two nonagenarian student friends met up again before Harris's death the following year. See also Rollin Smith, *Stokowski and the Organ*, New York, Pendragon Press, 2004.

occasions. Parry was very keen on broadening a student's musical experience beyond their chosen discipline. Paul Spicer, in his book *Sir George Dyson: His Life and Music*, quotes the occasion of a "Grand Concert by the Orchestra" conducted by Parry: 'Dyson was in a generous percussion section of five players (not including the timpanist) amongst whom was his exact contemporary William Harris...'[34]

He completed his studies at the RCM in 1902, and now set out to gain experience at a number of London churches, whilst studying externally for the B Mus degree at Oxford, which he obtained two years later in 1904. He then went on to gain his D Mus, again externally from Oxford, in 1910.

His B Mus Exercise (1903) was a setting of the poem *Veni creator spiritus* by John Dryden (1631-1700) for Soli, SATTB & strings. The D Mus Exercise (1909) was a *Nativity Ode : Some stanzas from On the morning of Christ's Nativity* for Tenor solo, 8-part chorus & orchestra. *On the morning of Christ's Nativity 1629* was a major work by John Milton (1608-1674). Both Exercises are extant in the Bodleian Library in Oxford. Harris's choice of texts is another sign of his lifelong interest in the metaphysical poets which 15 years later would produce *Faire is the Heaven*.

This D Mus Exercise also shows that, following a 67 page overture, the 25 year-old was not shy about attempting double choir writing. The first choral movement (160 bars) is for unaccompanied 8-part chorus.

Opening of the first chorus from the 1910 D Mus Exercise.

[34] Spicer, Paul, *Sir George Dyson: His Life and Music* Martlesham, The Boydell Press, 2014

A DANCE SUITE, for Toy Orchestra.
(Composed specially for this occasion)

1.	Introduction, Theme and Gigue	*William H. Harris*
2.	Minuet	*Richard H. Walthew*
3.	Air, air raid and raid on an Air	*Harold E. Darke*
4.	The Ambitious Cuckoo	*Thomas F. Dunhill*
	Solo Cuckoo : Mr. T. F. Dunhill.	
5.	Thé Dansant	*Herbert Howells*
6.	March	*H. Walford Davies*

Harris returned to the RCM to participate in a concert on 4th July 1919 – an "At Home" of the Royal College of Music Union. Part One of this concert, in which WHH and Harold Darke played the piano duet accompaniment to Brahms' *Liebeslieder Waltzes* along with some vocal solos, was marginally more serious than Part Two where the first (and probably only) performance was given of a newly-composed *Toy Dance Suite* performed by a Toy Orchestra. The orchestra contained many well-known names including Adrian Boult, Henry Cope Colles, Walford Davies, Thomas Dunhill, Herbert Howells, Harold Darke, Cyril Rootham, Henry Ley, Ivor Gurney, Leslie Heward, George Ball (before he added Thalben to his name) and Harris himself.

An added sense of irony was that the conductor of the toy orchestra was Major Geoffrey Toye (1889-1942), recently back from war service, who went on to make his name at the D'Oyly Carte Opera Company and Sadler's Wells Theatre.

As can be seen, Harold Darke's contribution harks back to WWI, still very much in the consciousness of British people, and much of the material relating to Germany in the programme notes would make slightly uncomfortable reading in today's politically correct society.

Harris composed his piece *Introduction, Theme and Gigue on 'Cruel Barbara Allen' (with alterations and altercations)*[35] in June 1919, whilst still in Lichfield and his own synopsis reads:

a)   "Cruel Barbara Allen"
b)   An organ fugue of Bach[36]
c)   Combined Counterpoint [37]
d)   An interrupted rehearsal of a Beethoven Overture[38]
e)   Finale[39]

The programme note (by H C Colles) relating to Harris's movement reads:

'1. INTRODUCTION, THEME AND GIGUE.

The brilliant Organist of New College seems here to picture for us his sensations on taking up his new appointment. Some psychologists believe that the *aura* of a human being may cling to the places he has frequented after his bodily presence is withdrawn. Dr Harris is evidently in sympathy with this view. The old English folk melody, "Cruel barbarous Allen" is his principal theme. Played broadly at the outset, the cuckoo makes

---

[35] This full title on the *ms.* [EGG A]
[36] A 12/8 jig fugue. This section also uses the Mirliton – a kazoo-like instrument.
[37] He combines Barbara Allen with the fugue subject of Bach's *Fantasia and Fugue in G-minor* BWV 542. The cuckoo and quail make their appearance in this section.
[38] Motor horns, police whistles, rattles and castanets appear in this section.
[39] Basically a general hullabaloo!

a vain attempt to finish the last two notes (the cuckoo's vanity, by the way, gets fuller scope in a later moment of the Suite), and the composer's joy at finding himself in possession of the organ loft is vividly depicted when the cruel and barbarous theme is later metamorphosed into the measure of a merry Gigue. He tries to play a Fugue by Bach, on the organ; the dance and the fugue become inextricably mixed. At the height of the revelry a fanfare sounds as once it sounded from the walls of Florestan's prison. Is the cruel and barbarous One returning? Perish the thought! Or on second thoughts, possibly the *whole* is a biography of the cruel and barbarous One, his joyful activities at the organ and as a conductor representing an epoch in the musical life of the University.'

One suspects that Colles' clear allusion to Hugh Allen, WHH's immediate predecessor at New College, is his own mischievous humour. Whilst in the Edwardian era it would seem unlikely that the young Harris would deliberately call his senior 'barbarous', all these men were reputed to have a good sense of humour. Both the composition and this concert took place before WHH even arrived at New College.

"Barbara Allen" combined with Bach's G-minor Fugue BWV 542

Harris was to return to the RCM in 1923 as a lecturer in harmony and organ. Amongst his pupils were Benjamin Britten (briefly), Lennox Berkeley and Herbert Howells, who was later to pay Harris a 90th birthday tribute in 1973 and sadly, in the same year, a memorial tribute. Harris also gave an occasional organ lesson to the young Percy Whitlock, usually when his regular tutor, Henry Ley, was away from the RCM, and was later to dedicate A Fancy to 'the memory of Percy Whitlock, for whom it was written'. This piece was not published until 1947, so it is not certain whether it was a posthumous offering, which is most likely, or had been composed for Whitlock at an earlier date. Harris and Whitlock certainly kept in touch. Whitlock visited Harris at New College in 1928, but it is a particular visit from Harris to Bournemouth which is recorded in Whitlock's diary for December 1938, which reads: 'Dr Harris took me out to lunch at the Regent, & was v sweet.... He asked me to write him a piece "just for him"'. As far as the authors are aware, no such piece was forthcoming before Whitlock's untimely death in 1946.

How successful was Harris as a lecturer at the RCM? Thomas Armstrong makes the following observation: 'Harris was too self-effacing to be really effective.'[40] One wonders how demanding he was in his expectation of students' exercises. Armstrong observes 'Gross errors in a harmony exercise might be treated as interesting evidence of originality.'[41] Harris is also recorded as saying that he had nothing more to give to an organ student who could already play Mozart's *Fantasia*. Was his natural shyness and modesty a handicap in these situations? Perhaps this was so regarding the students under him, a diffidence most likely arising in a one-to-one situation, but there is no evidence that this was the case when dealing with choirs where 'everything was direct and authoritative.'[42] Harris finally relinquished his professorial post at the RCM in 1955.

The Temple Church

The Temple Church[43] is a late 12th century church in the City of London built by the Knights Templar as their English headquarters. During the reign of King John (1199–1216) it served as the Royal Treasury, supported by the role of the Knights Templars as international bankers. It is jointly owned by the Inner Temple and Middle Temple Inns of Court, bases of the English legal profession. It is a round church, a common design feature for Knights Templar churches.

Being in London gave Harris the opportunity to attend a variety of churches, both great and small, including the Temple Church, where Dr Walford Davies, appointed in 1898, was in charge of the music. As well as Walford Davies' own pupils, Henry Colles and Leopold Stokowski, other young organists, including William Harris, Harold Darke, Gerald Bullivant, Rutland Boughton, Sydney Toms and George Dyson, used to foregather at the Temple Church console on Saturday afternoons to improvise on the organ with Walford Davies. Davies' predecessor at the Temple Church was Dr E J Hopkins who had a reputation as a gifted improviser, and Davies' improvisations by all accounts were in the same mould.

> '…like so many of my contemporaries, [I] gained valuable experience through attending the Temple Church services and practices and studying the methods of Walford Davies who was then in his prime and at the height of his powers.'[44]

Interior of the Chancel facing west toward the Round Church

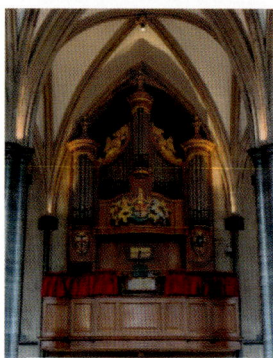

The organ in the Temple Church.

Interior of the Round Church facing east towards the Chancel

---

[40] Parker, Timothy James, *Sir William Henry Harris (1883-1973) His life and work with particular reference to his anthems.* (MMus Thesis), Sheffield, University of Sheffield, 1997

[41] *ibid.*

[42] *ibid.*

[43] Photographs by Diliff https://commons.wikimedia.org/w/index.php?curid=33466962, used with permission.

[44] Harris 1948 (February) *Op. cit.*

Some sources have stated that Harris was an assistant organist at Temple Church, but there seems to be a little uncertainty as to whether this was ever an official appointment - or just that he was part of a team of assistants. It was probably more a case of helping out as required. Such were Walford Davies' other musical commitments, that he had a number of deputies to rehearse the choir and play for services, the chief of whom was Harold Darke. Later (in 1915) it was agreed that Darke should receive £200 (half the organist's salary) and a key to the church in return for standing by and doing Walford Davies' job whenever he was away. Darke was himself helped on occasions by Harris, Stubbs[45], Scott Goddard[46], H C Colles[47] and Gerald Bullivant.[48]

Dr Harold Darke

Harold Edwin Darke (1888-1976) was a pupil of Sir Walter Parratt and Sir Charles Stanford at the RCM. He was organist at the Presbyterian Church in Stoke Newington, at Emmanuel Church in West Hampstead and at St James's in Paddington before appointment to St Michael's, Cornhill, in the City of London. He was well known for the weekly organ recitals he gave there during his fifty years (1916 to 1966) of service, a series still running today and the longest-running lunchtime organ concert series in the world.

His time at St Michael was interrupted only by deputising as organist of King's College in Cambridge from 1941-1945 whilst Boris Ord was serving in the RAF.

Harold Edwin Darke
Above: c 1923
Below: c 1968

Darke and Harris were lifelong friends and Darke is mentioned many times in this book, not least for acting as 'best man' at WHH's wedding. The two men also collaborated on many musical projects, often together with Henry G Ley of Eton College. Darke founded the St Michael's Singers in 1919 soon after arriving at Cornhill where he also instituted a regular music festival at the church. Harris and Ley would regularly give recitals in (and take their choirs to) Darke's festivals at Cornhill and Darke performed both in recital and as director of the St Michael's Singers in Windsor and Eton festivals.

Harris dedicated two pieces to Darke – the 1922 organ *Fantasy on the tune "Babylon's Streams"* and the 1956 anthem *The eyes of all wait upon Thee, O Lord*, the latter to celebrate Darke's 40th anniversary at Cornhill.

---

[45] Harry Hearn Stubbs (1892-1969), organist of the Old Charterhouse from 1911, and a professor at the RCM.

[46] Scott Goddard (1895-1965), author and music critic for the *News Chronicle*.

[47] Dr Henry Cope Colles (1879-1943). Colles studied (contemporary with Sydney Nicholson) at the Royal College of Music with Walford Davies, Hubert Parry and Walter Alcock. He went on to Worcester College, Oxford as organ scholar. He was on the Council of the SECM from 1930 until his death. Editor of both *Grove's Dictionary of Music* and the RSCM's publication *English Church Music*.

[48] Rennert, Jonathan, *George Thalben-Ball*, Newton Abbott, David & Charles 1979.

The Temple Church choir, renowned for its 'suppression of *personal* characteristics'[49] consisted of 12 boys and 6 men, 'supplemented by probationers, a few old boys, and one or two occasional members.' (ibid) The phrase "suppression of personal characteristics" is particularly significant. Walford Davies had been a boy chorister at St George's Windsor under Walter Parratt who, as we shall see later, was an advocate of suppressing emotion in the performance of choral music. Services at the Temple around this time consisted of Sunday morning and afternoon during the ten months of the year when the church was open:

> '...with some extra services on week-days, principally on Fridays at 5pm, during Advent and Lent. The third Sunday of the month is known as Cantata Sunday, when a cantata or selections from an oratorio are sung in place of the sermon at Evensong. There are no services during August and September.'[50]

The custom of singing part of a cantata or oratorio in the place of the anthem, with a shortened evensong or litany, was started in January 1899, as a once-a-month event. From 1901, an entire cantata was performed once a year, usually in February.

The music repertoire, apart from these cantatas, was mainly English, of the traditional cathedral type:

> '...but not excluding selections from foreign masterpieces "from Arcadelt to Brahms" and choice specimens of ancient ecclesiastical music are not infrequently rendered.'[51]

Perhaps "*infrequently* rendered" would be a more accurate statement, as Harris was to comment in the 1930's on music at the Temple:

> 'Ah yes, very beautiful, but a very limited repertoire – not much of the glorious Tudor school.'[52]

When Walford Davies decided to retire from the Temple, the choir committee considered three strong candidates to succeed him. They were Henry Ley, Harold Darke and William Harris. Walford Davies had intimated to Darke that he was his preferred choice as successor. However George Thalben-Ball was appointed instead. This caused some ill-feeling at the time, in particular Stanford felt that Darke had been poorly treated over the appointment.

Sir Henry Walford Davies

Left: c 1905;   Right: c 1940

Below
Walford Davies at the BBC in the 1930's

---

[49] *The Cathedral Quarterly* Easter 1915
[50] *Ibid.*
[51] *Ibid.*
[52] Lewer, David, *A Spiritual Song: The Story of the Temple Choir London*, The Templars' Union, 1961.

Henry Walford Davies

Born in Oswestry in 1869, the seventh of nine children, Henry Walford Davies grew up in a very musical family. His early talent for singing led to a choristership (at the age of twelve) at St George's Chapel, Windsor, first under Sir George Elvey and then under Walter Parratt, with whom he studied for five years before becoming his assistant organist. When Davies' voice changed in 1885, he left the choir and was appointed organist of the Royal Chapel in Windsor Great Park. In the same year he also became the Dean's Secretary, a post which proved to be significant in that the Dean at that time was Randall Davidson, who subsequently became Archbishop of Canterbury and in that capacity influenced Walford Davies' later career.

HWD was organist of St John's, Soho (1890-1891), Christ Church, Hampstead (1891-1898) and then of the Temple Church (1898-1917). His wartime service included giving concerts for servicemen and, upon the creation of the RAF, became its Director of Music with the rank of Major, composing the well-known *RAF March Past* in 1918.

He was appointed Professor of Music at the University of Aberystwyth in 1919, became chairman of the National Council of Music for Wales and was knighted in 1922. He resigned his professorship in 1926, but continued as chairman of the National Council until his death. In 1927 he returned to St George's, Windsor, as organist. He had been offered the job on the death of Parratt in 1924, but his many other commitments precluded his acceptance of the offer. The Revd Dr Edmund Fellowes acted as temporary director of music until HWD was able to take up the post. It is widely thought that Archbishop Davidson his influence to keep the door open for his former secretary.

Davies was Music Advisor to the embryo British Broadcasting Corporation and his regular radio broadcasts to schools on music and his recorded lectures on 78rpm records proved very popular. Between 1924 and 1939 he gave over 400 broadcasts, aimed at the average listener with the intention of clarifying their understanding and appreciation of classical music.

His five years at Windsor, his last full-time post and begun when he was already 58, were soured by problems with the relationship between himself and the Dean and Chapter. Differences over the contract and design of the organ rebuilding project (see Chapter 6) and his choice of repertoire for the liturgy being the most difficult areas. As a very successful and mature musician, and no doubt used to getting his own way, the politics of dealing with Deans and Chapters was perhaps not an area he was used to. Davies resigned as organist in November 1932 and it is not clear whether this was voluntary or under pressure but the Chapter minute reads:

"…while regretting the resignation of Sir Walford Davies they [the Chapter] do not question the wisdom of his decision and accordingly accept it with a deep sense of gratitude for his services to St George's throughout an important period in its history."

In 1932 he was appointed Commander of the Victorian Order (elevated to Knight Commander in 1937) and in 1935 received an honorary Doctorate in Music from Oxford University. On the death of Sir Edward Elgar in 1934 he held the office of Master of the King's Music until his own death.

On the outbreak of war in 1939, the BBC Symphony Orchestra and the BBC music administration department moved to Bristol and, still its music advisor, so did HWD. He died at his home in Wrington, near Bristol, in 1941 and is buried in the graveyard of Bristol Cathedral.

Other London musical activities

Whilst studying the organ under Walter Parratt, the sixteen-year-old Harris helped out at St Barnabas, South Lambeth. Vaughan Williams had taken the post of organist at St Barnabas in 1895, the year that he had returned to the RCM as a student following his Cambridge degrees. By all accounts RVW did not enjoy the job, and when he got married in 1897, he was happy to leave the work to Harris, who covered for him during the summer holidays. Sometimes Harris

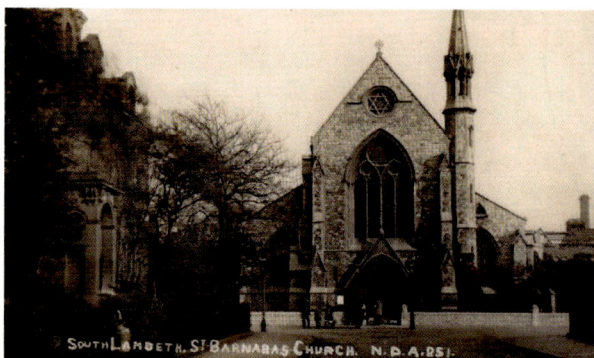

An undated postcard of St Barnabas, Lambeth

would play with RVW conducting the choir[53]. Gustav Holst also filled in as a deputy for a while and RVW finally resigned from St Barnabas in 1899.

This early contact was the start of a long friendship between Vaughan Williams and Harris. He was one of a number of musicians who assisted RVW by harmonising tunes for the 1906 first edition of *The English Hymnal*. Alastair Sampson, a former chorister at St George's, Windsor, during the 1950's recalls RVW attending the trebles' practice at St George's before evensong on more than one occasion. Both men had a deep affection for the music of the 'Tudor School'.

As well as the Temple Church, and St Barnabas, referred to above, Harris gave assistance at a number of other London churches, including St John the Baptist in Holland Road, Kensington (where Healey Willan was organist); Holy Cross Church in St Pancras; St Mary's Parish Church in Wimbledon (1903-1906) and St Mary's Parish Church in Ewell (1906-1911).

It was during his final year at Ewell that Harris composed his first hymn tune, naming it 'Ewell'[54]. It was first used at a festival of choirs in St Paul's Cathedral but not noted in the press until after he had moved to Lichfield when *The Lichfield Mercury*[55] reported that:

> '...the processional hymn "Divine, Majestic Maker" was sung to an admirable setting by Dr William H Harris, the assistant organist of the Cathedral. The words are by Marion M Scott , who was present at the service. The hymn has previously been sung at a festival of choirs in St Paul's Cathedral.'

Ewell set to Scott's text was published in 1912 in the USA in *Hymns of the Church: New and Old* by A S Barnes Co. of New York. Neither text nor tune seem to have been taken up in the UK, somewhat surprising as this is a strong tune and Scott's text is straightforward and not the flowery prose so prevalent in that era.

Harris also became organist and accompanist to the London Bach Choir in 1908[56], a post he held until 1921 and which brought him into direct contact with Hugh Allen, its Director, who was also organist of New College, Oxford. The experience gained through all these various London posts would give him a valuable grounding for the next stage in his career.

---

[53] Ursula Vaughan Williams, RVW: A Biography of Ralph Vaughan Williams, London, Oxford University Press, 1964
[54] See p. 215.
[55] 21st June 1912
[56] The Bach Choir was founded in 1876 to give the first complete British performance of Bach's Mass in B-minor. Otto Goldschmidt (1827-1907), the husband of soprano Jenny Lind and a former pupil of Felix Mendelssohn in Leipzig, was the first musical director and was succeeded by Charles Villiers Stanford in 1885, Walford Davies in 1902 and Hugh Allen in 1907.

London churches served by WHH whilst studying at the RCM.

St John the Baptist in Holland Road, Kensington

Church consecrated 1876 but not completed until 1891.

Organ by August Gern 1896, 4-manual, 32 speaking stops.

Healey Willan (1880-1968) was organist here from 1903 to 1913, when Harris served as assistant.

Photo: © Copyright John Salmon
www.victorianweb.org/art/architecture/brooks/6.html

Holy Cross Church, St Pancras

Church consecrated in 1888.

Nothing is known about the organ in use when Harris played here.

Photo: © Copyright John Salmon
www.geograph.org.uk/photo/2736020

St Mary the Virgin Parish Church, Wimbledon

Church consecrated in 1842, the work of Sir George Gilbert Scott.

3-manual organ by J Walker in 1843, rebuilt in 1876 by Hunter & Son.

Harris served here from 1903 to 1906.

Photo: ©Jacqueline Banerjee.
www.victorianweb.org/art/architecture/scott/8.html

St Mary the Virgin Parish Church, Ewell

Church consecrated in 1848. Organ by Henry Willis 1865, rebuilt to 3-manuals and 38 speaking stops by Norman & Beard in 1903. This organ was destroyed by fire in 1973.

Harris served here from 1906 to 1911.

Photo: Wikimedia © Richard Blanch
www.surreychurches.org.uk/epsomewell/ewellstm.html

Chapter 4: Lichfield

The choral foundation at Lichfield dates back to the 14th century. Like many of the choral foundations over the passage of years, there were low points. Before the Reformation the number of boys had dropped to six, only rising to eight in the reign of Henry VIII. (Being a cathedral of the Old Foundation, the cathedral's constitution remained unchanged at the Reformation.) Years of neglect followed. In 1726 the Sacrist's Roll records 'but five *old* prayer books "for ye boys" and four Service and Anthem books.' Towards the end of the eighteenth century, the antiquary John Carter, on paying a visit to Lichfield, commented: 'Certain deplorable children in dirty ragged stuff gowns flitted by me – not robed in decent surplices, as is the custom in other cathedrals.' The state of affairs was such that it prompted the Choristers' Friend, Maria Hackett, to pay a visit to the cathedral in 1826 in order to see what could be done for the boy's welfare. At the time of her survey, there were twelve Vicars Choral, eight choristers and two probationers.

> 'The Organist is Master of the boys in music, and instructs them daily after morning service. Beyond this, 'till within a recent period, there has been no establishment in this Cathedral for any other branches of education. There is an old foundation of a free Grammar School in the adjoining city, and also a modern National School, but in neither of these could the choristers be conveniently received on account of their attendance in the choir and in the Music School. A school for their separate use was wanted...'

Hackett goes on to report that a master, employed by the Dean and Chapter had now been engaged to instruct the choristers in reading, writing and arithmetic. It would seem that here, although notice was taken of her *Account* and its recommendations, the Cathedral authorities had already started to put reforms in motion.

Harris was appointed Assistant Organist to John Browning Lott[57] at Lichfield Cathedral in 1911, his name having been put forward by Walter Parratt. The number of choristers had recently been increased, and Lott had requested of the Dean and Chapter that he might be given more help, especially in the training of the boys. As a result of this request the Dean and Chapter decided to rebuild the Choristers' School on the site of the former school. Demolition of the old building began in 1913.

Lichfield Cathedral

---

[57] John Browning Lott (1849-1924) was a former chorister at Canterbury Cathedral and a pupil of Dr William Longhurst there. He served as organist successively of St Dunstan's and St Paul's churches in Canterbury and was assistant organist of Canterbury Cathedral before appointment as full organist at Lichfield Cathedral in 1881.

Statistics compiled for *The Cathedral Quarterly* a short-lived publication lasting from 1913 to 1916, with the somewhat cumbersome sub-title "A record of the work at, and in conjunction with the Cathedral Churches in Communion with the See of Canterbury", show that in 1914 the choir consisted of 24 choristers, six probationers, nine lay clerks (on the Foundation) and four priest vicars, with the boarder choristers having eight week's holiday a year, and the "town boys" (i.e. day boys) having four weeks.

Lott had been appointed organist as far back as 1881, and was to continue in the post for 44 years until just before his death in 1924.

Harris described Lott as:

> '...an organist of the old school and one of the kindest and best of men. When I first met him he said: "You and I are to be colleagues. I am so glad you have come and I am sure we shall be very happy together". And so it was.'[58]

Lott had been both a chorister and assistant organist at Canterbury Cathedral under William Longhurst. Harris described Lott's accompanying of services as:

> '...small-scaled and within its limits had a quiet beauty. He could rise to an occasion, and at times surprised everybody by his playing of such things as Wesley's *Wilderness* (not the easiest of anthems to play) which was remarkable for clearness, accuracy and appropriate registration.'[59]

Here again, as at St Davids, Harris was coming under the influence of an organist whose accompaniments were "small-scaled".

By all accounts, Lott had an engaging sense of humour. Harris recalled how Lott, on being asked whether it was true he had worked under a Precentor named Abraham, replied (evidently relishing the reference to his own surname): 'Yes, but he had *all* the Cattle'[60], this being a reference to the Book of Genesis, Chapter 13. As we shall see, Harris too had a sense of humour, which tempts one to speculate on a later quote from Harris, when asked for his favourite psalm verse, replied 'The lot is fallen unto me in a fair ground: yea, I have a goodly heritage.'[61] (Psalm 16) The sincerity of the words chosen would certainly fit with his natural sense of humility, but could equally refer to Lott [the Organist] - and 'fair ground' is open to more than one interpretation. Was Harris thinking back to Lott's answer? But perhaps not, as it was this same psalm, which had been chosen for Hugh Allen's funeral service in New College Chapel in 1946, at which Harris played. It was also a favourite psalm of Allen's, by virtue of it being one of the set psalms on the occasion of Allen's first service in New College Chapel in 1901.

A report in *The Cathedral Quarterly* for Easter 1914 records the following entry for Lichfield:

> 'The musical training of the choristers is in the hands of the Assistant Organist, Dr W. H. Harris. The usual number of boys singing at the week-day services is 14 or 16, and these are practised for 45 minutes before each service. When these leave for the service the others are taken for 30 or 40 minutes. All, however, are practised together when Dr Harris plays the service, those not required at the cathedral returning to school.'

Matins and Evensong were sung daily by the choir throughout the year with day-boy choristers singing some of the holiday services, and other services using men's voices only. This was the pattern of worship, not uncommon in cathedrals at this time, which was to last until the

---

[58] Harris 1948 (February) *Op. cit.*
[59] *ibid.*
[60] *ibid.*
[61] Brockway *Op. cit.*

outbreak of the Second World War in 1939. A survey entitled *The Present State of Cathedral Music*[62] notes that only three English cathedrals were still singing daily Matins, one of which was Lichfield – the other two being Wells and St Paul's. Matins at Lichfield was at 10.00am in the summer, and half an hour later in the winter months. Evensong was sung daily at 4.00pm, with Tuesdays being sung by men's voices.

A further glimpse of life at Lichfield just prior to the First World War can be obtained from the same report in *The Cathedral Quarterly* which reads:

> 'The Cathedral Choristers gave a concert in the Guildhall on February 5th. The programme included "Sumer is icumen in" and other rounds, "The Death of Trevor," Brahms, Eight Nursery Rhymes by Walford Davies, choruses, songs, recitations, piano duets, and a violin solo. The concert was directed by Dr Harris, the Assistant Organist, and he and Mr Lott, the Organist, presided at the piano. On February 12th, the Choristers paid their annual visit to the pantomime at the Theatre Royal, Birmingham, and spent a very enjoyable day. They were accompanied by their Master (Mr Bailey), Dr Harris, and the Sub-chanter.'

The same year [1914] also saw the completion of the new Choristers' School.

As part of a series of recitals in August/September 1915, organised to support the war-time British Red Cross Fund, Harris gave a recital at Christ Church, Oxford. Other recitalists in this particular series included Dr Alan Gray, Dr Basil Harwood and Dr Walford Davies.

Conscription following the outbreak of the First World War in 1914 began in March 1916. Prior to his joining up, Harris had applied for the post of Organist at Salisbury Cathedral. He was not successful, the position being given to Walter Alcock, appointed in January 1917. This would explain the delay in Harris starting his army duties until that year, as the post of cathedral organist would, in all likelihood, have been regarded in terms of a 'reserve occupation' should he have been successful in his application. In all probability he asked for a deferment until the results of the appointment were made known. Incidentally, this was the only post that Harris applied for in his life. All other appointments were offered to him.

He joined the 28th (County of London) Battalion, a volunteer light infantry unit known as the "Artists' Rifles", his place as Assistant being covered by E. Dunhill[63] from August 1917 to August 1918. However, on joining up, the army downgraded his health status, and he was declared only fit for service on the Home Front. He was released from the army fairly soon after the war, and returned to Lichfield.

During his eight years as assistant in Lichfield, Harris received much encouragement from Granville Bantock, for whom he took on some teaching at the Birmingham and Midland Institute[64], becoming Professor of Harmony and Counterpoint there. Harris acknowledged that he owed much to Bantock[65], describing him as being one of the most inspiring and vivid characters he had met. In a memorial tribute, he commented that;

> '... he had extraordinary vitality and his output was immense. No one was more generous-minded than he, and his friends and pupils have cause to remember many kindnesses [...] his sense of humour was irresistible. And what a fine teacher he was!'[66]

62 *The Present State of Cathedral Music Op. cit.*
63 About whom the authors have been unable to trace any information.
64 The Birmingham and Midland Institute was founded by Act of Parliament in 1854 "for the Diffusion and Advancement of Science, Literature and Art amongst all Classes of Persons resident in Birmingham and the Midland Counties".
65 Harris was a founder member of The Granville Bantock Society in 1946, after his death. Jean Sibelius, who had dedicated his 3rd Symphony to Bantock, became President of the Society. The initial idea of the founders was to promote recordings of Bantock's works.
66 Harris 1948 (February) *Op. cit.*

Sir Granville Bantock (1868-1946)

Born in London to a medical family, Bantock studied at TCL and the RAM in London. In the earlier years of his career he was a conductor in musical theatre and burlesque. As a person he was energetic, eccentric and reluctant to conform to conventions, making him somewhat of an outcast from the general musical establishment. In 1900, whilst engaged in musical theatre in the Wirral, he was appointed as Principal of the Birmingham and Midland Institute School of Music, on the recommendation of Mackenzie, Stainer, Parry and Stanford, amongst others. He was also offered a post at the RAM but declared (quoting Milton's *Paradise Lost*) that he would "rather reign in hell than serve in Heaven".

Bantock c. 1913

Edward Elgar was the Peyton Professor of Music at Birmingham University and on his retirement in 1906, Bantock accepted the post, serving until 1934 when he was elected Chairman of the Corporation of TCL in London. Vincent Budd, in his essay *A Brief Introduction to the Life and Work of Sir Granville Bantock*, added:

'... with his natural and commendable distrust of personal honour, rejected a number of academic awards (though he did accept an honorary doctorate from Edinburgh University): but, there was one award conferred upon him, it seems through Elgar's influence, that he could not resist and did seem to accept gladly - though, so he said, more for his wife than for himself - that of a knighthood in 1930 in recognition of his services to British music.'

The Birmingham and Midland Institute

Along with the post at Lichfield, Harris also became organist of The Church of St Augustine of Hippo in Edgbaston, Birmingham, from September 1913, remaining there until his move to Oxford in 1919.

> 'As my week-ends and most of my evenings were free, I became organist of St Augustine's Church, Edgbaston, Birmingham – a church with a good musical tradition – where I had a competent choir of twenty-four boys and twelve men, and what is very much to the point, a kind and sympathetic vicar.'[67]

How important that still is today for any organist! The photograph seems to show that the church had five clergy during Harris's time there.

The Clergy
of
S. Augustine's, Edgbaston.
1916.

W. COOKE.
M.A. Oxford. 1898.

J. M. La F. McANALLY.
M.A. Oxford. 1913.

ROSSLYN BRUCE.
D.D. Oxford. 1908.
(M.A. 1897).

E. ALBANY T. CLARKE.
M.A. London. 1884.

S. BURGESS.
M.A. Cambridge. 1873.

St Augustine of Hippo, Edgbaston

Designed by Birmingham architect Julius Alfred Chatwin (1830-1907), the church was consecrated in 1868 with a tower and spire (185 feet high and the tallest in Birmingham) added in 1876.

The original organ, by William Hill of London, was rebuilt by Frederick Rothwell in 1914 during Harris's tenure. The choice of Rothwell may well have been brokered by Walford-Davies who was an enthusiastic supporter of Rothwell's work – see p. 50.

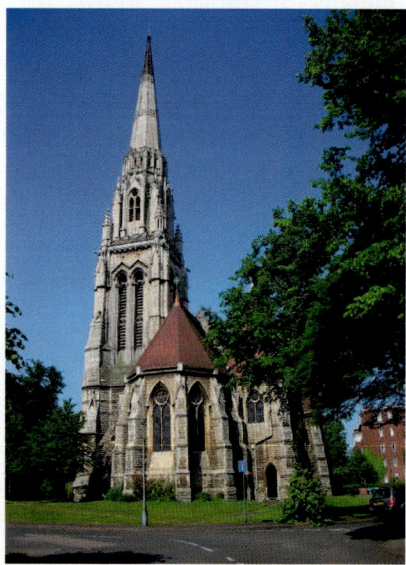

Harris succeeded Alfred Gaul (1868-1913) to become only the second organist of St Augustine's. Gaul, a former chorister at Norwich Cathedral, was subsequently assistant organist there under Zachariah Buck. He was appointed as the first organist at St Augustine's in 1868, holding the post for 45 years. Later organists at Edgbaston include Thomas W. North (1919-1955), Philip Moore (1956-1960)[68] and Roy Massey (1960-1965) – an impressive line-up. Roy Massey recalls:

> 'One night I was playing with the CBSO at the Town Hall and in the interval Fred Ledsam [see following page] came round to see me and conveyed the news that Philip Moore was leaving Birmingham to become Director of Music at BBC Bristol and would

---

[67] ibid.
[68] See p. 91 regarding Moore. This is not Philip Moore (b. 1943) former organist of York Minster.

I be interested in the St Augustine's job? To cut a long story short I was auditioned by WHH. [Roy describes the audition in his Foreword] Two days later I heard I'd been appointed. Afterwards I was told that there had been thirty applications, as at £325 per annum, plus fees, this was the best paid organist's job in the City - better even than the cathedral or St Martin's Parish church at that time.'

Two other men were to inspire the young Harris whilst at Lichfield; Royle Shore[69], well-known in his day as editor of the *Tudor Cathedral Music* series, and Edwin Stephenson[70]. Stephenson was organist at Birmingham Cathedral where Harris heard many of Shore's editions of Tudor music, directed by the organist.

'He and Royle Shore were closely associated, and I was able to hear at Birmingham Cathedral for the first time some of the finest examples of English Tudor Church music under Stephenson's direction. It was a revelation to hear such flexibility of phrasing, and to be conscious of so high a standard of musical intelligence in the interpretation of sixteenth-century music.'[71]

One wonders how much Tudor music was in use at Lichfield Cathedral at this stage. Harris's comment "hear...for the first time" regarding his visits to Birmingham Cathedral may be significant.

Frederick Ledsam

Of the many friends Harris made whilst at Lichfield, mention must be made of Fred Ledsam, who was a partner in the accountancy firm of Harris, West, Ledsam & Co of Birmingham. The Ledsam family was associated with St Augustine's over several generations, from its consecration. Roy Massey recalls that Fred Ledsam was the means by which he became acquainted with WHH.[72]

'Fred's main passion in life was music, about which he was very knowledgeable. He loved the organ repertoire and works for chorus and orchestra and was a great supporter of the CBSO concerts at the Town hall and the Handel operas at the Barber Institute of the University. He was also married (in middle age) to Margaret, a lovely person and a talented Viola player who played in a string quartet at their home on a regular basis, so Fred was also well acquainted with the chamber music repertoire.'

WHH often stayed with the Ledsams for a day or two and I was often invited to join them for supper on these occasions and WHH seemed to take a considerable interest in what I was doing at the church. Years later, Fred told me that after Matins one Sunday morning which WHH had attended, he said to Fred "By Jove, Massey's certainly put his foot behind that choir." WHH used to give Fred a signed copy of everything he had published. He [Harris] also owned two finely bound 18th century volumes of Handel's Overtures and concertos inscribed on the flyleaf "one day for Fred - WHH."

Fred duly inherited them and, eventually, they came down to me, together with one or of the signed choral and organ copies. I moved on from St Augustine's in 1965 to my RSCM job at Addington and in 1968 returned to Birmingham as cathedral organist, but

---

[69] Samuel Royle Shore (b. 1856, Edgbaston; d. 1946, Hindhead) was a lawyer by profession and a pupil of A R Gaul. He was Diocesan Lecturer in plainsong, assistant organist of Birmingham Cathedral and organist of St Alban's in Birmingham. Ordained priest in 1911, he edited and published much Latin church music and in retirement was an organist in Hindhead.

[70] Edwin Stephenson (1871-1922) was organist of Cartmel Priory in Cumbria at the age of 14 and studied in London at the RCM. After serving as an organist at churches in Brighton, he was organist of St Philip's Cathedral in Birmingham from 1906 to 1914 and then of St Margaret's Church in Westminster from 1914 until his death. He was a keen promoter of Tudor church music.

[71] Harris 1948 (February) *Op. cit.*

[72] Personal email Sept 2017.

throughout this time my friendship with the Ledsams continued to thrive and so did the periodic invitations to supper with WHH in Edgbaston.'

Roy Massey remained a life-long friend of the Ledsam's and played for Fred's funeral – at St Augustine's.

Not only was the friendship between WHH and Ledsam also long-standing, but Fred was able in his professional capacity to assist the Harris's with their financial affairs when they retired to Petersfield as neither of them had adequate money nor any idea about how to manage their affairs. Harris dedicated his *Miniature Suite* for organ (1957) to Ledsam and also gave his name to a hymn tune, annotating the *ms*. "For FCAL on his 70th Birthday from his old friend WHH." (See Appendix 2)

Chapter 5: Oxford

New College

New College, originally called The College of St Mary of Winchester in Oxford, was founded in 1380 by William of Wykeham, Bishop of Winchester. It opened its doors to students in 1386 including '…sixteen poor and needy boys less than twelve years of age, of good standing and honest conversation, who are sufficiently competent in reading and singing, who would form the top line of the College choir.'

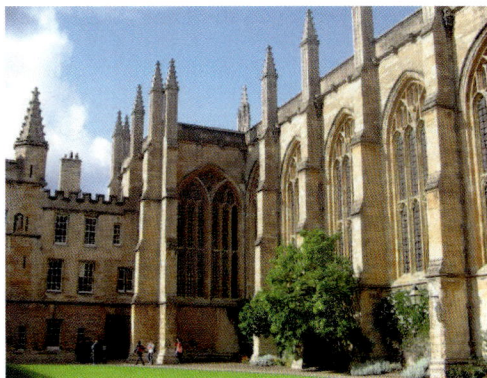

The name 'New College' was to distinguish it from Oriel College, also dedicated to the Virgin Mary but founded earlier in 1326.

During Harris's time the organ, an 1884 Willis with 3-manuals and 47 stops, rebuilt in 1906 by Gray & Davison, was further reconditioned in 1926 by Rushworth & Dreaper.

Music in the chapel at New College has had, like so many similar choral foundations, a somewhat chequered existence over the years. A visitation of 1566, during the reign of Elizabeth I, examined the choristers' ability to sing. 'Only three of the sixteen could, and it was clear that no one had really attempted to teach them.'[73] And again, in 1781, diarist John Byng, Fifth Viscount Torrington, on a visit to Oxford, records the following rather scathing account:

> 'We hurried away from our dinner in hopes of hearing an anthem sung by a famous singing boy of New College… We were baulked of our intention as the anthem was very ill sung, and the service most idly perform'd by such persons as I should suppose had never learnt to sing or read…'[74]

The organist at that time was Philip Hayes, who had been appointed to New College in 1776. Later, he also held the posts of organist at St John's and Magdalen Colleges concurrently. It would seem that he had spread himself somewhat thinly as in addition he was a Professor of Music and a Gentleman of the Chapel Royal. A nephew described him as 'a lazy dog, fond of good living, in fact a gourman.' (sic) He has also been described as "the largest man in England" in its most literal sense. In view of all his commitments, the term 'lazy' seems a little unjustified.

Maria Hackett's *Account* of 1827 gives a good report on the provision for the choristers' education at the College; 'they are instructed in Grammar, in the Latin and Greek classics, in Writing, Arithmetic and Music … the Organist attends them personally three times a week.' Her *Account* goes on to say that the choir '…is one of the largest in the kingdom, and there is no place which has been more remarkable for supplying the various Cathedrals with valuable and efficient members.' However, it is not clear whether it is singers or clergy to which she refers.

---

[73] Jenkinson, Matthew, *New College School, Oxford – A History*, London, Bloomsbury Publishing, 2013.
[74] Hale, Paul, in *Music and Musicians*, in *New College Oxford 1379-1979* ed. Buxton, John & Williams, Penry, Oxford, New College, 1979

By the time of Revd John Jebb's survey[75] of choral services in cathedrals and collegiate foundations published in 1843, he notes that New College, under Stephen Elvey's musical direction, still retained the choir prescribed by its founder:

'It consists of ten chaplains, most of them in orders, one being Precentor, three clerks and sixteen choristers. The service is performed twice daily [during term] all parts being chanted, including the prayers and litany, with a solemnity perhaps unequalled in England.'

It may be that Jebb had chosen a particularly good day for his visit, for we read in Tuckwell's *Reminiscences* that 'Choral services in the chapels were not of a high order, though individual voices of special sweetness kept up their popularity.' He goes on to complain that the choristers ran wild.[76] Dr Stephen Elvey (1805-1860), who's organ-playing was considerably hampered by his having a wooden leg, has been described as having an uncertain temper, and who had difficulty in keeping order with the choristers. The full choral daily Matins was to be shortened considerably in 1867, when a committee set up by the College decided to omit the canticles at Morning Prayer.

Ten years later (in 1877), a visiting cleric (Revd Coker Adams) voiced a comment on the newly-reduced morning service, saying 'it was a most monotonous performance to my mind, and frequently sung flat.'[77] A music list of 1879 does show that the situation had improved somewhat, from what had been a preponderance of eighteenth century music, with morning canticles by Parry and an anthem by Sterndale Bennett and evening canticles by Garrett and an anthem by Sullivan, two of the four composers listed (Parry and Sullivan) being contemporary, and the other two only recently deceased.

James Taylor (1833-1900), a pupil of Sterndale Bennett, had been appointed organist in 1865, a post he was to hold for 35 years until 1900. Taylor, recognised as a remarkably fine pianist and piano teacher, has been described as 'exceptionally shy [...] and content with adequate achievement for the New College Choir.'[78] Taylor's quoted diffidence may perhaps be significant, as the standard of singing when Hugh Allen took over was held to be somewhat "second rate". Also, by this time, he was aged 67. Sydney Nicholson, who had gone up to New College, Oxford as an undergraduate in 1893, records in his memoirs that he visited the various colleges for matins and evensong; namely Magdalen – under Varley Roberts, Christ Church – under Basil Harwood, and New – under James Taylor, whom he describes as 'an elderly gentleman with a long white beard [...] a fine organist of the old-fashioned school.' Nicholson was a student under Taylor. He goes on to say that 'his choir was excellent: perhaps less highly finished than Magdalen, but I think more natural and spontaneous.'[79] Magdalen seems to have been the most famous of the three choirs at this time, and attracted the music-loving undergraduates, while '...New College under the "gentle" and aging Dr Taylor had a little dropped behind the others.'[80]

In order to put Harris's achievements at New College in context, it is useful to examine what went before, especially the powerful influence of his immediate predecessor, Hugh Allen, and the legacy which Harris inherited.

---

[75] John Jebb (1805 – 1886) was an Anglo-Irish Anglican priest. His survey of 1843 was an enquiry into the low state of services and music in cathedrals and collegiate churches. Towards the end of his life he was appointed a Canon of Hereford Cathedral.

[76] Tuckwell, Revd. William. *Reminiscences of Oxford*, London, Cassell, 1900

[77] Edmunds, Jonathan, *New College Brats: a History of the Life and Education of the Choristers of New College, Oxford*, Oxford, New College School, 1996.

[78] Shaw, Harold Watkins, *The Succession of Organists*, Oxford, Clarendon Press, 1991.

[79] Henderson, John; Jarvis, Trevor, *Sydney Nicholson and his Musings of a Musician*, Salisbury, RSCM, 2013.

[80] Bailey, Cyril, *Hugh Percy Allen*, London, Oxford University Press, 1948.

Allen had been appointed as organist of New College in 1901, after the death of James Taylor[81]. Following his appointment, it was not long before Allen brought the choir back to its former standard '...and even surpassed them' [i.e. Magdalen and Christ Church][82].

Allen has been described as having an 'unusually powerful personality which cloaked great kindness.'[83] Allen's memorial in the cloisters of New College echoes this description, describing him as a 'devoted musician and wise counsellor who used his talent and the singular force of his personality in strenuously promoting the love and practice of his art.' One boy chorister described Allen as; 'an energetic and enthusiastic perfectionist with a wicked sense of humour.'[84] In many ways, this perceptive comment sums up Allen's character. One example of this 'wicked sense of humour' comes from a report when the choir were singing Purcell's *Thy Word is a Lantern*. On reaching the line "The ungodly have laid a snare for me" sung by a not very talented alto, Allen shouted from the organ loft, "wish to hell he'd got you!"[85] The choir could also retaliate. On one occasion they pointed out 'the piquancy of the hymn *Dark and cheerless is the morn unaccompanied by Thee*, when Allen once again failed to appear at an 8 am matins service.'[86] There are echoes of Herbert Morris of St Davids here, regarding the non-appearance of an organist at matins!

Sir Hugh Allen

Sir Hugh Percy Allen GCVO (1869-1946) studied as a boy in his home town of Reading with Frederick John Read (1857-1944) who was then organist of Christ Church prior to his appointment to Chichester Cathedral. At the age of eleven Allen was organist of St Saviour in Coley near Reading later serving in nearby Tilehurst and Eversley. He became Read's assistant at Chichester Cathedral in 1887 and studied for his Oxford University musical degree. From 1892 he was organ scholar of Christ's College in Cambridge during which time he graduated with his Oxford B Mus in 1893! His Cambridge degree in 1895 was a BA. After brief service at St Asaph Cathedral and Ely Cathedral, during which time he obtained an Oxford D Mus, he applied to New College and won the post in competition with Edward Bairstow (and others) in 1901.

Walford Davies, Hugh Allen and Cyril Rootham c.1932[87]   **Hugh Allen c. 1905**

---

[81] The appointment was by competition. Edward Bairstow and Hubert Hunt were also competitors.
[82] Bailey *Op.cit.*
[83] Shaw, Harold Watkins *Op. cit.*
[84] Jenkinson *Op. cit.*
[85] *ibid.*
[86] *ibid.*
[87] Photo: Jasper Rootham - family album. (Wikipedia)

The lot of the choristers in Allen's time seems, on the whole, to have been a happy one.

> 'Allen was much respected and there was great devotion to him. He taught far more than was required and did so with energy and enthusiasm.'[88]

Although Allen has been praised for his high expectations, which had helped raise standards in the Chapel, there were also criticisms.

> 'He did have fits of temper at poor singing, and used physical punishment. No singing technique was taught and you learned to sight-read as you went along, from your seniors.'[89]

Something a modern choir-trainer would find difficult to reconcile, if this last statement is to be taken at face value!

Harris must have felt that Allen was quite a hard act to follow. One wonders to what extent Allen had, by his behaviour, deliberately made himself that "hard act to follow". He certainly displayed a reluctance to let go his connection with the choir. Andrew Carwood comments that the strength of Allen's character forced Harris to assert himself on several occasions, and quotes the following example: 'The lock on the New College Song Room door had to be changed so as to prevent Allen wandering into the rehearsals and taking over.[90]' Allen's biographer noted that all his energy was coupled with a restlessness which could lead to impatience with others; but any outburst was usually followed by Allen saying '…how I wish I hadn't said that' when he got home[91]. There was an underlying humanity and sensitivity about the man, albeit on occasions well-camouflaged; and Harris, in spite of some problems along the way, always regarded him as a personal friend.

A student, Randall Ellison[92], who spent much time in the organ loft with WHH and even occasionally deputised for him recalls:

> 'Above the console was a photo of the 3 chief Oxford organists of the day, Henry Ley, Varley Roberts and H P A [Hugh Percy Allen]. Harris used to refer to them as "The World, "The Flesh" and "Dr Allen"!'[93]

When Harris succeeded Hugh Allen as organist of New College in 1919, Allen was well-acquainted with Harris's work as a pianist, through Harris having served as an accompanist for the London Bach Choir from 1908 to 1921, which Allen conducted. Allen had resigned his position at New College on being elected both Professor of Music at Oxford (the Heather Professorship of Music in 1918 – the vacancy following Sir Walter Parratt's resignation) – and also Director of The Royal College of Music following the death of Sir Hubert Parry, in 1919. There is some evidence that Allen was reluctant to leave the city of Oxford for London, for in a letter to a friend he wrote:

> 'I have been more than ordinarily troubled in spirit and feel as if it was impossible to give up the things that have meant so much to me and to Oxford. I only go away from a real sense of duty and from no inclination.'[94]

The post of Organist and Master of the Choristers at New College gave Harris his first taste of being in charge but, as has been shown, his predecessor exhibited a reluctance to let go the

---

88 Edmunds *Op.cit.*

89 *ibid.*

90 Carwood, Andrew, CD Notes for *Harris: Faire is the Heaven*, ASV CD DCA 1015, ASV, 1997

91 Bailey *Op.cit.*

92 Randall Erskine Ellison (1904-1984) worked in education administration in Nigeria from 1928 becoming Director of Education for the Northern Region in 1956. He retired back to London in 1961 to be Assistant Secretary of the Church Assembly and then Chairman of the Africa Committee of the Church Mission Society.

93 Ellison, Randall, Letter from Randall Ellison to Paul Hale June 1977, by courtesy of Paul Hale.

94 Letter quoted in Bailey *Op.cit.*

reins. In fact Allen maintained a physical presence at Oxford for at least another six years in his role as conductor of the Oxford Bach Choir, as Professor of Music and as a Fellow of New College. Allen had been elected a Fellow of New College back in 1908 – then a significant honour for a College organist. In fact, as a Fellow, Allen was to retain his old rooms in New College, and return from London to spend long week-ends there.

Another area where life was not that easy for Harris was his standing in the university hierarchy. Although Harris held both Mus B and Mus D degrees from Oxford, because of a change in Oxford's regulations, these degrees were not sufficient to establish membership of the university because they lacked the requirement of residency which had by then been brought in. This meant that in order to engage more fully in academic activities at the university, as well as being able to sit on top table whilst dining in hall and become a member of the Senior Common Room, Harris had to begin the process of studying towards the Oxford BA degree. Until he achieved this status he had to sit at a separate table for one when dining in college[95].

This must have been a considerable commitment of time on his part, taking into account the many other professional calls on his time. Both his BA and MA degrees were conferred in 1923. Now, at last, he was a full member of the university, and was able to enjoy all the appurtenances that ensued; he enjoyed Oxford life all the more, not least the dinners. Harris was, and remained until retirement, a collegiate-minded person; living, as he did for most of his life, in provided accommodation, in gracious surroundings and among his work colleagues and friends, and partaking of formal dinners. In all probability, this may well have been part of the reason why Harris was to agree to take on, at a later stage, the post of Director of Studies of the RSCM at Addington Palace – also renowned for its gracious surroundings – and dinners.

As mentioned in "The Early Life" section of this book, Harris had a life-long affection for the theatre in general, and opera in particular. It is for this reason that his work as one of the founders of the Oxford Opera Club gave him so much pleasure. Hugh Allen, having failed to prevent Harris founding the University Opera Club for some unspecified reason, then did his best to stop Harris putting on a pioneering production of Monteverdi's *Orfeo*, but he was thwarted. We can only speculate on why Allen should try and prevent this from taking place.

Orfeo

The staging in Oxford of *Orfeo*, regarded by many as the first fully developed opera to be performed regularly[96], on the 7th, 8th and 9th of December 1925 was its first British staged performance, though there had been concert versions performed previously.

The genesis of the *Orfeo* project was described in *The Times*[97] by librettist Robert Stuart in 1965. By then a Presbyterian priest in Fraserburgh, Scotland, Stuart wrote:

'...in the Easter vacation of 1925[98], I had decided to persuade my friends to stage *Orfeo* in Oxford, my intention was to sing it in Italian and use the edition by Malipiero... I went down to London to discuss the project with Professor E J Dent, at that time a journalist living in Panton Street. He went with me to Messrs. Chester to examine the Malipiero score which he considered unscholarly. He advised me most earnestly to perform the opera in English and to get some musical scholar in Oxford to make a new edition following more nearly the ideas of the composer. We then visited Sir William Harris, then organist of New College, who was teaching that afternoon at the RCM. The three

---

[95] Henry Ley had been in a similar position, having to sit at a separate table for one in Hall, as he was appointed organist at Christ Church whilst still an undergraduate.

[96] Whether it was actually the first 'opera', as we know the genre, is much debated by scholars!

[97] 30th December 1965.

[98] Stuart was an undergraduate at Corpus Christi College.

of us decided in Dent's flat that evening that Harris should conduct the work and edit the score and that I should try my hand at translating the libretto.

When Sir Jack Westrup, then an undergraduate at Balliol, heard that we were thinking of staging *Orfeo*, he began to make a transcript of an early printed copy of the score in the British Museum and completed it from another copy in the Bodleian after the Trinity term had begun. As time went on Harris, being very busy, left more and more of the editing to Westrup who finally edited and orchestrated the whole work. The realization of the continuo, however, was by Harris.'

In comparing the 1925 edition with Raymond Leppard's 1965 edition, Stuart goes on to say:

'..there is no doubt but that the simpler, more homophonic realization by Harris makes our edition far more suitable for amateurs, whilst the straightforward alternative version to the florid passages in the great Styx recitatives has a quality of emotional and dramatic appeal which is lacking in the more complicated variant.'

A review of the performances by Dyneley Hussey[99] on 19th December in *The Saturday Review of Politics, Literature, Science and Art* called the occasion:

'one of the most important events of recent years' and that the production had 'indicated at once Monteverdi's claim to rank among the great geniuses who have written dramatic music.'

Harry Colles in his article on Harris for *Grove's Dictionary* (1954 edition) describes the performance in 1925 as 'a most interesting revival'. Another reviewer wrote '...the conductor, Dr William Harris, kept everything alive and played the continuo as though he had a life's experience as Kapellmeister at an Opera House.'[100]

The Westrup edition of *Orfeo* was revived in December 1929 at the Scala Theatre[101] in London, however the three performances there 'resulted in a financial disaster, and the opera was not seen again in Britain for 35 years'[102]

Formed after the Oxford success of *Orfeo*, the Oxford University Opera Club performed Gluck's *Alceste* in the Oxford Playhouse in the following year – seven performances in period costume – in December 1926. This time Sir Hugh Allen gave his blessing to the project and also helped to engage some of the soloists. Harris again conducted though with Sidney Newman[103], a Christ Church undergraduate, directing some performances. *The Times*, in its review of the performance, noted that:

'Dr W H Harris conducted, but had to share the credit for the excellence of the choral singing, which was the outstanding feature of the opera, with Mr S T M Newman...who did much of the preliminary training.'

---

[99] Dyneley Hussey (1893-1972) was a poet, journalist and critic. He was music critic for *The Times* from 1923 to 1946 before working for the BBC Third Programme. He was the author of several books about opera.

[100] Brockway *Op. cit.*

[101] The Scala Theatre in Charlotte Street near Tottenham Court Road was demolished in 1969, after being destroyed by fire.

[102] Fortune, Nigel. "The rediscovery of Orfeo" in Whenham, John (ed.): Claudio Monteverdi: Orfeo. Cambridge, Cambridge University Press. 1986

[103] Sidney Thomas Mayow Newman (1906-1971) CBE, MA(Oxon), Hon D Mus (Dunelm.), Hon RAM, FRCO, FTCL, so only aged 20 when he made this opera conducting debut, was sub-organist at Christ Church before attending the RCM. He became Reid Professor of Music at the University of Edinburgh in 1941 in succession to Sir Donald Tovey.

Harris was appointed President of the University Music Club in 1921[104] and he directed the Balliol Sunday Evening Concerts in succession to Ernest Walker[105] from 1925 to 1933. It was the custom to invite well-known and respected musicians to perform at these popular evening concerts.

Harris was also actively involved with the Oxford University Dramatic Society (OUDS), conducting Grieg's *Peer Gynt* in 1925[106] and writing incidental music for some productions. The latter include a setting of the song *You spotted snakes* from 'A Midsummer Night's Dream' for "Jean Forbes Robertson (Titania) and her Fairies"[107] in the OUDS summer production of 1926 in Magdalen Grove and incidental orchestral music for *King John* performed at the New Theatre in Oxford Feb 21st-25th 1933. WHH noted on the *ms.* of *King John* that "This was the last production and the last music to be played in the old New Theatre in Oxford before its demolition in March 1933". Harris himself conducted the last night of the production.

Harris's love of Wagner 'sprang from the time he accompanied Marie Brema in her various roles in *Parsifal* and *The Ring*.'[108] Marie Brema was a well-known mezzo-soprano[109], who was the first English singer to appear at the Richard Wagner Festival in Bayreuth. This led to Harris making further visits to Bayreuth and Salzburg – very often calling in at St Thomas's, Leipzig, on the way home in order to pay a visit to the church where Bach had been organist[110].

In his presidential address to the RCO in 1948, Harris was to recount how he had lately tried to '…fill the gaps in what I must now consider to be a defective musical education by going a good deal to Italian opera.' To this end, he heard the early operas of Verdi, citing *Rigoletto, La Traviata, Macbeth* and *Aida*, and commenting that these were works that he in his youth '…had been rather dissuaded from hearing.' One wonders who the dissuader was!

In 1926 Allen finally handed over the conductorship of the Oxford Bach Choir to Harris, a post in which he was to continue until leaving Oxford in 1933. During his tenure he gave public performances of many large choral works; Brahms, Verdi, Stanford and of course Bach[111]. This appointment elevated Harris's standing among his colleagues at the university. Although he had a successful tenure, it cannot be said that Harris was ever quite as effective with a large choir as with a smaller one. However, he maintained the high standard of the college chapel choir, especially the boy choristers, which had been achieved under Allen. William Hayter, an undergraduate at the time (later to become Warden of the college) remembers the notable pianissimo singing of the choir, which he describes as 'almost a whisper, especially in the responses.'[112] Randall Ellison, who was an undergraduate at the College between 1922 and 1925, notes – with fulsome praise – that Harris:

> '…was a fabulously talented musician, a composer of outstanding gifts…a first-rate organist…who could play at sight an eight-part anthem with all the parts, but for the bass, in the C clef, and with only a figured bass to guide the accompaniment.'[113]

---

104 Note that there was also an Oxford University Musical Union. The Oxford University Musical Club was founded by Sir Hubert Parry and C H Lloyd in 1874. It subsequently merged with 'Union' to become 'The Oxford University Musical Club and Union'. Both had similar aims, but all performers at the 'club' were amateurs.

105 Ernest Walker had been Director of Music at Balliol from 1901 to 1925, and continued these Sunday concerts, started by his predecessor John Farmer, until he handed over to Harris in 1925.

106 For which he had Grieg's orchestral parts with the composer's own markings brought over from Germany.

107 This dedication is on the *ms.*

108 Brockway *Op. cit.*

109 She sang Ortrud in *Lohengrin* at Bayreuth in 1894. It was for her that the role of The Angel in Elgar's *Dream of Gerontius* was created and she gave the first performance in 1900.

110 See also the *Prelude in E-flat* p. 247 which was composed whilst sitting in the nave of the Thomaskirche.

111 His first concert with the choir was Bach's *Christmas Oratorio* on 5th Dec 1926. The critic in *The Musical Times* of January 1927 noted good choral singing, impeccable rhythm and a pleasing variety of tone and expression but commented that the solo singing, with one exception, was very poor.

112 Hale *Op.cit.*

113 Ellison *Op.cit.*

Ellison did not think that choir training was Harris's most successful skill, 'he was too nice and not really aggressive enough.' This observation from a student's perspective is at variance with observations from both the choristers and men at Windsor, as well elsewhere. Both Statham (from a boy's viewpoint) and Hodgson (from a choir gentleman's viewpoint) comment on Harris' strictness in rehearsal, when the occasion demanded.

Ellison made some other surprising observations on music at New College whilst he was a student from 1922 to 1925:

'It [New College] was not, apart from its choir and chapel, a musical college by normal standards. There was no musical scholar to assist Doc H at the organ... There was no College Musical Society. I can't remember any concert having been given in hall. The choir however, did give concerts in the ante chapel from time to time, and these might also include some solo instrumental contributions.'

He also recalls the antics of another student, John Hewlett Alden (1900-1976), subsequently Director of Music at Bradfield College in Berkshire:

'I remember one occasion when we were both in the organ loft for a Sunday Evening Service and the anthem was *In the Beginning* from *The Creation*. Doc H was giving a very vivid account of the "Representation of chaos" and at the climax Alden pulled out the Tuba stop on the solo organ and did a glissando on it from bottom to top! Doc H wasn't all that amused!'

Another of Harris's achievements whilst at New College was his appointment at the Royal College of Music as a Professor of Harmony and Organ in 1921.

Throughout his career and in common with most of his cathedral colleagues, Harris was a participant in the usual treadmill of giving recitals, adjudicating at musical festivals, advising on organ projects, giving the opening recitals of new organs and so on. A few examples during his time at New College include: directing a hymn festival at Wadhurst Parish Church in Sussex in September 1923, conducting 400 children at a Festival in Sevenoaks in May 1925, conducting community hymn-singing in Banbury in July 1925 and directing the third annual Deddington Deanery Hymn Festival in June 1928. He also began broadcasting recitals on the BBC from St Michael's, Cornhill, during 1925.

The New College choir made its first recordings on 22nd March 1927 for HMV. Two 10" 78rpm records were issued: one[114] containing *Lord, for Thy tender mercy's sake* (Farrant) and *O Lord my God* (Wesley); the other[115] *Justorum Animae* (Byrd) and *Beati quorum via* (Stanford). There was also a recording of *My soul, there is a country* (Parry) which was not released. This may well have been a test pressing which for some reason, whether technical or performance-wise, was judged not suitable for release.

Paul Hale recounts the episode of when Vaughan Williams brought Jean Sibelius to New College on a visit about this time. Sibelius asked to hear the organ, and Harris played Bach's *Prelude and Fugue in A minor*. 'At the conclusion of this, the great composer [Sibelius] came upstairs and putting his arm round Harris's shoulders exclaimed "Artiste!"'[116]

Probably Harris's most well-known composition *Faire is the Heaven*, written for unaccompanied double choir, was published in 1925 whilst at New College, and dedicated to Hugh Allen[117]. Herbert Howells, many years later, was to comment in a BBC Radio 3 talk given on 28th March 1973: 'Stylistic propriety has been Sir William's strength in all his creative

---

[114] HMV B2446
[115] HMV B2447
[116] Hale *Op.cit.*
[117] Interestingly, *Faire is the Heaven* was first published by the Year Book Press in their Part-Song series, and not in their Church Music Anthems series.

work [...] his setting of Edmund Spenser's *Faire is the Heaven* is a supreme and flawless example of the ordered beauty of his church works.'

Another composition from 1925, but for boys' voices, is a setting of George Herbert's hymn *King of glory, King of peace* which was dedicated to "Cullis, Gooderson and all other New College Choristers." Perhaps this is an indication for the regard in which he held his choristers.

It seems that Harris had an especial affinity with this choir. Paul Hale wrote: 'shortly before he died, Doc H told me that he considered his New College Choristers the finest he ever had anywhere.'[118]

Harris had enjoyed friendship and a good working relationship with the Warden of New College, Revd Dr William Spooner[119], but when Spooner retired in 1924, Harris didn't seem to have the same close association with his successor, historian and politician Herbert Fisher.

Politics at New College continued to be not always sympathetic to Harris, so he took the opportunity to move to Christ Church Cathedral in 1929 when a vacancy occurred following the sudden death of Noel Ponsonby in 1928. Here, conditions suited him better. However, he was later to comment on his time at New College in a favourable light, perhaps given the intervening passage of years, as being a place '...where I was fortunate in spending ten uncommonly happy years serving under the famous and now almost legendary figure, Dr Spooner, and Herbert Fisher.'[120] Of Harris's tenure of the post of organist, Grove's *Dictionary of Music* (1954 edition) includes a generous and doubtless merited summing up, which also gives us a glimpse of the repertoire:

> 'He had brought the choir of New College Chapel to a high level of efficiency and had given with it a number of special performances of the masses and motets of Palestrina and Lassus, the Passions of Obrecht and Schutz, as well as much English music of the Tudor school.'[121]

Harris was succeeded at New College in 1929 by John Dykes Bower, a Cambridge graduate who served as organist at Truro Cathedral from 1926 until his appointment in Oxford[122].

The dress of an Oxford Chorister (college unspecified) from a series of watercolours by James Roberts (1753–c.1809) published in 1792.
Note that only a surplice is worn.

---

[118] Email from Paul Hale.

[119] William Spooner (1844-1930) was the Spooner famous for his accidental transposition of the initial letters of words, known as 'Spoonerisms'. It seems that most of those now quoted are apocryphal. Spooner was at New College for more than sixty years, as an undergraduate, Fellow, Lecturer, Tutor, Dean and as Warden from 1903 until 1924.

[120] *The Musical Times* February 1948 & August 1948.

[121] H C Colles in *Grove's Dictionary of Music and Musicians* 5th Edition, 1954

[122] He was subsequently organist of Durham Cathedral 1933-1936 and of St Paul's Cathedral from 1936 until retirement in 1968.

Christ Church Cathedral

Christ Church Cathedral, Oxford, founded in 1542, has a choral foundation dating back to 1546. The first list, appearing in the Cathedral records of 1549, states that there were eight choristers. This number appears to have remained constant over the year. Dean Aldrich[123], who was Dean at Christ Church from 1689 to 1704, set about raising the standard of the choir: 'He never admitted a boy chorister unless he had been previously instructed, and had given sufficient proof of his abilities.' He also brought in other changes, namely '…giving the choir boys an academic dress, and a place at College table.' Maria Hackett, in her account of 1827, notes:

> 'The Choristers are in the sole nomination of the Dean [...] and he appoints at any age he thinks proper; the time of their dismissal is also at his discretion.'

It would appear from this quote, and the preceding one[124], that the organist did not have much say in the matter!

Revd John Jebb's survey of 1843 is disparaging about the long university vacation during which the choral service at the cathedral 'by a strange anomaly is either suspended or but half performed.' An account in *The Cathedral Quarterly*, dated July 1915, notes that 'In former days the boys took holidays in relays, but now they all go together for a fortnight at Christmas and Easter, and a month in August. During these holidays the services are sung by the men only, or are plain.'

In 1855, soon after the appointment of Dr Henry George Liddell as Dean, the number of choir boys was increased to 16, although the statutory eight choristers were termed as being on the Foundation as King's Scholars, and the additional eight boys as probationers. The choristers

were boarded out in the town until 1878, but from that year they were gradually collected under one roof, at Wolsey House in Brewer Street, and from 1879 onwards, were required to board there. This accommodation proved to be inadequate, so a new choir house was built further along Brewer Street, coming into use in 1894.

Matins and Evensong were sung daily, with the exception of Wednesdays, but by the time of a survey entitled *The Present State of Cathedral Music* we see that there was no longer a week-day service of choral Matins, and Evensong was said on Thursdays.

Top: The Great Quadrangle of Christ Church
Bottom: The choir stalls

---

[123] Revd Henry Aldrich (1648-1710) was a well-known theologian and musician, composing a number of service settings and anthems. He also adapted the music of Palestrina and Carissimi to English words – not very successfully.
[124] E F A Suttle, *Henry Aldrich, Dean of Christ Church, Oxford*, 1940.

Harris was appointed Organist of Christ Church Cathedral in 1929 following the sudden death of their newly-appointed organist, Noel Ponsonby. Born in 1891, Ponsonby had been a chorister at St George's, Windsor under Sir Walter Parratt, organ scholar at Trinity College, Oxford, entering the world of cathedral organists at Ely in 1919. He was appointed organist at Christ Church, Oxford in 1926, to succeed Henry Ley, but died two years later at the early age of 37. There is a discrepancy with some sources as to the actual year in which Harris started at Christ Church. Following Ponsonby's death in 1928, Harris had been asked to help cover some of the Christ Church services and rehearsals, whilst still carrying on with his New College duties. This, in all probability, would have given Harris his first taste of life at the cathedral. In 1929 Harris made the move. The appointment must have been offered to him during this transition period.

It was about this time that one former chorister recalled his first attempt at a voice trial for New College, conducted by Harris, who had just been appointed to Christ Church. The boy had prepared Reger's Maria Wiegenlied to sing from memory. When Harris asked for the music, he was told that the boy had not brought it, so he said he thought he could play it from memory. The boy then recounted the following:

> 'Halfway through I stopped him and told him he was playing it wrong! This caused loud guffaws from the Dons at the back of the Song Room.'[125]

A few months later he took a second voice trial, presumably this time with music [!], under John Dykes Bower (Harris's successor at New College) – and passed.

As we have seen during the Lichfield years, Harris had only once applied for a position (Salisbury Cathedral). This change of post within Oxford seems to have been welcomed by Harris, who appeared more at home with cathedral routine rather than in the academic environment of the purely university college setting of New College. New College choir only sang during university terms, and so were not present for the major festivals of Christmas and Easter. At Christ Church, Harris was able to provide music for the whole Christian Year.

It has been noted that 'the acoustic properties of the cathedral are not favourable, and therefore a musicianly style, not aiming at loud or extravagant effects, is the more to be appreciated.' Nicholson, too, comments on the unrewarding acoustic of Christ Church in his memoir: 'His [Basil Harwood's] choir always suffered from the poor acoustics of the Cathedral, but it was very efficient and its repertoire was probably the most interesting of the three [New College and Magdalen College being the others].'[126] This, in all probability, reinforced Harris's penchant for restraint. A report in The Cathedral Quarterly, dated April 1913, stated that 'experiments are being made to improve the acoustic properties of the cathedral, and a temporary glass screen has been placed behind the choir stalls. It is hoped that some means may be found to overcome the disadvantages of the building in the matter of sound, and allow the choir to be heard to greater advantage.'

During Harris's time as organist, Albert Einstein paid a visit to Oxford, and expressed a wish to hear the Christ Church Cathedral organ. Harris wrote:

> 'I played him the Passacaglia [Bach]. When it was ended he turned the pages back to the fourteenth and fifteenth variations (where all is thinned down to a "one dimensional" arpeggio figure) and said: "so little, but so much; it is all there in the background".'[127]

Harris was impressed with Einstein's complete understanding.

---

[125] Wallin, Peter, 'A Lifetime of Singing', in New College Choir Association Newsletter – July 2012, Oxford, New College Choir Association, 2012
[126] Henderson/Jarvis Musings Op. cit.
[127] Harris 1935 Op. cit.

Harris was later to recall his time at Christ Church under the Dean, The Very Revd Henry White (1859-1934), appointed in 1920, and 'a remarkably fine Chapter' in some amusing detail:

'These many changes of scene brought me into touch with an extraordinary number of people of every variety. One could write a book on the vagaries and whims of Deans and Canons, Heads of Colleges and Dons who formed the governing body of these ancient foundations. Their views and opinions were certainly not always those of the professional musician and often quite unaccountable. There was the Dean who would do away with all music but Bach; the Canon who liked nothing but sixteenth-century music; another who saw little good in anything but the music of the eighteenth century; the one who called himself 'something of a purist' and was inclined to be intolerant of everything but the music of Palestrina; another who wondered why we didn't do a little Gounod. All these dignitaries made their lively contribution to the life and activities of a small community, and if not taken too seriously could be very entertaining.'[128]

Among Harris's compositions whilst at Christ Church were: *The heavens declare the glory of God* 1930, *O what their joy and their glory must be*[129] 1931 and *Most glorious Lord of Life* 1932. Harris resigned his post as organist in 1933, in order to take up his position at St George's Chapel in Windsor. He was succeeded at Christ Church Cathedral by (Sir) Thomas Armstrong who moved to Oxford from Exeter Cathedral.

Four organists of Christ Church (date unknown)

(left to right)

Dr Sydney Watson	**(1955-1970)**
Dr Henry Ley	**(1909-1926)**
Sir Thomas Armstrong	**(1933-1955)**
Sir William Harris	**(1929-1932)**

---

[128] Harris 1948 (February) *Op. cit.*

[129] Based on the tune "O Quanta Qualia", this highly complex example of the hymn-anthem form was performed with orchestral accompaniment at the Three Choirs' Festival in Gloucester in 1934.

Chapter 6: Windsor

King Edward III founded the "Royal Free Chapel of Our Lady, St George and St Edward the Confessor within the Castle of Windsor" in 1348. The foundation was established by statute in 1352, with a Warden, twelve secular canons, 13 presbyters or vicars, four clerks [probably young men whose voices had recently broken] and six choristers, also clerks. There were possibly six junior boys as well. The Grammar Master was required to teach the boys Latin for four hours daily, and for the rest of the day the Teacher of Music was to instruct the choristers in singing and the playing of musical instruments. They were also required to be trained in the performance of liturgy, namely text, chant and ceremonial.

The number of choristers fluctuated over the years. For example, in 1478, during the reign of Edward IV who had ordered the rebuilding of the Chapel in 1473, the number of choristers had been increased to 13. By the time of Edward VI it was back to ten.

Maria Hackett, who first visited St George's in 1818, noted in her survey of 1827: 'there are now twelve choristers, who are boarded with a respectable Dame in the Cloisters. They are kindly treated…but their education is of a most limited character…' By the time Walford Davies joined the choir as a boy in 1882, there were still twelve choristers. This number later rose to 24 in 1894, after the choristers took up residence in their newly-acquired building (Travers' College, now St George's, the present-day choir school.) in September 1893.

As with many ancient foundations, St George's had its own time-honoured traditions. One of which being "Spur Money". This was a custom whereby any person entering the Chapel wearing spurs could be fined by a chorister for doing so. King Henry VII and King Henry VIII both paid the fine, the latter on several occasions. The offender however could demand that the chorister prove his worth by singing his "gamut" (scales), before handing over the fine, which in Thorndike's time was 5 guineas. Unfortunately for the modern chorister the fine is no longer imposed.

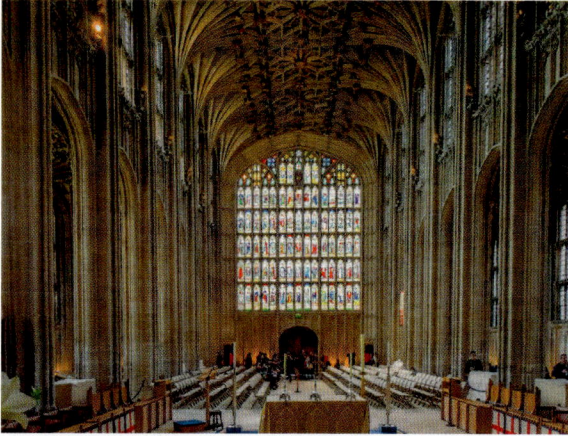

(Left) The Nave of St George's looking West[130]

(Below) The Quire looking East

Harris was recommended for the post of Organist and Master of the Choristers at St George's Chapel, following the early death on 14th November 1932 of Charles Hylton Stewart. Stewart, formerly organist at Chester Cathedral, had arrived in Windsor early in September 1932, and in less than twelve weeks in post, had been struck down by a sudden short unspecified and fatal illness. The Revd Dr Edmund Fellowes, one of the Minor Canons, was put in charge of the choir in the interval between Hylton Stewart's death and the arrival of Harris in 1933. This was the second time that Fellowes had been asked to step in, the previous occasion being on the death of Sir Walter Parratt in March 1924. On that occasion Fellowes was to stay in charge of the choir for three and a half years, until the appointment of Walford Davies in the autumn of 1927. Walford Davies did not stay long at Windsor. He resigned in 1932, after only five years, opting for retirement to Cookham Dean, his health at this stage giving some concern. His ideals of what cathedral music should be did not exactly coincide with Chapters' views. 'In particular he did not see eye to eye with Dr E H Fellowes.'[131] C L Graves also makes reference to Davies' tenure at St George's being '…not altogether a bed of roses.' However, Graves goes on to say 'On Sundays we generally went over to Windsor for the service in George's Chapel, where his genial and gifted successor Dr Harris has so worthily maintained the traditions of Sir Walter Parratt.' Walford Davies must have thought highly of what Harris was achieving, even if he disapproved of some of the Canons.

Incidentally, it was during the time of the interregnum following Davies' retirement that Fellowes, having been asked by the Chapter to "hold the fort", took eight gentlemen of the choir, along with twelve boys from Westminster Abbey choir, to Canada on a tour organised by Sydney Nicholson in 1927. The original intention had been to take twelve St George's choristers but, apparently the Dean and Canons of Windsor, who had initially given their consent, then declined permission through the intervention of the Senior Canon who persuaded the Chapter against the boys going. This decision is somewhat puzzling, as the Chapel was closed for restoration from March 1921 until the autumn of 1930, and all services suspended for two months over the winter period of 1927. However, the Dean (Dr A V Bailey), who had been out-voted by the Chapter, did accompany the choir on the tour.

---

130 © Jack Pease 2015, used with permission.
131 Graves *Op. cit.*

Edmund Horace Fellowes CH, MVO

Fellowes was born in Paddington, London, in 1870, and showed considerable musicality as a child. Indeed he was so proficient on the violin that, at the age of eight, the virtuoso violinist Joseph Joachim offered to take him to Berlin to train as a professional violinist. Instead it was decided that he pursue a career in the Anglican Church. He studied theology at Oriel College in Oxford and was ordained priest in 1895, becoming Precentor of Bristol Cathedral two years later. In the interim, he studied music at Oxford, gaining his B Mus degree in 1896.

In 1900 he and his wife moved to Windsor, taking up the post of Minor Canon, a position he continued to hold until the end of his life, through the reigns of five monarchs. His involvement with the music at Windsor was very considerable and he features throughout this book.

He was on the Council of the Plainsong and Mediæval Music Society from 1931 to 1946 and today he is chiefly remembered as a musicologist, not only through his books, especially *English Cathedral Music* (published in 1941), but mainly through his numerous editions of Tudor music, both sacred and secular. He did much to raise the profile of sixteenth and seventeenth century church music.

He died in 1951, after 51 years unbroken service at St George's.

1927 Canada Tour: The Gentlemen of St George's with the Revd Dr Edmund Fellowes

Andrew Carwood mentions that Harris had received a message from Henry Ley asking him why he hadn't been in contact with the Chapter at Windsor, as they were waiting for him to apply for the position of Organist[132]. Harris accepted an invitation to lunch with the Chapter on 22nd December 1932. This lunch meeting must have formed the occasion of the formal offering to Harris of the vacant position, as the Minute in the Chapter Records of St George's, Windsor of Harris's appointment is dated 22nd December 1932, and Harris's acceptance was announced at a Chapter meeting on 31st December of that year. Although Harris would have had no immediate connection with Charles Hylton Stewart, he did however have connections with two of the organists before Stewart; Sir Walter Parratt (1882–1923) and Sir Walford Davies (1927–32).

Moving to take up residence in Windsor, he began work on 25th March 1933. Alwyn Surplice, Assistant Organist at the time, remembered the first Evensong for which Harris played. It was *Stanford in A*, not the easiest of accompaniments, being an organ reduction of a full orchestral score.

> 'I received an unforgettable impression of his brilliant technique and command of the organ when handling the testing accompaniment of *Stanford in A*.'[133]

On his appointment to Windsor, Harris relinquished all of his Oxford duties, but he retained his post as Professor of Organ and Harmony at the Royal College of Music until 1955, an appointment which had been made as long ago as 1921.

Undated postcard of the Horseshoe Cloisters

On arrival at Windsor, the Harris family moved into the organist's house in the fifteenth century Horseshoe Cloisters. This house had been Walter Parratt's, and was provided as part of the organist's remuneration. The post of organist was for life and they were usually expected to remain and die "in post". The actual organist's salary proved insufficient for the Harrises, who did not have an extravagant lifestyle, to be able to save enough to purchase a property on his retirement. Edmund Fellowes and his wife lived next door, in a house once (erroneously) thought to be the former home of John Merbecke. Harris's daughter Margaret recalled that living in the cloisters in the Castle, life was always in the shadow of the Royal family. Queen Mary had a disconcerting habit of visiting at very short notice, whereupon she would throw open cupboards to see how people lived.

---

132 Carwood *Op. cit.*
133 Surplice, Alwyn, 'Sir William Harris – A personal appreciation', *Organists' Review*, October 1973.

The daily round of sung services, shown in the survey entitled *The Present State of Cathedral Music*[134], lists Matins being sung each day except Tuesdays and Wednesdays, and Evensong each day except Wednesdays, plus a full round of sung services on Sundays, namely Matins, preceded by the Litany sung in procession, Holy Communion and Evensong – a not inconsiderable workload! Michael Statham (son of Heathcote Statham), a St George's chorister from 1939 to 1943, recalled[135] that the boys were singing for nearly three hours a day, on six days of the week. School lessons had to be slotted around a routine dominated by rehearsals and services – both twice a day. In addition to this were all the additional services connected with royal occasions. Former chorister Allan Ledger recalls that:

> "Sir William lived in what is now part of the Chapel Archives. It was considered to be a privilege to be invited for tea on a Sunday by Lady Harris, and Doc H would play some of his compositions on his baby grand in the drawing room. (...) During my first few terms at St George's, the choir rehearsed in the old music school, now part of Vicar's Hall, which was next to where Doc H lived. As we practised for Matins and Evensong, we boys surreptitiously carved the shield of the Cross of St George, which we coloured in blue, red and white, on the ancient wooden stalls at which we sat. When we moved to the new music school for our rehearsals, still used today, it was made abundantly clear that carving would no longer be permitted on the new stalls.

> During the services in the Chapel, DocH could, by means of mirrors in the organ loft above the choir stalls, keep an eagle eye on us. If we were caught slacking or misbehaving, especially when Her Majesty was present, we would be duly summoned to the organ loft."

Another feature of Harris's work at Windsor was the continuance of the annual Festival of Church Music held in the Chapel. This summer Festival of Church Music had been set up by Walford Davies during his last year at Windsor (1932) in which church music, both *a cappella* and accompanied by organ and strings, was performed, using the choirs of St George's Chapel, Eton College, the Windsor and Eton Choral Society and, in the first of these festivals, the London Bach Choir. The St George's Chapel choir played the principal part in these performances, and, in addition, sang Choral Evensong between concert sessions. These festivals were remarkable for the diversity of styles represented in the programmes.

A surviving programme for the 1935 Festival, which seems to by then have been moved to the autumn, listed the following participants:

8th November (two concerts): St George's Chapel Choir (Dr W H Harris with Alwyn Surplice)[136] & Eton College Choir (Conductor Dr Henry Ley)

9th November (two concerts): St George's Chapel Choir, Bach Choir (Conductor Reginald Jacques[137]), St George's Special Choir, (Conductor Geoffrey Leeds[138]) and the Windsor & Eton Amateur Orchestral Society

10th November (one concert): St George's Chapel Choir and The Fleet Street Choir (Conductor T B Lawrence[139])

---

134 *The Present State of Cathedral Music Op. cit.*

135 Statham, Michael, 'Sir William Harris: A choirboy's memories', *Musical Opinion,* October 1983

136 Two motets by Harold Darke and two anthems by WHH were given their first performance. The latter may have been *From a heart made whole* and *Love of Love and Light of Light* but this is conjecture.

137 Dr Reginald Jacques (1894-1969) directed the London Bach Choir from 1932 to 1960, founded and directed his own Jacques Orchestra in 1936 and was conductor of the National Youth Orchestra of Great Britain from 1948. His name is best-known to most singers as co-editor, with David Willcocks, of *Carols for Choirs* [Bk.1] in 1961.

138 Geoffrey Leeds (1891-1965), pupil of Sir Walter Parratt at St George's Chapel, was a music master at Eton. Organist of both Eton and Windsor Parish churches for twenty years, and then in London of St James', Sussex Gardens and of Holy Trinity, Prince Consort Road.

The 1939 Annual Festival of Church Music, consisting of the customary five sessions, was held from June 9th – 11th, seemingly moved back at some stage to its summer slot.

Harris also became President of the Windsor and Eton Amateur Orchestral Society in March 1935, succeeding Sir Frederick Dyson. This society, which according to the minutes was founded in 1883, lasted until 1947. It may well have been the aftermath of the war that devastated the membership. Harris was also Conductor of Windsor & Eton Choral Society, which had been founded in 1841 by George Elvey, from 1944 to 1949. During his tenure, and presumably because of his natural modesty, he conducted only two of his own compositions: *Song of May Day* in June 1941 (repeated in May 1951) and *Psalm 103* in June 1948. This latter work is an extended setting of the words *Praise the Lord, O my Soul* for eight-part unaccompanied choir written in 1938.

Another enterprise, in which Harris was involved, presumably through his former connection with St Davids Cathedral, was his appointment as music assessor of the Church in Wales' new Welsh language hymn book, *Emynau'r Eglwys*. Another Dr William Henry Harris, a coincidence of names which has led to some confusion in the past), the father of Llywela Harris (a former Warden of the RSCM at Addington Palace), was the secretary, compiler, translator and also author of some of the hymns.

Llywela[140] recalls how much her father enjoyed the trips to Windsor to see his namesake for regular discussions and consultations. The words edition of the hymn book was published in 1941, followed by the music edition in 1951. The hymn tune *Alberta*, set to the text "Lead kindly light", was Harris's only contribution to the book. This would seem to be yet another example of his self-effacing reluctance for the limelight.

The Revd Dr William Henry Harris (1884-1956) was Professor of Welsh at St Davids College in Lampeter where he first graduated with a B.A. in Welsh in 1910. A degree from Jesus College in Oxford preceeded his ordination as deacon in 1913 and as priest in 1914. Following parish appointments, he taught at St Davids College from 1919 until his death, also acting as Precentor. In addition he was Precentor of St Davids Cathedral from 1933, Canon of the Cathedral from 1937 and Treasurer from 1948. In contrast to "Doc. H" of Windsor he was known to his students as "Pa Bill"!

The Revd. Dr. William Henry Harris
Precentor of St Davids College Chapel

In addition to his many chapel music commitments, Harris was also an active director of the Theatre Royal in Windsor for many years. In 1946, he took on the role of President of the Royal College of Organists, a post he held for two consecutive years.

Harris, affectionately known as Billy by his friends, and Doc H by generations of choristers and men of the choir, was, by all accounts, a strict disciplinarian. Frederick Hodgson, a lay clerk in

---

[139] Thomas Bertie Lawrence (1880-1953), educated in his home town of Liverpool, was founder and conductor of the Fleet Street Choir in 1929 and of the London Madrigal Group in 1931.

[140] Personal communication May 2017. Llywela kindly provided the photograph of her father.

the choir, records in his memoirs[141] that Harris '…drove himself hard as he drove his singers. He was fastidious to a degree, and was completely dedicated to his work. No slackness was tolerated, full attendance was demanded, and he was rarely absent.' He goes on to recall that there were many tense early morning practices, with Harris in a critical mood, and an aggrieved lay clerk would retaliate – with the inevitable fireworks. But on another occasion, Harris had said to the choir "you are turning out every note like sausages from a machine." A voice from somewhere queried "Harris's?"[142] Fortunately on this occasion, Harris's sense of humour prevailed, and the tension was relieved.

Nevertheless, the choristers seemed to have a genuine affection for him. Lionel Dakers recalled that 'One remembers the exhilarating way in which the choristers would run down the hill to greet Doc H as he emerged from 12 The Cloisters to take boys' practice, and the Sunday tea parties over which his wife Doris presided with such charm.'[143] Bruce Nightingale, who had been a chorister at St George's during the Second World War, described Doc H as having 'a fat, usually jolly face with a few wisps of hair across an otherwise bald head.'[144] Michael Statham refers to a feeling of apprehension felt by the boys on hearing Harris's footsteps on the spiral staircase approaching the practice room, concerning what sort of mood he would be in. 'If he was in a good mood he would wave cheerily as he came through the door, his circular face beaming, and almost trot round to the piano […] If he was in a bad mood there would be no doorway greeting and his progress would be a somewhat tetchy stalk which augured a difficult half-hour.'[145] The same chorister makes reference to Harris, on occasions, arriving a few minutes late for the morning practice. When this happened, the senior chorister would start the rehearsal, looking at some of the music for that day's services. Statham goes on to mention that Harris gave the impression of caring how the boys sang more 'than of almost anything else in his life'. He also noted that during his voice trial, Harris had 'a characteristically withdrawn, attentive expression on his face.' The juxtaposition of the words "withdrawn, attentive" are, in many ways, a good indication of WHH's character, already noted by his daughter's comment about living 'in a world of musical vision.' However, a badly-sung evensong would reduce him 'to irascible misery.'

There seems to be no doubt that on occasions, Harris could be not only a hard task-master but also somewhat unorthodox in his approach, especially in the case of poor intonation. He was known, during a service, to give 'a corrective peep on the organ if he thought someone had strayed off the note, and this was not always accepted without strong protests from minor canons and lay clerks.'[146] He was also known to pass audible comments from the organ console on the rare occasions of a mediocre performance during a service. Harris would scold the choristers in 'a loud stage whisper from the organ loft.'[147] This too must have been an irritation to the clergy! However, these were relatively mild eccentricities compared with one of his predecessors, Sir Walter Parratt, who was also fastidious about tuning. He used to make the senior chorister responsible for 'pitch and time' in unaccompanied services as, presumably, Parratt remained in the organ loft.[148] Russell Thorndike, recording his time as a chorister under Parratt in his memoirs *Children of the Chapel*, recounts the following:

[141] Hodgson, Frederic, *Choirs and Cloisters: Sixty years of music in Church, College, Cathedral and Chapels Royal* London, Thames Publishing, 1988.

[142] Harris's Sausages were once a well-known household brand. Based in Calne, Wiltshire, where both of Harris's daughters were educated, the joke would not have been lost on him.

[143] Dakers, Lionel, St George's Chapel Centenary Concert Programme 19th March 1983.

[144] Nightingale, Bruce, *Seven Rivers to Cross: A Mostly British Council Life*, London, Radcliffe Press 1996

[145] Statham *Op.cit.*

[146] Hodgson *Op. cit.*

[147] Nightingale *Op.cit.*

[148] Wridgway, Neville, *The Choristers of St George's Chapel*, Slough, Chas. Luff, 1980

'I remember that if the choir dropped the fragment of a tone in the Litany or Confession, he would stump about the organ loft, tearing at his hair, and shaking his fists in full view of the congregation. On one occasion when we had been guilty of dropping a whole semitone, he let us know our crime by playing the note we had started on upon the tuba stop.'[149]

Although possibly an amusing anecdote, one can't help wondering if a little youthful hyperbole on the part of Thorndike is being employed here.

As has already been mentioned, Harris retained his professorship at the Royal College of Music, to which he had been appointed in 1921, whilst he was still at New College. This necessitated many trips to London, normally on Mondays, which had to be slotted into the Windsor timetable. The music for matins and evensong would be left in the hands of the assistant on these days. Lionel Dakers, who went on to become Director of The Royal School of Church Music, was appointed Assistant Organist of St George's in 1950. He wryly notes that on the Mondays, when Harris was away at the RCM, he tended to put down on the music list 'non-demanding and somewhat unadventurous 18th and 19th century settings such as *Kempton in B flat, Nares in F* or *Elvey in A.*'[150] However, one may view this as prudence on Harris's part, until such time that the assistant had proved his competence. Dakers also makes reference to Harris testing him out in the early days of his apprenticeship.

'Having said he would not be at Evensong, there were occasions when, if I looked down the nave from the organ loft, I would catch sight of him in the distance listening to my efforts.'

Although they seem to have had a good working relationship, enjoying frequent walks in the Home Park, Dakers also notes that Harris could be both difficult and unpredictable on occasions.

The War Years: 1939-1945

The Second World War presented Harris with a number of problems, not least of which was the continuing threat of air-raids.

'For several weeks [in 1940] air-raid warnings occurred repeatedly, sometimes as many as six times in one day. The choir had to come down from Chapel in the middle of services, anthems and psalms having to be abandoned in mid-verse.'[151]

Later, air-raid warnings during services were largely ignored. 'Matins and Evensong continued to be sung with unruffled peace-time dignity.'[152] The maintenance of an uninterrupted round of services was probably regarded as a form of war work. The bombing threat returned in 1944, with the new hazard of flying bombs. As a safety measure against the threat of air-raids, the time of Evensong was moved from 5.00pm to 3.00 or 3.30pm. A chorister during the early war years remembers that night after night he would hear the sound of ack-ack guns being fired during the blitz on London 25 miles away. The choristers had now to sleep in ground-floor classrooms, which had been turned into dormitories, for safety.

Another problem, which had surfaced back in 1938, was financial. This came to a head in February 1942, when the Chapter was forced to look at ways of making changes at the choir school, as an economy measure. The Chapter, being the governing body of the school, called a meeting at which William Harris and Edmund Fellowes were invited to attend. This meeting was convened to consider the possible reduction in the number of choristers. At this meeting

[149] Thorndike, Russell, *Children of the Garter: Being the Memoirs of a Windsor Choir-boy, during the Last Years of Queen Victoria*, London, Rich & Cowan, 1937.
[150] Dakers, Lionel, *Places where they sing: Memoirs of a Church Musician*, Norwich, Canterbury Press, 1995.
[151] Wridgway *Op. cit.*
[152] Statham *Op.cit.*

it was decided to invite Sir Sydney Nicholson, Director of the School of English Church Music, to visit the school and offer any recommendations he may make on its future constitution. Following on from this meeting, it was decided in January of the following year that the number of choristers would gradually be reduced from 24 to 18. However, by Easter 1949, the numbers were increased to 20. This invitation to Nicholson may well have come about at Edmund Fellowes' suggestion, as they had both enjoyed a long association. Harris was on the Council of the Church Music Society during the war years and the CMS was chaired by Sir Sydney Nicholson, who had succeeded Walford Davies.

Nicholson would certainly be known at Windsor, not only through his work with the SECM, but he had also taken part with his choir at the reopening service of the restored Chapel in November 1930. Furthermore, Nicholson and his choristers had been invited to sing morning service in the Private Chapel in February 1938, at the invitation of the King and Queen. During this visit Kenneth Jones, one of Nicholson's choristers from Chislehurst, recalls[153] meeting Harris, and that, after the service [Evensong in St George's], both Harris and Nicholson improvised for 15 minutes on the two consoles in the organ loft. Apparently the Queen (later Queen Elizabeth, the Queen Mother) was delighted. These two consoles, set at right-angles, were used on various occasions. Applicants for the post of Assistant Organist were required to play one, whilst Harris played the other. On 13th December 1939, the BBC broadcast an organ recital from St George's, with William Harris and Henry Ley playing duets. Many years later, former Addington student Lionel Sawkins and his fiancée were invited into the organ loft on Christmas Day 1958, and witnessed (and turned the pages) for Harris and his assistant [presumably Richard Greening] playing the accompaniment to Bach's *Christmas Oratorio* (part 1) on both consoles. Harris also used the twin consoles when giving an organ lesson '…frequently playing the piece being studied at the same time as his pupil, … I was attempting to play Bach's little G-minor fugue and at some point became aware that Doc H was playing it with me. I remember desperately wondering whether to continue to play and thus ensure that my innumerable wrong notes became glaringly obvious or whether to disengage hands and feet completely and hope that Doc H would not stop before the end.'[154]

Harris, in common with all who worked at the Chapel, was of course subject to the authority of the Dean and Chapter at St George's. 'In November 1942 the Chapter had written to Dr Harris to advise him that practices for the boys must not be held on Sundays, the reasons then were not given.'[155] In fact it was not until October 1943 that the reason became known. It was apparently because a number of parents had complained that their boys were suffering from "overwork and strain."[156] One questions why Harris was not told of this at the time. Was this overwork and strain a reaction to the reduction in chorister numbers?

On another occasion choral Evensong had to be cancelled at a moment's notice when Harris discovered 'that all the choirboys had gone to the cinema with the Dean, after he had given them a party, and the organist had not been informed.'[157] One can only surmise what Harris must have felt by what seemed a cavalier attitude on such occasions. Hodgson recounts another incident when the choir was lined up ready to process into evensong, but the Dean and all the Canons were absent. 'No Canons?' said Dr Fellowes, 'then there will be no service.'[158] One wonders why Fellowes, a cleric, did not take the service himself. Fellowes had a reputation of being a law unto himself; neither did he suffer fools gladly, so perhaps a point

---

153 Personal communication April 2017
154 Statham *Op.cit.*
155 Wridgway *Op. cit.*
156 *ibid.*
157 Hodgson *Op. cit.*
158 *ibid.*

was being made here. Again this must have been somewhat galling for Harris, with a fully-rehearsed evensong ditched at the last moment.

The system of choral scholarships, awarded to the top 12 choristers, had also caused some problems through 'the Organist's habit of changing the position of boys in the choir order as it suited him'[159] Not an unreasonable thing for Harris to do, it may be thought, but it resulted in unrest among the parents of boys who had been promoted to the top twelve, without receiving the corresponding remission of fees awarded to scholars. This led to the cessation of choral scholarships, under the old arrangement in 1948.

An initiative of Harris's dating from 1939 which has now become an oft-repeated format up and down the country, was when he held a "Come and Sing" event in St George's on the 16th December, in which he invited 'anyone who wanted to sing Handel's *Messiah* to turn up and sing the work unrehearsed. Over 350 singers attended.'[160] The fact that this was only a few months into the war, may well have served as a morale-boosting exercise. The BBC also broadcast series of organ recitals for the same reason. Harris gave a number of these, not only from St George's, but also from St Luke's Church in Chelsea, St Margaret's in Westminster and from the concert hall at Broadcasting House between 1937 and 1944.

As regards the Royal Family, the official line was that the King and Queen would remain in residence at Buckingham Palace during the Blitz, but the two princesses would, from May 1940, live in the safer environment of Windsor Castle for the duration, being quartered in the relative safety of the Lancaster Tower, with easy access to the cellars below during air raids. What was not made public at the time was that the King and Queen, whilst remaining in the capital during the day, would travel to Windsor every night, if at all possible, to be with their children.

Amongst Harris's duties was the tutoring of the princesses in music, especially singing. It was at the Queen's suggestion that the two princesses should once or twice a week have music lessons at the Harris's house in Horseshoe Cloister. During 1944 and 1945 Harris, together with between four and eight of the senior choristers, attended musical gatherings known as 'Madrigal Parties' in the Red Drawing Room of the Castle to assist in the singing of madrigals, part songs and rounds, with a small choir of friends, ranging from senior boys from Eton College, guardsmen and members of the Windsor and Eton Choral Society, together with the two teenage princesses. For two years (1943-1944) the two princesses donated jars of Argentinian honey to the choristers as a Christmas treat. Another treat occurred on 20th December 1944 when, through the influence of Harris, the choristers staying on for Christmas were invited to the Waterloo Chamber in the Castle 'to see a pantomime in which both Princess Elizabeth and Princess Margaret acted.'[161]

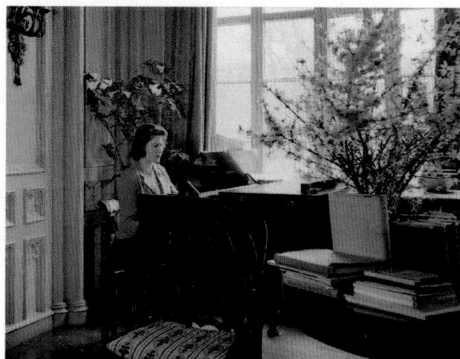

Princess Elizabeth at the piano in 1942

[159] Wridgway *Op. cit.*
[160] Dakers 1995 *Op.cit.*
[161] Wridgway *Op. cit.*

The musical education of the princesses and the 'Madrigal Parties' were described in detail by Betty Spencer Shew, author of *The Royal Wedding* published in 1947, a book both approved of by Princess Elizabeth and to which the Princess willingly contributed details of her meeting and falling in love with Philip Mountbatten. Shew also wrote an article published in the *Dundee Evening Telegraph* on 30th January 1947 under the headline "THE PRINCESS LIKES BING AND SWING".

She noted that:

'Mabel Lander[162] gave the Princess her first pianoforte lesson in May 1930. That lesson consisted mainly in screwing the music stool up and down! To-day Princess Elizabeth, like her sister, is still Miss Lander's pupil. Both sisters play with accomplishment... Their interest owes much to the encouragement of the Queen. As small children, they would stand by her side whilst she played the piano them, and they would join their voices to hers in English ballads. negro spirituals, and old Scottish airs. ... Nowadays Princess Elizabeth's preferences in classical music lean rather towards Beethoven, Brahms, Chopin, Haydn, Handel, Schumann, and Tchaikovsky. The Princesses have had formal voice training, but singing comes as second nature to them. Both have agreeable light soprano voices, clear and true in quality. You can often hear them singing in the corridors, and in the lift, as they come in with their dogs from a walk in the Palace gardens, and they nearly always sing together when they are out riding... The Princesses' love of singing was taken a stage further when the madrigal singing parties, which have since become regular institution, were started in May 1943, at the Queen's suggestion. It all began when Her Majesty asked Dr William H Harris, organist of St George's Chapel, Windsor, to talk to the Princesses about music for a short while each week. With him they learnt to read a musical score. He introduced them to the famous "Ladye Nevells Booke", the 16th Century collection of virginal music. Here was a new source of delight to them. The Queen, noting their newly-awakened interest in Old English music, suggested they might enjoy and come to understand it even better if they got their friends to join them :n singing madrigals and part-songs. So the weekly parties started. I have been present at some these parties, and can speak of the atmosphere of happy informality. Those are not "performances" for the benefit of an audience. They are essentially musical parties at which the guests sing for their own enjoyment. Dr Harris generally chooses the programmes. Some of the songs he accompanies on the piano; more often than not he stands beside it and conducts - without a baton. Although the singing itself is taking seriously and the standard is remarkably high, the guests have fun too. There are often unrehearsed incidents which cause a great deal of laughter. Dr Harris "brought the house down" when, after sitting on a rickety chair, which collapsed under him, announced with mock gravity that the next item would be "Chairs to mend".'

Shew goes on to say:

'But I would not like to give the impression that the Princess lives only on the musical heights. She likes to play records of good light cabaret artistes, and jazz of all kinds. Both she and Princess Margaret have many Bing Crosby recordings. They are very fond of the Andrews Sisters. Princess Elizabeth often gives her sister gramophone records as birthday and Christmas presents. One of her gifts was recording of " Sentimental Journey." One of Princess Elizabeth's favourite records is the famous Cole Porter number "Night and Day".'

---

[162] Mabel Lander was a pupil of Theodor Leschetizky and teacher of pianists Benno Moiseiwitsch and Artur Schnabel as well as composer John Ireland.

If the King and Queen were entertaining guests up at the Castle, there would sometimes come a request for organ music in the Chapel after dinner. The Royal Family and guests 'would wander about the Chapel, illuminated only by moonlight, and Harris would play by the light of a small electric torch' (because of the war-time black-out regulations). 'The audience would come and go in the dark. It was so informal that you might have been sitting next to the King without realising it.'[163]

However, Royal interest in Harris's playing pre-dates the war. Percy Whitlock notes in his diary entry for December 1938 the following: 'He [Harris] says the Queen and the young princesses go to hear him play sometimes in the loft, after lock-up, but the King says he's only interested in Wurlitzers!'[164]

The Organ of St George's Chapel

Mention must be made of the rather unusual organ at St George's. In the decade before Harris's arrival in Windsor, not only had the fabric of St George's Chapel undergone major restoration work, but a major rebuilding of the organ had been completed. It had been noted for some time that the main walls supporting the chapel vaulting were slowly moving outwards and expensive remedial work was begun in 1921. In order to repair the Quire and Transepts it was necessary to remove and store (in the Nave) the organ, this work being undertaken by J W Walker & Sons. As a temporary instrument, Walkers installed a small 7-stop, 2-manual 1905 Foster & Andrews instrument in the Nave adjacent to some temporary choir stalls. As Roger Judd notes in his comprehensive account of the Windsor organs:

> 'One can't help but feel sympathy for [Sir Walter] Parratt, ending his working life at St George's with such a poor thing.'[165]

Following the appointment of Walford Davies as organist in 1927, planning began for the restitution of the main organ. The planning of the case and the new instrument, incorporating some complex ideas from the new organist proved to be a long-winded process, beset with political storms involving the Chapter and the various organ builders. A full account of this can be found in Chapter V of Judd's book.

Sir Walford was very (almost obsessively) keen to have two independently working consoles of a design patented and built by Frederick Rothwell of London. They were designed for two players to use the instrument simultaneously, but with completely independent control except for the swell boxes. It had been hoped that Harrison & Harrison of Durham would provide

---

[163] Personal reminiscence from Harris's Grandsons Robert and Duncan Eggar April 2017.
[164] Riley, Malcolm, *Percy Whitlock: Organist and Composer*, London, Thames Publishing, 1998.
[165] Judd, Roger, *The Organs in Windsor Castle: Their History and Development*, Oxford, Positif Press, 2015

the pipework with Rothwell constructing the keyboards and action. In the end Arthur Harrison felt unable to accept this partnership and the organ was built jointly by J W Walker and Frederick Rothwell. The two consoles, pictured below in Rothwell's workshop, were inaugurated at a morning service on 4 November 1930.

Walford Davies at the Rothwell console (L) and a close-up of one of the consoles (R).

Frederick Rothwell (1853-1944)

From the age of 22 Rothwell learned his trade whilst working for the London firm of Gray & Davison, eventually becoming a skilled voicer and tonal finisher. He set up business on his own around 1890. He was joined in the business by his son George and the firm continued until the death of George in 1960.

He became acquainted with Sir Walter Parratt whilst working (for Gray & Davison) on the organs at Magdalen College in Oxford, and had also worked on the 1882/1883 Gray & Davison organ in St George's Chapel.

Walford Davies's relationship with Rothwell was also longstanding. The rebuilding of the Temple Church organ in 1910 was entrusted to Rothwell and used his patented stop-key control system whereby stop-keys placed above each manual replaced the conventional stop-knobs on either side of the console.

H C Colles wrote in his biography of Walford Davies that the Temple organ was:

> 'the organ of Walford's dreams, and on it he made his dreams come true'. For George Thalben-Ball it was 'the most beautiful organ in the world'. Walford Davies became an enthusiastic advocate of the Rothwell control system which enabled the player, in Walford Davies's own words, "to glide from stop-key to stop-key while still playing, without the slightest break in the musical thought and without the slightest turn of the head or any irrelevant muscular effort".'

William Harris must have also admired Rothwell's console design for, shortly after he was appointed to St Augustine in Edgbaston in 1913, the organ there was rebuilt by Rothwell with one of his new consoles.

When complete the cost of the St George's organ was around £1000 over budget, largely because of the extra console required by Walford Davies, but, in March 1931, Sir Walford sent a personal cheque to the Canon Steward for the overspend[166]. The new organ was first used in November 1930. Quite early on in Harris's tenure there were problems with the organ, mainly due to dirt and moths (eating the felt) and complete cleaning and repairs were required in 1940 and again in 1954. Around 1958 the second console was disabled and was cannibalised for spare parts.

Sir Walford's enthusiasm for the double console included the argument that they would make possible antiphonal accompaniment of the choir by two organists. He and his assistant Malcolm Boyle enjoyed accompanying in this way and Sir Walford wrote:

> 'When we both left, we seemed to stand at the beginning of discoveries that await future students of antiphonal accompaniment, and antiphonal playing generally. It is too early to predict how far-reaching for good its reverent and persevering use may prove.'[167]

With hindsight we now see that Davies' initiative has left no legacy.

Judd mentions a personal letter from Lionel Dakers[168], latterly Director of the RSCM, but who was appointed from Finchley Parish Church as assistant to Harris in 1949. He sheds light on the use of the two consoles. Services in the Quire were accompanied from the south facing console but without the aid of mirrors or CCTV. He says:

> In order to have some visible contact with the choir below you could draw back the curtains which went across the screen and peer down as best you could. This prompted the Duke of Edinburgh, being a naval man, to offer Sir William a periscope, a suggestion which was not taken up!'

The second console was at the west side of the screen facing east. It was used for Nave services (the Sunday Eucharist) and for recitals. Dakers mentions that:

> 'Sir William, having accompanied Evensong in the Quire, would often use the second console for his voluntary. Using this second console was even more difficult, even impossible, as to visibility, as you had your back to the musicians below. If there was a conductor in the Nave my task was to relay the beat by tapping on Sir William's shoulder.'[169]

---

[166] £1000 in 1931 is equivalent to about £70,000 in 2017. A year later Walford Davies was repaid the money following a generous gift to the Chapter.

[167] From Walford Davies's *Memorandum and Report to the Chapter of St George's Chapel on Musical Questions (1927-1932)*. This quotation given in Judd *Op. cit.*

[168] Judd *Op.cit.*, pp.131/132

[169] Dakers 1995 *Op.cit.*

Regarding Harris's improvisations he recalled:

'In those days Matins was sung on most weekdays, after which Sir William delighted in getting me to improvise with him using both consoles. While he enjoyed modulating into remote keys, and as I did not have perfect pitch, he would get annoyed if I lost my whereabouts; he eventually gave me up as a lost cause. When Henry Ley was Precentor of Eton College they managed with far greater success.

Strange though these console arrangements were, it was an invaluable experience for a young fledgling like myself.'

Harris at a Rothwell console (undated, source unknown)

One surviving link between Harris and this organ is an arrangement of the slow movement of Mendelssohn's *Octet* Op. 20 that he made specifically for these two consoles.

Harris during the early years at Windsor

Windsor Recordings

The first recording by St George's Choir was made in 1924 by Columbia Gramophone Company, under the direction of Revd Edmund Fellowes, who "held the fort" as interim Master of the Choristers following the death of Sir Walter Parratt, and before Sir Walford Davies had taken up the post. To call this a recording of the choir is slightly misleading, as it was recorded in the company's studio at Hayes, with only six boys and one each of alto, tenor and bass grouped around a recording horn. The recording was of a complete choral evensong. *The Church Times* of March 13th 1925 reported: 'A unique achievement has been accomplished by Dr E H Fellowes and a choir from St George's Chapel in recording for the gramophone the Church of England service with the evening canticles.' It is historically significant, however, being the last acoustic recording made of a choir. Electric recordings using a microphone came in the following year and in 1926, the Columbia Gramophone Company recorded the choir in the Chapel over two days in December, including the *Magnificat* from *Stanford in G* with John Anderson as the boy soloist. A number of recordings of St George's choir followed, made during the time of Sir Walford Davies, one of which was in July 1930, again for Columbia. The first broadcast from St George's Chapel was on 22nd February 1931, prior to Harris's arrival.

In 1948 Harris and the choir were asked to record a hymn for use in a film sound-track. The film was *Once a Jolly Swagman* (in the USA the title was *Maniacs on Wheels*) starring Dirk Bogarde, released in January 1949. The film, a story of speedway riders, uses the hymn, "The strife is o'er" – one verse full choir and the start of the second verse sung by the lay clerks. It occurs, to a backdrop of St Paul's Cathedral, at the end of WWII[170]. Despite Harris's dislike of recordings, this recording was made, probably at Easter 1948 in the Chapel, and this was followed up by a choir visit to Pinewood Studios, only seven miles from Windsor.[171]

Between 1949 and 1954 Columbia Records embarked upon a series of recordings, using leading cathedral and chapel choirs of the day. This series, entitled *An Anthology of English Church Music*, involved St George's choir under the direction of William Harris, and with Edmund Fellowes as the artistic director. Surprisingly, Columbia issued the series on 78's, rather than on LP's which had already started to take over.

Music-making beyond the chapel

Of all his organist appointments, Harris was probably happiest at Windsor. His tenure lasted almost three decades during which he composed a considerable amount of music both for choir, organ and also larger-scale pieces for the Three Choirs Festival; *O quanta qualia* at Gloucester in 1934, and *Michael Angelo's Confession of Faith*, which was premiered in 1935, when the Festival was in Worcester – with Harris conducting. His organ piece *Flourish for an Occasion* (1948), was performed at the Hereford Festival in 1955 by WHH himself, was included at the organ recital given at the opening Festival Service at Gloucester in 1959, played by John Sanders, and again the following year at Worcester, played by John Birch. The *Saraband Processional* of 1949, was played by Michael Burton at the Hereford Festival in 1961.

Harris also had two premières at the London Promenade Concerts. His *Overture: Once upon a time* was performed on 5th September 1940 at the Queen's Hall by the London Symphony Orchestra, conducted by the composer. Sir Henry Wood commented afterwards that 'the overture was a nice, clean, clever work, a great success.'[172] The reviewer in *The Musical Times* described it as "...a charming work of light calibre suggested by some recollections, exclusively pleasant, of youthful experiences"[173] The *Liverpool Daily Post* reported[174] that:

---

[170] The film is available on YouTube. The hymn is at 1 hour and 19 minutes.
[171] For a complete list of commercial recordings by WHH see Appendix 3
[172] Pound, Reginald, *Sir Henry Wood: A Biography*, London, Cassell & Co, 1969
[173] *The Musical Times* October 1940 p.424.

'[the overture] purports to recall memories of the composer's youth, of holiday in the Highlands, of a Jack-in-the-Green in England, and so on. From the music we deduce that all of them are pleasant memories, with never a disturbing thought. In other words, it is pleasant, easy-flowing music, agreeable to the ears but, frankly, not particularly exciting.'

Other items in the concert included the first piano concerto and fourth symphony by Tchaikovsky.

Two years later, on 4th August 1942 Harris conducted the BBC Symphony Orchestra in his *Heroic Prelude* at the Royal Albert Hall[175]. By coincidence, Tchaikovsky's fourth symphony was on the menu again; along with the double concerto for violin and cello by Brahms, Grieg's piano concerto and a curiosity by Eric Fenby entitled *Overture 'Rossini on Ilkla Moor'*. The piece received a second performance that year at the RCM when the College First Orchestra played it under the baton of Reginald Jacques on 10th December. The Proms' performance was described by one critic as:

'a short piece of elegiac character inspired by the valiant deeds of recent years. Unlike some of the composers invited to direct their own works, Dr Harris is an experienced conductor and a many-sided magician. His new prelude is commendably free from the kind of ponderous solemnity which real heroes are disposed to resent. If it may be described as academic, it is only in the best sense of that much abused word. In short, it is a distinguished page of music, not unworthy the kind of occasion for which it is intended.'[176]

Harris was not one to eschew modern music. In May 1951, in one of the organ recitals to celebrate the Festival of Britain, WHH gave the first London performance of Howells' *Chorale, Fugue and Epilogue*, which had been composed in 1940 but was not published by Novello until 1953.

Towards retirement

Not surprisingly, after so many years' constant service in the Chapel, there were, latterly, occasional signs of *anno dominie*. Whilst commenting on Harris's unfailing technique, Alastair Sampson, a former chorister at St George's during the 1950's, nevertheless makes mention of an unsteady control of pulse in later years:

'There would be consternation down in the choir stalls as long introductions to such anthems as Haydn's *Insanae et vanae curae* gathered speed before the time came for the choir to start singing.'[177]

Shortly before he retired, Harris recounted the following anecdote, when both the Duke of Edinburgh and Benjamin Britten had been with him in the organ loft during morning service:

'The Duke has asked Benjamin Britten to write something for St George's choir. I wonder what it will be like. I hope that it will be alright.'[178]

It certainly was, the result was Britten's now well-known *Jubilate in C*, given its first performance in the Chapel in July 1961. Incidentally, in a forthcoming performance scheduled for October, the Leeds Festival programme wrongly stated that they would be giving the first performance. This prompted Harris to write to *The Musical Times* in September, with the following correction:

---

174 6th September 1940
175 The Queen's Hall in Langham Place, Marylebone, was the venue for 'The Proms' from their inauguration in 1895 until it was destroyed by an incendiary bomb in May 1941. The Royal Albert Hall was used from July 1941.
176 *Liverpool Daily Post*, 5th August 1942.
177 Sampson, Alastair, CD Notes by Alastair Sampson for *Sir William Harris: Anthems* Naxos 8.570148, 2006.
178 Hodgson *Op. cit.*

'...Mr Britten was anxious that it [the *Jubilate*] should be ready for us to sing before my retirement in July. This it was our pride and pleasure to be able to do, and we sang it for the first time on Sunday July 16th.'

This premiere, together with Harris's final evensong, was a most fitting finale to his time as organist at Windsor. He retired from St George's in 1961 at the age of 78, having given 28 years' service to the Royal Chapel.

On retirement from Windsor, Harris attended Buckingham Palace for an "informal private luncheon party" on 8th November 1961, not his first visit to the Palace, for in 1942 he had received his CVO from King George VI there.

It is interesting to note that Harris had been appointed to St George's for life. It had long been the custom in many of the professions, and indeed the clergy, to make life-time appointments, expecting the post-holder either to announce their retirement when they considered the time to be right to do so, or to die "in harness" as in the case of Walter Parratt, at the age of eighty three. In some cases delayed retirement was of a necessity, the provision of a pension too often being inadequate; but one cannot help feeling that with Harris, it was to take a well-earned rest. However, it is worth observing that in Harris's case, he still had much to offer beyond the present-day statutory retiring age. One suspects that much talent is lost by having an inflexible arrangement such as this. Many musicians especially are able to continue bringing a wealth of experience to similar posts. In fact, having reached his 65th birthday, it was a further 13 years' service which Harris gave to both St George's and the RSCM.

Presentation to WHH on his retirement in 1961

Front Row (left to right):
Gerald Knight, WHH, Clement McWilliam

Back Row (left to right):
Tom Pinder[179], Robert Davies,
Bamfield Cooper, Philip Howell,
Frederic Hodgson, Cyril Ash, Arthur Raine

---

[179] This photograph was from the late Tom Pinder and is used in Hodgson *Op. cit.*

Chapter 7: Royal Occasions

The first state occasion in which Harris was involved, was the funeral service of Princess Victoria (sister of King George V) on 7th December 1935. Harris conducted a relatively simple service, at the King's expressed wish, which included the Croft *Funeral Sentences* and Walford Davies' *God be in my Head*. Following on shortly afterwards was the funeral service of King George V on 28th January 1936. The music for this was left entirely in Harris's hands. This too was a more modest service than the funerals of Queen Victoria and King Edward VII had been. On this occasion, Croft's *Funeral Sentences* and

The funeral of King George V. The cortege arrives at St George's Chapel.

Walford Davies's *God be in my Head* was supplemented by *I heard a voice from Heaven* by John Goss. The hymn *Abide with me* was also included, it being a particular favourite of King George. Harris also made a special arrangement of the *Dead March in Saul* by Handel for the occasion. For both the funeral of Princess Victoria and King George V, only the top 14 choristers were required to sing. Previously, for the funeral of King Edward VII, all 24 choristers sang – at the insistence of Sir Walter Parratt, whose rule was that *all* boys sang at *all* the major services. He objected to what he termed as "pet boys wrapped up in cotton wool."[180] Was this a case of Harris not being as insistent as Parratt had been?

Even more high profile was the Coronation of George VI in 1937, in Westminster Abbey at which Harris was a sub-conductor and for which he composed the Offertorium *O hearken thou*, with orchestral as well as organ accompaniment. At this service – all the St George's choristers attended. However on the occasion of the marriage of Princess Elizabeth to Lieutenant Philip Mountbatten on 20th November 1947, Harris was invited to send only his top six choristers to sing at the wedding in Westminster Abbey. That the Abbey choir was augmented by choristers from Windsor on this occasion, was reported in newspapers as being a tribute to Harris, who had taught music to the Princess. The choice of music was in the hands of Princess Elizabeth, however the King had stipulated that the service was to be a straightforward marriage service, and not a state ceremony, and that the service should not exceed 55 minutes' duration. Harris was invited to play for the two anthems, one of which was *Blessed be the God and Father* by S S Wesley. The following anecdote regarding the 1947 service and quoted in the biography of Sir William McKie, concerns one of the rehearsals at which Harris, who was on the organ, had been taking a boy's solo (presumably the middle section of the Wesley) at a slow pace. McKie then gave this passage to his "top eight" [Westminster Abbey choristers] saying to them privately, "'You come along with me and never mind Doc H." So they did. And William Harris, the perfect gentleman, came along too, but against his better judgement.'[181] An observer at the time noted 'while Doc H played, he looked more like the White Rabbit (from *Alice in Wonderland*) than ever, rocked slightly to and fro, and kept saying to himself quietly [...] "too fast, too fast."'[182]

On 25th August 1942 Prince George, Duke of Kent, aged 39, son of King George V and brother of King George VI, died when a military plane taking him to Iceland, crashed in

---

[180] Wridgway *Op cit.*

[181] Hollis, Howard, *The best of both worlds: A life of Sir William McKie*, Melbourne, Sir William McKie Memorial Trust, 1991.

[182] *ibid.*

Scotland. Three days later Sir Arnold Bax, only recently appointed as Master of the King's Music, sent a *Funeral March* to Harris saying:

> 'I have just orchestrated this short piece for incorporation into another work, and I wondered whether it might be suitable for the Duke of Kent's funeral (played by you on the organ).'

Bax felt the tragedy personally as he was a long-time friend of Lieutenant John Lowther, The Duke of Kent's Equerry, who was also killed in the crash. The music was subsequently used (retitled "The Ruins") in Bax's 1942 film score for "Malta G C " Sadly the score arrived in Windsor too late to be used at the Duke's funeral. To Bax's delight, Harris thought it would make a good organ piece and he proceeded to arrange it, as usual for a three-manual organ – he rarely wrote for less than three manuals, and it was published in 1945. Bax's original score is still in the Harris archive and WHH wrote on the cover 'I played this at King George VI's Funeral in St George's Chapel (AB was with me in the organ loft).'[183]

There were many other Royal funerals in Windsor. Two such were on 3rd November 1944 and 17th March 1948, those of HRH The Princess Beatrice, daughter of Queen Victoria and then her daughter, HRH Princess Helena Victoria. These occasions were generally reported in the 'Court Circular' of *The Times* with the addition of "The Music was rendered by the Choir of St George's Chapel directed by Dr William H Harris". Although a seemingly archaic way of describing a musical performance, a search of the internet shows that 'rendering' of music, still takes place today!

Then, in 1952, there was the funeral service for King George VI held, as is customary for the funeral of a Sovereign, in St George's Chapel. Lionel Dakers recalls[184] that before the start of the service Harris played the '…hauntingly beautiful prelude to Stanford's opera *The Travelling Companion*.' The choir began with Croft's *Burial Sentences*, as is the custom on these occasions and ended with Walford Davies' *God be in my head*. WHH played Bach's "Little" *Prelude and Fugue in E-minor* with great simplicity.

Harris was again appointed sub-conductor for the Coronation of Queen Elizabeth II in 1953, for which he composed the anthem *Let my prayer come up.*

The funeral procession for King George VI

> '22 choristers and 10 lay clerks from St George's Chapel, together with the organist William Harris and assistant Lionel Dakers [...] performed at what would surely be one of the greatest occasions of their careers. Each would receive a Coronation medal, along with other members of the College, as a memento of the event, and as a further commemoration, the choristers chose to put their expenses towards a new garden-seat for the playing fields..'[185] [Or was this choice made for them, one wonders?]

Former chorister Allan Ledger joined the choir just before the 1953 Coronation and recalls:

> "Even 65 years on when I hear Handel's *Zadok the Priest*, my eyes start to prick and my throat to quiver with vivid memories of the Coronation."[186]

---

[183] The story of this piece is recounted in letters from Bax to Harris.
[184] Dakers 1995 *Op. cit.*
[185] Eleanor Cracknell (Assistant Archivist) on www.stgeorges-windsor.org.
[186] Letter to the authors 3rd June 2018.

The 1953 Coronation choristers with Doc H

In the photograph above, Allan Ledger is the chorister on the front row at the left end and Alistair Sampson is standing to the immediate left of WHH. The choristers, Lionel Dakers (at the back on the left of Canon Christopher Hare) and Harris are all wearing their Coronation Medals. Harris is also wearing his CVO and his two war service medals.

The last of the magnificent royal occasions in which Harris took part was the wedding in Westminster Abbey of Princess Margaret to Anthony Armstrong-Jones on 6th May 1960. Six choristers from St George's were invited to take part, and Harris played the organ before the service, concluding with his *Processional*, specially composed for the occasion, on the entrance of the Queen.

Another tradition, unique to St George's Chapel, are the services for the Most Noble Order of the Garter.

The Most Noble Order of the Garter

The order of chivalry known as the Order of the Garter, a maximum of 26 members including the sovereign, was founded by King Edward III. The exact year is uncertain, but it was decided in 1948 to determine 1348 as the year of origin and to arrange sexcentenary celebrations during 1948. Originally a gift of the sovereign, for most of the last 300 years the Garter appointments were made on the advice of the government until 1946 when the appointments once again became a personal gift of the Sovereign. After investiture, normally in private, the recipients process in grand ceremony to St George's Chapel, the mother church of the order, for installation in one of the 26 specially designated stalls inside the chapel. In December 1946 Rear–Admiral Viscount Mountbatten of Burma and five others were invested at Buckingham Palace[187] rather than in Windsor because of bad weather and their installation was deferred, not taking place until 1948. The following year in November, HRH Princess Elizabeth was invested by her father in the order with Prince Philip's investiture following a few days later on the eve of their marriage.

On St George's Day, 23rd April 1948, and for the first time in 146 years, the first full chapter and installation service of the Order was held. After the private ceremony in the morning and

---

[187] The first ever investiture at Buckingham Palace, all previous ceremonies had been in Windsor.

lunch there was a procession, watched by 10,000 people, to St George's Chapel for the installation ceremony. For this occasion Harris composed his anthem *Be strong in the Lord*. Three months later the 600th anniversary celebration service took place on 18th July for which Harris composed his anthem *Ascribe unto the Lord*. The other music in the service included *Ecce Sacerdos Magnus* by Vittoria, during which the Archbishop of Canterbury processed to the sanctuary and *Stanford in C* canticles.

The anniversary celebration events were spread over eight days and, according to *The Musical Times*,

'The aim of this year's eight-day festival was not only to commemorate the sexcentenary year of the foundation of the Order of the Garter and of the College of St George, but also to concentrate on the work of English composers, especially those associated with St George's Chapel from the sixteenth century to the present day. The Chapel choir sang their daily services, contributed a programme and combined in another programme with Eton College chapel choir. The St Michael's Singers, the Cantata section of the Oxford Bach Choir, the Morley College choir and orchestra, the Windsor and Eton Choral Society, the Vivien Hind String Quartet, the Slough Philharmonic Orchestra (strings) all contributed programmes, and Dr Fellowes gave a lecture on English Cathedral Music. The conductors were Dr W H Harris, Dr Sydney Watson, Dr Harold Darke, Dr Thomas Armstrong, Mr Michael Tippett and Mr Anthony Hopkins; and the organists Dr Henry Ley, Mr Philip Moore and Dr Harris.'

There is also a second genre of Garter service, namely the "Annual Festival of the Friends of St George's and Descendants of the Knights of the Garter". This service, confusingly known as 'the garter service' falls on St George's Day. According to Fellowes[188], the music for the Garter service in 1937 was a marked improvement on the pre-war [WWI] services. There had been a lapse of 23 years since the last Garter Service in 1914.

The music in 1937 was chosen by Harris: *Let thy merciful ears* by Thomas Weelkes[189], *The righteous live for evermore* by C H Lloyd, *As the whirlwind passeth* by Walter Parratt and a specially written setting of the *Te Deum in B-flat* by Harris. This *Te Deum* was popular with the choristers who looked forward to singing it '...largely I suspect because it included a high B flat [below], a challenging rarity in our repertoire.'[190] The public were admitted after the service and WHH gave a public organ recital[191].

Many singers seem frightened of high notes, but clearly not the choristers of St George's!

---

[188] Fellowes *Op. cit.*

[189] At that time this beautiful short piece was thought to be by Weelkes. It is now considered to be the work of Thomas Mudd (1619-1667).

[190] Statham *Op.cit.*

[191] Together with guest artistes; violinists Jelly d'Arányi (1893-1966) and her sister Adila Fachiri (1886-1962).

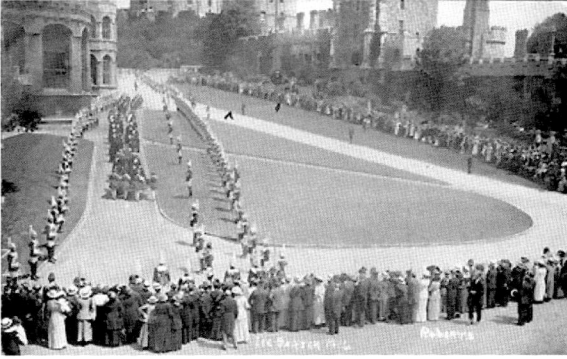

Procession following the 1914
George V Garter Service

The Princesses Elizabeth and
Margaret Rose attended the
1937 Garter Service.

Harris's musical input to the Royal Family, including the musical direction of many royal occasions, the Garter Services, and the sub-conducting of both the 1937 and 1953 Coronation services resulted in his appointment as CVO [Commander of the Royal Victorian Order] in 1942[192], and a KCVO [Knight Commander of the Royal Victorian Order] in 1954.

He received his CVO at Buckingham Palace from King George VI on July 18th 1942 and received the KCVO from the Queen at Windsor Castle on the morning of 15th June 1954. Her Majesty then went to the Ascot Races in the afternoon.

King George VI and Queen Elizabeth
leave the 600th Anniversary Service for
the Order of the Garter, 18th July 1948

---

[192] Most major honours require parliament's consent, and so Queen Victoria established the Royal Victorian Order in 1896 as a junior and personal order of knighthood that allows the Sovereign to bestow direct honours for personal services to him/herself or to members of the Royal Family. The first and second classes of the RVO were knighthoods (Knight of the Grand Cross, GCVO and Knight Commander, KCVO), whereas the third (Commander, CVO), fourth (Lieutenant, LVO) and fifth (Member, MVO) were not.

Royal Command Concert on Empire Day 24th May 1938

In 1935, by command of King George V, a concert was organised for Empire Day[193] and in 1938 King George VI and Queen Elisabeth issued a similar command:

'It is Their Majesties wish that the concert shall fulfil the same two aims as that of Jubilee Year [1935] – to exemplify and encourage the nation's music making at its best and to benefit musicians in need.'

Both these concerts were masterminded by Walford Davies, Master of the King's Music, and there were contributions by sectional choirs, quartets and solo singers as well as mass choral items with orchestra. The 1938 concert was broadcast to the Nation and to the Empire.

Invitations to send a specific number of singers were sent to 288 Choral Societies around the country and the 1700 'delegates' so recruited received a 127pp. music book published by Novello. With the addition of the Royal Choral Society and other London singers, the choir numbered almost 2000. One of the features of these concerts was the performance of national songs of the four nations and so Welsh texts were heard in addition to English and Latin, though the Scottish folk-songs were sung in their English dialect form and Ireland was represented by *Heraclitus* by Stanford. The music book does not include Harris's contribution or George Dyson's *Homage Anthem*, written the previous year for the King's Coronation and which also featured.

Harris, who by then was in his fifth year at St George's Chapel, was asked (presumably by Walford Davies) to contribute something. He chose to set war poet Siegfried Sassoon's *Everyone Sang*, written in April 1919, shortly after he had been discharged from his commission. It is widely assumed to represent the front-line soldiers' reaction on hearing that the war was over.

The official dedication of Harris's offering reads "Specially composed for the Royal Command Concert, Royal Albert Hall, Empire Day 1938" but Harris also subsequently wrote on his copy "for Owen Morshead who first showed me the poem. WHH October 1938"[194].

Set for tenor solo, two part female chorus and orchestra, Harris also noted on his copy - "Sung by Walter Widdop[195], conducted by Malcolm Sargent". Sargent conducted most of the massed choir with orchestra items but Sir Hugh Allen also took part.

The Times reviewer of the concert mentioned 'There was another new work in the form of a spirited song by W H Harris, which Mr Walter Widdop introduced [and sang]. This was *Everyone burst out singing* [the opening lines of *Everyone sang*] and, coming near the end, the words seemed a just comment on the whole occasion.'[196]

---

[193] Empire Day in the UK was instituted in 1904, although it had previously been observed in Canada from 1898. From 1958 it was renamed Commonwealth Day and is still exists on the second Monday in March, marked by a multi-faith service in Westminster Abbey.

[194] Major Sir Owen Frederick Morshead GCVO KCB DSO MC (1893-1977) was a British Army officer and librarian, who served as Royal Librarian in Windsor between 1926 and 1958 and became a close personal friend of King George V.
Harris's 1939 3-part song "May" is also dedicated to Morshead – inscribed "For Owen who sent me this poem from somewhere in the East". Their friendship was rooted in their mutual love of reading and poetry.

[195] Walter Widdop (1892-1949) was best known as a Wagnerian operatic singer.

[196] *The Times* 25th May 1938

Chapter 8: Addington

Addington Palace near Croydon was the former country residence of the Archbishop of Canterbury and in 1953 became the new home of the Royal School of Church Music, serving as its headquarters until 1996. The College of St Nicholas, formerly based in Chislehurst, Kent, before WWII and at Canterbury post-war, was a full-time residential college for training church musicians with a boys' choir on which the students could hone their skills. It was based at Addington until the College's closure in July 1974.

Harris had been appointed Director of Studies at the Headquarters of the Royal School of Church Music at Addington Palace in 1956[197]. The following announcement appeared in *English Church Music*, the RSCM's quarterly magazine, in May of that year:

> 'We also congratulate ourselves on our further good fortune in securing Sir William Harris as Director of Musical Studies. Sir William visits Addington from Windsor once a fortnight and we have quickly come to value highly his friendly association with us. It is a great honour to have with us one who has achieved a world-wide reputation as choir trainer, organist and composer.'[198]

Interestingly, the editor of ECM here puts "choir trainer" first, rather than organist.

Why should Harris even contemplate taking on another commitment at this stage in his career, having just relinquished his duties as professor at the RCM? The answer may well be that he was already missing the contact with trainee church musicians.

Several people have implied that the appointment of Harris was more a cosmetic one, to add credibility to the RSCM's educational credentials. Nonetheless many of the better students benefitted from his occasional one-to-one lessons. Harris's contact with the RSCM however, goes further back than his appointment as Director of Studies. During the Second World War Harris had been on the Council of the Church Music Society (CMS), and would have known Sir Sydney Nicholson, founder of the School of English Church Music (forerunner of the RSCM), who had replaced Walford Davies as Chairman. Harris had also been appointed one

---

197 For a history of the RSCM at Addington Palace see *The Royal School of Church Music: The Addington Years* by John Henderson and Trevor Jarvis, Salisbury, RSCM, 2015.
198 *English Church Music,* Croydon, RSCM, May 1956.

of the first Fellows of the College of St Nicolas in 1937[199]. He was the SECM examiner, along with Sir Ivor Atkins from the RCO, and Canon Crawley from Lambeth Palace for the newly-introduced Archbishop's Diploma in Church Music in October 1937. In addition, Harris was on the Music Advisory Board of the RSCM at its inception in 1946 retiring three years later as required by the board's constitution.

Just as Harris had acquired a nickname among the choristers and gentlemen at St George's (Doc H) and was known as Billy to his friends, so he was to acquire yet another at Addington among the students, who referred to him as Sir Bill [but probably behind his back].

> 'Every fortnight we enjoyed a visit from Sir William, who gave a chosen few an organ lesson and provided an evening's entertainment with a short talk followed by a sing–along, which he directed from the piano in the Great Hall – all very memorable, if not of the highest musical standard!'[200]

One student was less complimentary about Harris, observing that some students from the Commonwealth felt that Harris regarded them as "second best." However, this may be that some were not necessarily "first division" students. Gerald Knight, when Director of the RSCM, was keen to add to the number of overseas students studying at Addington, and one may speculate that he might have been more generous in his acceptance of them[201].

It is on the occasion of one of Harris's visits to Addington, when it was the custom of students and staff to gather in the Great Hall and sing through a choral work, that Martin How remembers being introduced to Carissimi's *Jeptha*, and being moved by its poignant last chorus. Martin also remembers the occasion, during an organ accompaniment session; when Harris was asked to play his own composition *Behold the Tabernacle of God* (written for the opening service of Addington Palace in July 1954), and noted the legato, unhurried cantabile style which was so typical of Harris's generation[202].

Martin goes on to recount the following anecdote: 'At one of these evenings Harris was talking about the possibility of singing through Handel's *Judas Maccabeus* on a subsequent visit, and asked if anyone had copies.

> Marjorie Spence, wife of the Warden, said, "Sir Hubert Langley – who is coming next week - has copies."
> "Well ask him to bring them," replied Harris.
> Marjorie continued, "Poor Sir Hubert, he has had shingles."
> Harris, either mishearing or misunderstanding [or perhaps mischievously misunderstanding] replied, amid much laughter, "Well, ask him to bring them."'

Such Harris anecdotes abound. Perhaps another one here will suffice:

Student:	(sharpening pencil during harmony and counterpoint session)
Harris:	What is that?
Student:	It's a pencil sharpener, Sir William
Harris:	It's a what?
Student:	A pencil sharpener
Harris:	Oh yes, what does that do?
Student:	It sharpens pencils, Sir William
Harris:	Fancy that!

---

[199] The original 1936/1937 Fellows of the College of St Nicolas were appointed as a governing Council. There were three categories of Fellowship, 1) Life, 2) By appointment and 3) Ex-officio (such as the organists of York Minster and Canterbury Cathedral) and Harris fell into this third category.

[200] Personal communication from Guyon Wells, Addington student 1957/1958.

[201] Lionel Dakers also admitted, when considering the future of residential courses at Addington, that not enough first class students were applying to keep numbers at an economically viable level.

[202] Martin How, Personal communication 2016

… and one of Harris's jokes, again recalled by Martin How:

> A man went into the post office and said, "Have you any stamps?" The person behind the counter showed him a large sheet of purple stamps, and after pondering over them for a minute or two, the man pointed to the middle stamp and said, "Oh yes, I'll have that one."

Harris rather liked the punch-line of this joke, and repeated it on a number of subsequent occasions, accompanied by a pointing gesture, and could be observed through the rear window of his departing taxi still making the same gesture.

Here, and in the previous anecdote, one can't help but feel Harris is rather putting on an act of "a doddery old man" – probably for his own amusement as well as that of his audience. An example of this is on his arrival at Addington, he professed never to remember the way to the dining room, and would approach a passing student with the words, "Oh yes, where do I go?" on every occasion. One student recalls a particular female student who would wait breathlessly for Sir William Harris's chauffeured arrival from Windsor, and Harris '…was never so frail and wobbly as when Ann [the student] was there to help him up the long grand staircase ascent, each clinging to the other for dear life.'[203]

Commenting on Harris's visits, Lionel Dakers wrote in the RSCM's *Church Music Quarterly* magazine[204]:

> 'Addington in those days was an unduly inward–looking community, so his [Sir William's] visits had particular importance; and not only for that reason, but because his complete musicianship fitted him so perfectly for this task. However, he had a strange propensity for dissembling this.'

He relinquished his post of Director of Studies at the RSCM in 1961, at the same time retiring from his post as Organist at St George's Chapel. Dr Gerald Knight, Director of the RSCM, attended the presentation ceremony at Windsor following his retirement. The RSCM quarterly magazine *English Church Music* for June 1961 announced the news of his standing down from both Addington and Windsor: 'As organist, choirmaster and composer, he has made his name, and all of his very many friends will wish him health and happiness in his well-earned retirement.'

Ten years after Harris's death Canon Cyril Taylor wrote the following:

> 'In the evenings [at Addington Palace] he sometimes presided at the piano over the 'singing through' of some major work in the Great Hall, and on other occasions he came to our large sitting–room, which provided a superb acoustic for the then new hi–fi recordings, and introduced students to some work on disc. They were much amused, I recall, when his final introductory comment on the Elgar *Enigma Variations* was, "I knew Dorabella". It was in the same room that he accepted the suggestion that he should write an anthem on *This Joyful Eastertide*, which Novello in due course published and where, in 1958 I think, he handed me the manuscript of *Bring us, O Lord* with the characteristic words, "Do you think this will do?" A few weeks before my wife and I left Addington in 1958 for Cerne Abbas in Dorset, we received a postcard in his hand, written in the village, enthusing over its beauty, asking to be considered for the next vacancy on the organ–stool, and signed Henry G Ley, William H Harris: organ–blowers (unpaid).'[205]

---

[203] Henderson/Jarvis Addington *Op. cit.*
[204] *Church Music Quarterly* July 1983
[205] *ibid.*

Chapter 9: Petersfield

Retiring with his wife to Petersfield, Hampshire in 1961, to live with their daughter Anne Eggar, must have been quite a sea-change for Harris, now aged 78, suddenly being without the commitment of the daily round of services in the Chapel, and the fortnightly trips to Addington Palace. He was not at all practical about the house. The domestic routine was maintained by his wife and even during his years at St George's she organised his days. He normally had a rigid routine, breakfast, coffee and biscuits and afternoon tea all arranged at fixed times. All he needed to think about was his music. In retirement it was breakfast, composing, coffee, composing, tea, composing etc. – all organised for him.

However, he was not one to remain idle and he continued to compose right up to the end of his life. He also attended the local Petersfield Music Festival, where he was 'expected to be seen, but played no active part in it'.

The Petersfield Musical Festival

The origins of the Petersfield Musical Festival lie in the inspirational effect of the Mary Wakefield Festival of Music at Kendal in 1897 on two sisters: Edith and Rosalind Craig Sellar. The history is recounted in *Petersfield Music Makers* by Marjorie Lunt and Mary Ray, published by the Petersfield Area Historical Society in 1986. The sisters hailed from Compton in West Sussex and their enthusiasm and drive to bring a similar event to Petersfield resulted in the first Petersfield Festival taking place in the old Drill Hall in 1901, attracting six choirs, various individual and group competitions and a hall full of music lovers. Edith Craig Sellar was one of the conductors involved in the first performances, while her sister Rosalind took on the role of accompanist. The Petersfield WI joined the Festival competitions with a choir in 1902. Later, as Mrs Alexander Maitland, Rosalind conducted the Children's Day choirs (in 1913-14 and 1921-23).

He received many visitors in Petersfield. 'Both he and his wife made many friends throughout his working life, and many used to visit them in retirement, including the Dyson and Dakers families.'[206]

The death of his wife Doris in 1968 was a considerable blow, affecting him deeply. He was supported through this sad time by his family, and especially by his daughter Anne, with whom he was living, and many local friends.

Sir William lived on, reaching ninety on 28th March 1973. Herbert Howells wrote an appreciation of him on the occasion of his 90th birthday in *English Church Music*, a collection of essays published by the RSCM:

> 'Petersfield is but another name in the long list of centres and places – London, Lichfield, Oxford, Windsor among them – to which he [Harris] has given vital and devoted service. [...] with undiminished confidence and technical alertness, he still goes to his work-table: ready to demonstrate that eight-part counterpoint and double choir texture can achieve shining clarity...' [207]

The BBC also marked Harris's 90th birthday on the 28th March 1973 with the broadcast of a recital given by Nicholas Danby on the organ of St George's Chapel, the programme being introduced by Herbert Howells. The music was *Fantasia on a tune by Campion*, *Prelude* (the E-flat piece written in the Thomaskirche), the Slow movement from *Sonata in A minor* and

---

[206] Personal reminiscences of Duncan and Robert Eggar.
[207] Howells *Op. cit.*

finishing appropriately with *Flourish for an occasion*. Furthermore, Choral Evensong that day, which was broadcast live from Salisbury Cathedral conducted by Richard Seal, included an introit, *Let the lifting up of my hands* and anthem, *Bring us, O Lord God*, both by Harris.

Howells' introduced his Radio 3 programme with brief tribute to WHH in which he said:

'And I have in mind an imagined miracle. It's just this: that if this present year were *1573*, and a mature Harris a part of it, famous Tudor musicians would be saluting him – birthday or *no* birthday – they would know him as a composer of their own kind, enriching (as they themselves were enriching) music dedicated to the service of the Church. They would be acknowledging him as an equal in their own illustrious company.'

In announcing Nicholas Danby's recital, Howell's went on:

'...a select few of Sir William's organ works – works that will be a reminder of the composer's own brilliance as an organist. Those works will do even more. They will stress the fact of his unfailing stylistic gifts; and may even rebuke some of us who may be writing for a noble instrument as if it were a substitute for a one-man orchestra.'

Also resident in Petersfield was the well-known tenor Wilfrid Brown (1921-1971), who would often visit Harris, and they would play and sing together. In July 1962, soon after Harris arrived in Petersfield he composed *Three George Herbert Songs* for Brown and these were given their first performance on the BBC Home Service on 29th May 1964 by Brown accompanied by Edna Blackwell[208]. There were other musicians who visited and played piano duets with him, but many were terrified at the speed he took things. There was obviously no loss of finger dexterity.

One of Harris's last compositions, written at Petersfield, was *Prevent us, O Lord*, written for the Petersfield Choral Society, and published in *The Musical Times* in the September 1973 issue. However, Harris's final major composition, written for the 1,300th anniversary of Hexham Abbey, was *In Christ Jesus*. Harris's daughter Margaret Brockway recalls that he had been working on it for some months and, having posted it off, said with great pleasure, 'Now they will have it in good time.'[209] Only just, as it turned out as Harris died soon after on the 6th September 1973. His last dated *ms* is a hymn tune for the text "Love divine, all loves excelling" signed 7th August 1973.

For some time there has been a "Chinese whisper" circulating that Peter Phillips, founder and director of *The Tallis Scholars* was present in the house when Harris died. Peter writes:

'The story has done the rounds a bit, and I have long wanted to nail what actually happened. In early September 1973 I was 19, living in a house which gave onto the lake at Petersfield, as did the house of Anne Eggar. Staying with me at the time was the (now) composer Francis Pott, whose family I knew well. He must have just passed his 16th birthday. We had recently moved into this house, and my mother was keen to make new friends around the lake. Since we knew very well that Harris was living in the house, we decided to go to meet Anne Eggar, and hope to meet him. In the event he was too ill to receive us, so we sat downstairs and he lay upstairs. History does not record the exact date of our visit, but it must have been very close to the day he died since we only moved into the house in the late summer of that year. However I never actually met him.'[210]

---

[208] Subsequently Head of Music at Stonar School near Bath, she was musical director of the Bath Cantata Group for 38 years until retirement in 2013.

[209] Brockway *Op. cit.*

[210] Email communication to the authors July 2017.

The October issue of *Promoting Church Music*, the RSCM's quarterly magazine, announced the news of his death to the membership. RSCM Director, Lionel Dakers, wrote:

'[He] was one of the last surviving members of a generation whose eminence, derived from the powerful influence of composers such as Parry, Stanford and Charles Wood, and did much to guide succeeding generations in paving the way for the best in church music today. For future generations, when the personal memory [...] will of necessity has passed, there will be his music. The depth of sincerity, let alone the craftsmanship underlying its message will, without any doubt, continue to enhance the repertoire of English church music.'

In 1977, following his own death, a wrought-iron gate, together with a memorial plaque, was installed at the entrance to the Addington Palace gardens. The plaque has now been returned to the family. Also, a set of water colours, depicting the five major places where Harris had worked, were placed in the music room. These were given in memory of Sir William Harris by his gifted painter son-in-law, Michael Brockway. They were eventually returned to the family when the RSCM moved into smaller accommodation.

It is fitting that both he and his wife are interred at the foot of the organ loft stairs in St George's Chapel.

WILLIAM HENRY
HARRIS
K.C.V.O. M.A. D.MUS.
1883-1973
FOR TWENTY-EIGHT
YEARS ORGANIST OF
THIS CHAPEL AND
KATHLEEN DORIS
HIS WIFE
1889-1968

Centenary Concert

On Saturday 19th March 1983 a concert was arranged by the Friends of St George's and held in the Chapel to mark the centenary of Harris's birth. The Queen, Queen Mother and HRH Princess Margaret were all present. The Chapel Choir was directed by Christopher Robinson with assistant organist John Porter at the organ. The programme was:

1.	(i)	O what their joy and their glory may be	
	(ii)	From a heart made whole	
	(iii)	Strengthen ye the weak hands	*Harris*
2	(i)	Prayer of King Charles I	*Henry Ley*
	(ii)	King of Glory	*Walford Davies*
	(iii)	Collect for St George	*Harris*
3.		Flourish for an occasion	*Harris*
4		Latin Magnificat	*Stanford*
		Interval	
5	(i)	Sicut cervus	
	(ii)	Super flumina Babylonis	
	(iii)	Exultate Deo	*Palestrina*
6		Four Short Organ Pieces	*Harris*
		Prelude – Reverie – Interlude – Scherzetto	
7	(i)	Bring us, O Lord	
	(ii)	Lord of love and light of light	
	(iii)	Faire is the heaven	*Harris*
8		Hymn (for all to sing)	
		Lead, kindly light. Tune – Alberta	*Harris*

Lionel Dakers wrote in the concert programme:[211]

> Tonight's recital ends with the hymn "Lead, kindly light" sung to the tune *Alberta*. Inspired by a journey through the Canadian Rockies, the music relays something of the breadth and spaciousness of the mountain splendour. Because of its superior qualities as compared with Dykes' tune, *Alberta* is now firmly established and widely used as one of the memorable hymn tunes of the 20th century.

Whilst many of us would agree with this sentiment and the tune is now in many hymn books, 35 years on *Alberta* still remains relatively unknown in parish churches where Evensong is an increasing rarity and the elderly congregations cling to Dykes.

Just over a week later, on 28th March 1983, there was a centenary concert broadcast on BBC Radio 3 which included the biographical talk by Herbert Howells already mentioned.

For the centenary, artist Michael Brockway, Harris's son-in-law, designed a postcard depicting St George's and a representation of two organ consoles.

211 Dakers 1983 *Op. cit.*

Chapter 10: His Music

The Ascension Opus 1

Harris began composing at an early age with his first extant work, proudly bearing the legend "opus 1", dating from 1891 when he was between eight and nine years old. His lifelong love of early poetry has already been mentioned, but is remarkable that a boy of this age would choose such poetry for his first substantial work – a 32-page offering in eleven movements. The text is *An Hymne of the Ascension* by William Drummond of Hawthornden (1585-1649). Many of the movements are joined with interludes including such subtleties as using the swell box and articulation. The overall effect is reminiscent of a Handel Chandos Anthem. The *ms.* is marked "William Henry Harris Jnr" – to distinguish him from his father.

Harris's lifelong restless self-critical urge to improve and revise his compositions is apparent even in this early work – pencil marks in the third and final bars.

Another early work is an *Evening Service in A*. The Bodleian Library copy is dated 24th September 1897 and the composer is again given as William Henry Harris Jnr.

EVENING SERVICE IN A. [1]

Set to Music

BY

WILLIAM H. HARRIS, JNR.

LONDON:
WEEKES & Cº, 14, HANOVER ST., REGENT ST., W.

Price 3ᵈ

The writing, whilst that of an untrained musician, is considerably in advance of what may be expected from a twelve or thirteen year old boy. Given the date, this piece must have been written and sent to the publisher before Harris went to St Davids. Therefore, it looks as if this Magnificat and Nunc Dimittis was his first *published* work, possibly written in Tulse Hill, where he would have been familiar with singing the Evening Canticles.

What of the adult Harris? As to be expected, a significant impact on his music comes from Parry, whose *Blest Pair of Sirens* (1887) influenced an entire generation of church composers. What might be termed the "big tune" structure encountered in this work (especially that sublime moment with the trebles' entry on the words *O may we soon again renew that song*) is found in several of Harris's anthems, notably *Vox Ultima Crucis* (a unison setting of the poem 'Tarry no longer', 1937), *The Lord my Pasture shall prepare* (1944) and *Laudamus* (written to celebrate victory after WWII, 1945). Looking at the dates of composition, one wonders whether there is a link with the employment of a strong tune, and the particular times through which the country was passing. More pronounced, maybe, is the use Harris makes of harmonic colour, especially in his enharmonic modulations. Examples here include *From a heart made whole* (1935), *Praise the Lord O my soul* (1938), *Be strong in the Lord* (1948) and, particularly, in *Faire is the Heaven* (1925) – which must surely remain one of his crowning achievements.

Dakers wrote in the 1983 Centenary Concert programme:

> As a composer, he was at heart a romantic, with his best works obviously influenced by the texts he elected to set. If he had written nothing more than *Faire is the heaven* he would have been assured an immortal place in the annals of English church music. His penchant for getting to the core of a text through double choir writing of great distinction was again revealed in his setting of John Donne's *Bring us, O Lord God at our last awakening*, written in 1959.

> Even if his settings of canticles come into a slighter and perhaps sometimes less inspired category, as with some other examples of his quicker moving music, the anthem *O what their joy* being a notable exception, it was poets of the calibre of Spenser and Donne who drew from him his best in contrapuntal writing. Not least in this was the influence of the 17th century Italian composers such as Palestrina.

> William Harris was also a not inconsiderable composer for the organ, with pride of popularity going to the *Four Short Pieces* (1938), Although *Flourish for an Occasion* is also frequently played, his earlier organ sonata deserves to be better known. The profound slow movement of this erudite work owes an acknowledged allegiance to the hauntingly beautiful Prelude to Stanford's opera *The Travelling Companion*, which he played at the funeral service for King George VI.'[212]

---

[212] Dakers 1983 *Op. cit.*

Harris composed at a fairly steady rate, completing around three pieces a year throughout the Lichfield and Oxford years, rising to four a year through the Windsor years, five a year during the Addington years and six a year in retirement. A generalisation of course, but it shows that, although he did not consider himself a composer, the urge to write was constantly present. Bryan Hesford described Harris' work as 'unpretentious and direct' and having a certain 'dignity and charm.'[213]

The Double Choir Motets

Although it is not the authors' intention to critically examine individual works, mention should be made of WHH's achievements in writing for double choir. It has been noted that he could play at sight with ease from eight part choral scores and it is clear that he could also think and compose on this broad canvas in a way that many have failed to emulate.

Faire is the heaven 1925

As already quoted from Lionel Dakers, *Faire is the heaven* alone would have assured Harris of "an immortal place in the annals of English church music." No *ms.* is extant, but the motet was almost certainly composed at New College and was "affectionately" dedicated to Sir Hugh Allen on publication in 1925, a year when Allen was actively trying to discourage Harris's involvement in the Monteverdi *Orfeo* production. Their relationship remains difficult to understand.

In 1948 Harris revised the piece – see Appendix 2 for a list of revisions – though the changes are so slight that even an expert ear in the audience/congregation would barely notice them. It is a further example of Harris's quest for 'endless perfectnesse' in the fine detail.

Love of Love and Light of Light 1934

Although Robert Bridges is not regarded as a metaphysical or mystic poet like George Herbert, one can see why this poem caught the eye of WHH. Both the Harrises and Bridges lived in Oxford through the 1920's and the authors suspect that they were friends or at least acquaintances. The motet is dedicated to Mary Monica Bridges in memory of her husband who had died in 1930. The piece is dated March 28th 1934. Harris was by then in Windsor and one wonders if this piece had been several years in gestation after Bridges' death before he regarded it as ready for publication. By the second bar it is clearly a work of WHH (or Parry) and, although shorter and with less enharmonic modulation than 'Faire', it is a worthy successor. The final climax on 'evermore' quickly fades to a quiet ending looking towards eternity – another Harris trademark. The only other text by Bridges to be set by WHH was the SATB part-song *Awake, my heart, to be loved* in 1946.

Praise the Lord, O my Soul (Psalm 103) 1938

Harris's next foray into 8-part writing was a large-scale setting of Psalm 103 – *Praise the Lord, O my soul* – published in 1938 for the Oxford Bach Choir who gave the first performance in the Sheldonian Theatre on 27th November 1938 under Thomas Armstrong. WHH notes on the score that he was unable to be present as it was his daughter Anne's confirmation that day at St Mary's School in Calne, Wiltshire. The piece is dedicated to the memory of Sydney Charles Scott who had died in December 1936 at the age of 87. Scott's eldest daughter Marion, author of the text of Harris's first hymn tune 'Ewell', was a lifelong friend of WHH and so the attribution was natural.[214] The setting is a little old-fashioned with the influence of

---

[213] Hesford *Op. cit.*

[214] Musicologist and violinist Marion Scott (1877-1953) studied at the RCM and probably knew WHH there. She was accompanied in concerts by WHH and they became lifelong friends. She was god-daughter to Margaret Harris (Brockway).

Parry and Stanford throughout and it is not until some way into the piece that the lush writing and enharmonic modulations appear.

O joyful light of the heavenly glory 1939

With 7th Century words from the Greek the opening bass solo conjures up an image of a bearded Eastern Orthodox cantor. This gives way to four part hymn-like homophony before a more lively section of imitative entries at 'Therefore we give thanks' which allude to polyphony of an earlier time. It is only halfway through that the double choir antiphonal entries begin. The constant juxtaposition of major and minor gives an unsettled feel to this short evening anthem.

The Beatitudes 1942

Dedicated to the memory of Walford Davies who had died the previous year, these short petitions rarely stray from E-flat. Charles Wood and Walford Davies seem to influence the earlier sections and the first mystery in G-flat is reserved for 'they shall see God'. 'The kingdom of heaven' sees the only fortissimo in the setting and the final page reveals another peaceful and timeless ending where all sense of bar lines is lost as the music drifts off. A thing of beauty but not perhaps his most inspired work.

Thou hast made me 1947

According to John Patton's monumental survey *A Century of Cathedral Music 1898-1998*, this anthem was not in the repertoire of the 84 choral foundations surveyed in 1958, 1986 and 1998 and a recent internet search failed to find any performances of it. Whilst not Harris at his most inspired, this setting of John Donne is surely unjustly neglected. There are moments of drama and some expressive imitations in the voice parts. It is ironic that Donne's text refers to the writer's work going to waste and this is certainly the case with Harris's music.

Bring us, O Lord God 1959

34 years on from *Faire is the heaven* and only two years before his retirement at the age of 78, Harris created another masterpiece with his spacious setting of John Donne's text 'from a sermon preached at White Hall' on 29th February in 1627 or 1628 in a version by Eric Milner-White.

> 'Bring us, O Lord God, at our last awakening into the house and gate of heaven, to enter into that gate and dwell in that house, where there shall be no darkness nor dazzling, but one equal light; no noise nor silence, but one equal music; no fears nor hopes, but one equal possession; no ends nor beginnings, but one equal eternity: in the habitations of thy majesty and glory, world without end.'

With such a text, was Harris thinking of his own mortality? Whatever his thinking his creativity peaked again with this musical vision of heaven, rich in texture, the text wonderfully dramatised and with magical moments such as the chords on 'dazzling' and the final cadence.

It is well-known that in 1958, on one of his fortnightly visits to Addington Palace to teach at the RSCM, Harris showed the newly-completed manuscript to chaplain Cyril Taylor with the comment 'Do you think this will do?'[215] Taylor's reply is never quoted, but, with retrospect we can reply – Yes, it most certainly will!

The beauty of heaven 1970

Lastly there is his unpublished setting of selected verses from Ecclesiasticus Ch 43. He finalised the text in March 1969 and initially composed an anthem for SATB with organ before deciding to rewrite it as an unaccompanied work for double choir. There are many drafts amongst

---

[215] Henderson/Jarvis Addington *Op. cit.*

Harris's papers. The final draft is dated 4th June 1970. It is extremely old-fashioned for its time but there is nonetheless skill in setting the rhythm and mood of his chosen text.

Other texts

Further examples of Harris's 8-part choral writing can be found in the *Magnificat in E* canticle of 1908, composed for Walford Davies and the Temple Church Choir whilst he was a RCM student, and in *From a heart made whole* of 1935, though the writing in this SSAATTBB anthem is divisi rather than truly double choir. The unpublished *My spirit longeth for Thee* is SATB with some splitting into Decani and Cantoris.

Finally there are two 8-part setting with organ – *The Heavens declare the Glory of God* (based on Gibbons' Song I) 1930 and *Offertorium: O hearken Thou* 1937.

The Hound of Heaven

Harris's most ambitious large-scale work was a setting of the allegorical Christian poem *The Hound of Heaven* by English poet Francis Thompson (1859–1907), Thompson's most acclaimed work. First published in the magazine *Merry England* in July 1890 edited by author Wilfrid Meynell (1852-1948). Meynell effectively 'discovered' this new young poet and published an anthology (including 'The Hound') of Thompson's poems in 1893. The poem was further reissued in the *Oxford Book of English Mystical Verse* in 1917 – the same year that Harris started work on his setting[216].

In 1917 the Carnegie United Kingdom Trust invited British composers to submit manuscripts of unpublished works to a competition called the Carnegie Publication Scheme. Only British born and resident composers were eligible and there were five categories of music:

  a. Concerted chamber music for three or more instruments.
  b. Concerto for one or more solo instruments, with accompaniment for large or small orchestra.
  c. Choral work, with accompaniment for large or small orchestra.
  d. Symphony or other orchestral work of an important nature.
  e. Opera or musical drama, including incidental music to plays.

Up to six pieces were chosen annually to be published by Stainer & Bell. The winners of the award secured two benefits; firstly the publication of their work at the expense of the Trust; and secondly the securing of copyright and royalties on their behalf.

The scheme allowed publication of several major works including the *London Symphony* by Vaughan-Williams. Harris won the award in 1919 with *The Hound of Heaven*. In that year there were 64 entries and five awards were made in total. Besides Harris, the others were – George Dyson: *Three Rhapsodies for string quartet*, Gustav Holst: *The Hymn of Jesus*, Percy Hilder Miles: *Sextet for strings in G-minor* and Sir Charles Stanford: *Symphony No.5*, the latter hardly new as it was composed in 1894.

World War I made the implementation of the Carnegie scheme difficult. Due to a shortage of engravers the winning composers had to wait several years before seeing their works in print. In the case of Harris, the vocal score was published in late 1920 and the full score in 1921, this sadly causing two further planned performances in Liverpool and Glasgow to be cancelled. The Trust's Ninth Annual Report in 1923, noted that Harris's work had sold 230 copies, Rutland Boughton's *Immortal Hour* 480 copies Edgar Bainton's *Before Sunrise* 568 copies. Not a commercial success in comparison with Gustav Holst's *The Hymn of Jesus* with 8500 copies sold.

---

[216] Composer Maurice Jacobsen (1896-1976) also set Thompson's THOH for tenor solo, S.A.T.B. and orchestra in 1953 with a first performance in Birmingham the following year.

In retrospect it is clear that panel of anonymous judges[217] who made the annual awards had somewhat eclectic tastes and, whilst admitting that a few masterpieces were discovered through this scheme, their choices, mostly from young lesser-known composers, were critically scorned in both the British and American general and musical press and the majority of works published in this so-called "Carnegie Collection of British Music" were destined to be forgotten. In lamenting any analysis or comment on both Harris's work and all the other works in the collection, Erpelding[218] notes that:

'There is no mention of the work's musical merits, even though such rudimentary information is available in the advertisements and press releases put forth by the Carnegie Trust in the 1920s[219]. Notably, the most thorough analysis of The Hound of Heaven to date is within a 1921 pamphlet by Percy Scholes, which was commissioned by the Trust to increase the dismal sales of the works within the collection.'

Erpelding writes that the work is approximately 25-30 minutes in length, although the Stainer & Bell listing of Carnegie works gives 40 minutes. The first performance was on 4th December 1918 by the Birmingham Festival Chorus under Allen Blackall, actually before official publication by Stainer & Bell. *The Birmingham Daily Post* reviewer Ernest Newman (1868-1959), one of the most celebrated music critics of the time, noted that:

'In his setting of 'The Hound of Heaven' Dr Harris has done one strikingly new thing: he has phrased English poetry with the nicest ear for its rhythms, its varied footfalls, its changing cadences. The accuracy of the prosody is remarkable; it is not the least exaggeration to say that no other English work, for solo voice or for chorus, shows anything like the same combination of elasticity of musical phrasing and regard for the natural rhythm of the spoken line.'[220]

The performance was first announced in the *Birmingham Daily Post* 29th July 1918 and so the work must have been complete or close to completion by then. A second performance with the same musical forces was given in Birmingham Town Hall on 4th February 1920 again with positive press reviews:

'...gave for the second time Dr William H Harris's fantasy for baritone solo, chorus, and orchestra, entitled 'The Hound of Heaven,' set to Francis Thompson's poem. The favourable impression created at its first hearing twelve months ago was even more emphasised at its second hearing. Mr Allen K Blackall again conducted a vivid and absorbing performance. Choir and orchestra were on their mettle, fully realising the deep-felt character of the music.'[221]

The third performance at Walsall Town Hall on 14th October 1921, during the Staffordshire Musical Festival was given by the Walsall Philharmonic Society and the City of Birmingham Orchestra. It was not a success, mainly due to inadequate preparation. Critic Sydney Grew in *The Musical Times* November 1921 was scathing about the festival in general and about Harris in particular saying:

'Harris' *Hound of Heaven* will not do for Francis Thompson's poem. I say this with regret, for Dr Harris is a very fine musician, and a genuine composer who will do good work in the future. His piece has many charming touches, and a considerable amount of beauty. But it is entirely away from the poem, as he himself, perhaps, now perceives. I

---

[217] We now know that the judges for 1919 were Donald Tovey, Granville Bantock and Hugh Allen. The latter two knowing Harris personally to a varying degree and Bantock already having heard the first performance of 'The Hound'.

[218] Erpelding *Op. cit.*

[219] Though the Carnegie Trust did issue an analytical pamphlet by Harris, with musical examples, about the work.

[220] Quoted in *The Musical Times* May 1919 p.138

[221] Reviewer Sydney Grew in *The Musical Times* March, 1920, p.195

am astonished the Carnegie adjudicators recommended the setting; either they had not read the poem, or, reading it, had not understood it.'

Harris himself was not happy with the work and in May 1919, even before it was printed, he had written to the Carnegie Trust to ask if he could revise part of it that he found "a little unsatisfying". He was never satisfied with the piece and when Stainer & Bell readvertised the Carnegie choral works in 1939, THOH was not included. Erpelding speculates that 'A more plausible theory is that Harris pulled *The Hound of Heaven* from Stainer and Bell's catalog'. Such a deliberate action is supported by Harris's daughter Margaret's assertion that he had no wish for it to be performed – adding that 'Nobody knows why'.[222]

THOH then lay dormant for many years, although in biographical sketches of Harris it was often referred to as his 'magnum opus'. The next known performance was given in Rochester Cathedral in July 1948 by Rochester Choral Society. As far as the authors are aware, there were no more performance until July 2015, when Paul Spicer directed THOH (with piano) at Dore Abbey and was much impressed by the work.

How did Harris come to write a work, which is in so many ways atypical? Thomas Armstrong suggests that it was through the 'stimulating influence of Granville Bantock, and the active musical life [at the Birmingham and Midland Institute] that surrounded him.'[223] (article from *The World of Church Music* – RSCM 1983) Armstrong describes the work as being of a 'fiery character, uneven perhaps, but rising to moments of real eloquence.' If Harris had pursued this path, of which THOH is a perhaps tentative, but none-the-less imaginative first attempt, then the world of church music would have been the poorer, and the name of Harris far less well known. The fact that Harris's devotion to providing music for the liturgy focussed all his compositional powers in one direction, has surely secured immortality.

The Songs

Although the authors have focused on WHH's sacred and organ music in this book, Harris's skill in setting texts extended beyond sacred music into his songs. His love of the written word, especially poetry, inspired a large output of song, from his early days at the RCM through to the *Three George Herbert Songs* composed for tenor Wilfrid Brown in his retirement years. Harris often composed for specific singers, but also contributed to the burgeoning epidemic of part-songs, unison songs and duets of the early 20th Century. Such choral singing, and especially in schools, is not extinct, but has declined to the extent that much of the repertoire is out-of-print. The texts of that time also appear dated to 21st Century audiences that they are unlikely to be revived in the near future. Whilst settings of Shakespeare and George Herbert are timeless, such titles as *Lines on the Massacre at Piedmont, Fairy flight* and *The hunt us up!* have little attraction for choir directors and singers of today.

Sir Thomas Armstrong wrote:

> 'Regrettable too is the fact that many [songs] have gone out of print, including some songs for children's voices, which show the composer at his best. There is real magic in *Someone* and *The Witches' Steeds*, beautifully and sparingly written and sensitive in feeling'[224]

Amongst the songs for children are two, *I know a baby* and *If the sun could tell us half*, composed by WHH for each of his two daughters which were included in a collection of unison songs boasting the title *Kikirikee*[225] and published in 1925 by The Year Book Press. The

[222] Parker *Op. cit.*
[223] Armstrong, Sir Thomas, 'William H Harris (born 28 March 1883)' *The World of Church Music 1983*, RSCM, 1983.
[224] *Ibid.*
[225] The strange title is from one of Rossetti's nursery rhymes. The anthology is still available from Banks Music Publications.

texts were all by Christina Rossetti (1830-1894) and many composers, including Herbert Howells, Charles Wood, George Dyson, C S Lang, Henry Ley and Edgar Bainton contributed a pair of short (two-page) songs to the collection. It was a follow-up anthology to *Kookoorookoo and other songs* published in 1916 – again texts by Rossetti with composers including Hubert Parry, Percy Buck, Sir Charles Stanford, Walter Parratt, Walford Davies, Frederick Bridge and Walter Alcock.

The Instrumental Music

Apart from the orchestral *Heroic Prelude* and *Overture: Once upon a time* mentioned earlier, WHH's instrumental music falls into two groups – the student works and later pieces written for individuals, mainly family and friends.

The early student exercises include *Theme with Variations* for string quartet 1900, a *Sextet* for string quartet, flute and clarinet of 1901 and the *Theme with Variations* 1901 for piano.

One work stands out as being worthy of revival – a grandiloquent romantic violin sonata in D, composed in Lichfield in 1915 and revised in Windsor in 1935. The score was returned to Harris by violinist Sybil Eaton[226] in 1957 "20 years late" suggesting that she must have performed it around 1935/36.

The Sacred Choral Music

Of the 75 published anthems, barely a handful are widely known but amongst the remainder there are many short introits, not too difficult for a good parish choir, though some have divisi. Many are unaccompanied though a few have complex organ parts such as the fine anthem *Prelude to a Solemn Music* ("Let God arise"). A glance through the first pages to be found in Appendix 2 should enable choirtrainers looking for new repertoire to judge the difficulty level of most pieces.

The Organ Music

In 1899, just as he began his studies at the RCM, Harris contributed two short organ voluntaries to the series *The Anglican Organist*[227] published by Dr Charles Vincent (1852-1934). Vincent taught harmony and was an examiner at TCL. Most of the compositions in this series were garnered by the two editors Vincent and Dr Edward John Hopkins (1818-1901), organist of the Temple Church in London for 55 years, an examiner for TCL and a founding member of the RCO. Some pieces were commissioned, or at least requested, by the editors and others were no doubt submissions by the composers themselves. Although Harris frequented the Temple Church during his RCM years, Hopkins had already retired from there in 1898, at the age of 80, and they probably did not meet there, although it is known that Hopkins would 'regularly drop in to see Walford Davies.'[228] Vincent was at TCL and so one wonders how a commission came Harris's way for, with his humble nature, he is unlikely to have pushed these pieces forward himself, especially as they are not ground-breaking. Hopkins was not an RCO examiner when WHH took his diploma examinations.

It is possible the *Andante in D* had been composed earlier than 1899 as the dedicatee was William Montagu Brooke (1861-1939), acting organist of St Davids Cathedral briefly before the appointment of Herbert Morris and the arrival of Harris. In triple time and visiting the relative minor in the middle section, there are no great surprises in its ABA construction, melody or harmonic language, but it is fluently written.

---

[226] See p. 279
[227] There were 20 Vols. of *The Anglican Organist* published between 1894 and 1900.
[228] Horton, Peter, "Edward John Hopkins: an organist and choirmaster re-examined (II)", *RCO Journal 2010*, p.34.

The *Allegretto in F#-minor* is typical of its time and of many other pieces in *The Anglican Organist*, a charming melody played in various registers. One slightly unusual feature is that he does require the melody to be "thumbed down" onto the Great manual at one point. It could be a piece by Hollins, Lemare or Wolstenholme and certainly does not give any indication of the spiritual or poetic Harris to come.

It would be over 20 years before Harris would again publish organ music – the *Fantasy on the tune "Babylon's Streams"*. Dedicated to his friend Harold Darke, the work was begun in Lichfield in 1916 but revised and published in 1922 whilst he was at New College, Oxford. The 1916 version is markedly shorter and different to the final published edition. Thomas Campion's tune "Babylon's Streams" has almost disappeared from the hymn books of today, but was formerly best-known set to the text "That day of wrath" – the *Dies irae* paraphrased by Sir Walter Scott. Whilst Harris conjures up plenty of wrath in his final ten-minute version, there is an indication on the early draft version that other thoughts were in his mind. An ink annotation under the title quotes Psalm 137: 4 "How shall we sing the Lord's song in a strange land" and Campion's original tune was a setting of Psalm 137 – "By the rivers of Babylon, there we sat down, yea, we wept, when we remembered Zion." Certainly and despite the Aeolian modality, this music is packed with angst, flourishes of disquiet and unresolved chords reminiscent of Parry, but ultimately resolving onto a major chord of hope, that of A-major, one of Harris's favourite keys for organ writing.

Three years later, still at New College, WHH published an *Improvisation on the Old 124th, (Genevan Psalter)*, dedicated to his friend Henry Ley down the road at Christ Church College. The work must have been composed at least a year earlier as Harris himself performed this and *Babylon's Streams* in 1924 at a recital in Westminster Cathedral. The five lines of the Genevan melody are quoted in the first five bars of the work. Only five bars are needed for the whole theme because this hypo Ionian tune is virtually without metre. The whole work is a complete contrast to the Babylon piece, it barely rises in dynamic above *mf* and features no dramatic flourishes, perhaps somewhat out of character with the work's dedicatee. The second variation with its sighing phrases in thirds and sixths reminds one of the preludes of Wood and Parry, both his teachers at the RCM, all published in the previous decade. In this second variation WHH also prefers the organist to have both tune and accompaniment in swell boxes so that both parts can 'played expressively and independently' At least the pedal part is non-legato in much of this section to enable the feet to control two swell boxes.

Harris gives no clue as to his inspiration for this piece but the text for Psalm 125 begins "If it had not been the Lord who was on our side..." Both the above pieces soon featured in recital programmes after publication with Charles Waters (1895-1975) in particular giving several performances of both works in and around London in the 1920's.

In 1930, now incumbent at Christ Church, he published a *Fantasia on an English folk tune*, the tune being "Monk's Gate" from *The English Hymnal*. Harris had by this time been teaching at the RCM for nearly a decade and, through his work there, he would have known [Sir] Walter Alcock, to whom the work is dedicated. Though equally flamboyant as *Babylon's Streams*, this is not so much a set of variations on a theme, but more a rhapsody in which fragments of the tune appear. There is even, unusually for Harris, a fugal episode using a new motive, later combined with "Monk's Gate", but which soon meanders off before the start of a long build-up to the final statements of the theme using double pedal reeds and the Tuba stop. Harris is always good at building towards climax, but whilst full of energy, this work is perhaps less successful than its predecessor – there is more rhetoric than substance.

Despite the aforementioned pieces, and of course *Faire is the Heaven*, Harris was essentially a miniaturist in both organ and choral compositions. His next work was the single page *Prelude in E-flat* famously written whilst sitting in the nave of the Thomaskirche in Leipzig, where his beloved Bach was Kantor, during a holiday in August 1931. A few years later in 1935, when the SECM (the School of English Church Music – later renamed the RSCM) was producing a limited edition *Gift Book* to raise funds, Harris was approached to provide a short piece. Along with Vaughan Williams, Alcock, Walford Davies, Bairstow, Harwood and Henry Ley, twelve living composers contributed pieces and Harris himself provided this *Prelude in E-flat*. Three years later in 1938 he composed three more miniatures and, together with the prelude, they were published by Novello as *Four Short Pieces*. The second of these, *Reverie* was a particular favourite of the composer. He frequently included it in his own recitals and also arranged it for piano solo and for oboe and piano. It is a pity that both this and the 3rd piece of the set, *Interlude in the form of a canon*, have key signatures of five sharps which surely deters amateur organists from experiencing these delightful pieces.

Whilst at Christ Church, Harris made two notable organ transcriptions – of *Nimrod* from Elgar's *Enigma Variations* and *Chaconne: The Grand Dance* from Purcell's *King Arthur*. The former, still in print and in many anthologies, has never been surpassed and the latter is a wonderful example of arranging, even though not perhaps registered according to 21st Century Purcell performance practice.

Published in September 1938, five years into his tenure at Windsor, the three-movement *Sonata in A-minor* was probably some time in gestation but, without any *ms.* sources, and this is the case with virtually all WHH's published works, we will never know. Whilst Harris was continually revising his music before he was satisfied, it would seem (confirmed by his family) that, once a piece had been sent off to the publisher, the project was deemed finished – he was disinterested in having the *mss.* returned and he moved on. His longest organ canvass, this sonata was published in a decade when British composers were still wanting to write in this classical form. Howells (1933), Whitlock (1936) and Bairstow (1937)[229] all published significant sonatas and, apart from a few exceptions, it would be the 1950's (seven composers) and 1970's (eleven composers) when new sonatas by UK composers appeared in publishers catalogues.

Harris's sonata is rather uneven in quality and has neither the melodic nor harmonic inventiveness shown by Bairstow or Whitlock. The first movement in sonata-form is hardly memorable, but the second fares much better[230]. This second movement was issued separately by Novello, though one has to admit that this was not because of its popularity but because 'It is a required piece in examination syllabuses from time to time' The Maestoso final movement in 5-time oscillates between major and minor but again is rather lacking in imagination.

Although Harris arranged and composed music for many royal occasions, his *Flourish for an Occasion*, published in September 1948 is not known to be linked with any specific event. Perhaps the Garter services in 1948 might have been candidates and more than one source makes this claim, but the authors have found no evidence for this. We do know that Harris performed the piece before publication at St Andrew's Parish Church in Rugby on 7th April 1948 together with his recently published *Fancy* – this was two weeks before the Garter Service on St George's Day. A newspaper report of the recital does not mention whether or not this was first performance but he also played it the following year at St Mary Redcliffe in Bristol when the newspaper[231] review specifically mentions 'the brilliant and rousing "Flourish for an Occasion" (no specific event disclosed)'. Harris also played the piece after the 1000-voice RSCM Festival of Britain service in the Royal Albert Hall in June 1951. A popular recital piece in the grand English style and, despite its coruscating arpeggios, 'Flourish' seems almost a

---

[229] Less well-known composers who published sonatas in the 1930's include Ian Parrott (1933), Ronald Chamberlain (1935), Gordon Phillips (1939) and Thomas Pitfield (1939).

[230] See Lionel Dakers' enthusiasm for this on p. 72

[231] *The Western Daily Press* 29th September 1949 – the review made the front page.

demeaning title for such a substantial ceremonial work. There is a restless Elgarian urgency throughout, especially in the pedals, which drives the work through a noble central section to a grand ending in this, probably Harris's best-known organ composition.

The remainder of Harris's organ pieces are miniatures ranging from 1 to 4 pages , some for specific occasions and some requested by Novello for their *Festal Voluntaries* series.

The majority of these pieces are romantic offerings in pastoral 'Evensong' style, rooted in the Elgar tradition with a whiff of Percy Whitlock and Alec Rowley. Very self-contained and introspective, they are notable for their fluency of movement and a dynamic ebb and flow that rarely reaches *forte*. Even in the 1950's this was rather backward looking music and of course he was in his 70's when he composed most of them. In an era where British organ music was becoming modernist, especially in cathedrals and that parish organists rarely have the three manuals and pistons needed for adequate performance, that these piece were never really fully adopted into the repertoire. A pity, because they are a joy to play. In contrast to his choral music when he sometimes uses existing melodies, only three of his organ pieces are based on hymn tunes. The *Epilogue on "Dix"* and *Fantasy on "Easter Hymn"* in *Festal Voluntaries* are reasonably ambitious in scope and extrovert[232], but the *Meditation on the Tune "Cheshire"* (No. 2 of *Three Opening Voluntaries*) is a stylistic oddity. Using only two manuals, a 3-part texture accompanies the hymn tune declaimed in unadorned long notes giving a rather baroque style piece. This is unique in Harris's output and perhaps his brief for this commission (for the 1956 IAO Congress in Edinburgh) required a simple piece for parish organists. It is a pity that the tune is little used today.

His *Processional March* was composed shortly before he retired from Windsor for the wedding of his former piano pupil, HRH Princess Margaret, which took place in Westminster Abbey in 1960. It is annotated "played by the composer at the Marriage of HRH Princess Margaret" but does not appear on the official order-of-service which states that the *Flourish for an occasion* and *Saraband Processional* were played before the service, perhaps an error by the printers.

The *Elegy & Postlude* in *Two-Stave Voluntaries Set 2* are somewhat slight pieces aimed at beginners, but the use of hemiola in the *Postlude* adds some vigour. Though indeed 2-stave, the use of the pedal, where marked, makes for a more interesting performance.

The *Miniature Suite* of 1957 might almost be short sonata if it weren't for the lack of any thematic links or key structure. The opening Introduction and Fugue (in B-minor) begins with an introductory sarabande followed by four pages of fugue – Harris's longest foray into this genre. A Pastorale (in G) in 12/8-time leads to a set of variations, Romance and Scherzetto (in F#-minor/major), though the short 4-bar theme on which the variations are based is so hidden in the texture that few will notice it.

The story behind the posthumously published *Fantasy-Prelude* can be found on p. 242.

---

[232] Archibald Farmer, critic of organ music in The Musical Times in July 1956 opined: "Sir William Harris has another impossible tune in 'Easter Hymn', and the tact with which he skates away from the melody every time another horror impends must be seen to be believed."

Chapter 11: Performance style

As an organist Harris had inherited from Parratt a wonderful sense of restraint, particularly manifest in his accompanying of the psalms, which were marked by their subtle yet imaginative interpretation. Hodgson, too, refers to Harris's upholding the Parratt tradition of 'an inhibited, impersonal style of singing in which any form of individuality was anathema.'[233] Parratt had insisted on considerable restraint being shown in singing. He would have anthems such as *Lord, for Thy tender mercies' sake* sung without any nuance or variation of tone, in a perfectly level, passionless style. 'That he succeeded in making his choir sing in this impersonal way (under much protest, I am told) is remarkable…'[234] Michael Statham also received the impression that Harris strove for this same style "the rather impersonal, disembodied tone" of the boys' voice[235].

Harris wrote the following pen-portrait of his teacher:

'Tall and spare, pointed beard, very active, quick moving – put on him doublet and hose and there would have been a very complete Tudor figure…'[236]

Thorndike, describing Parratt to his sister Sybil, also gives us a colourful picture:

'His chief characteristic was his hair, which he wore long. [...] it stood straight up on end.[...] What chorister serving under him has not seen him tear at it in rage should any note untunable offend his sensitive ear?'[237]

Of the many Parratt traits which influenced Harris, hair-tearing was not among them!

Parratt in the 1890's (without long hair)

Walford Davies, who was already a chorister at St George's when Parratt arrived on the scene in 1882, commented on his old master's organ playing in the following terms:

'He had a statuesque quality which his critics would call cold and his admirers sane. His proverbial love of Bach is, I think, typical. Those who look for colour and strong rhythmic sense as the signs of a great artist may declare him unemotional; but those who see greater things to love in the intensity and depths of polyphony, and in the stately, noble restraint of the old cathedral school, will claim Sir Walter Parratt as their faithful champion.'[238]

Here again is the term "restraint" which has so often been used to describe both Parratt's and Harris's playing. Harris refers to Parratt's 'economy of registration'. This was especially so in his accompaniment of the psalms.

'Remembering always that unvarying organ tone is apt to pall, he [Parratt] was at pains to vary it by carefully graded diapason, flute and reed, and more often than not in the use of single stops, seldom using two stops when one would do.'[239]

Harris was to continue in the tradition established by his mentor, in both his accompaniment of the psalms and in his playing of Bach. As we have seen in the chapter on St George's, two of

---

233 Hodgson *Op. cit.*
234 *The Musical Times* August 1947
235 Statham *Op.cit.*
236 *The Musical Times* August 1947
237 Thorndike *Op.cit.*
238 Tovey/Parratt *Op.cit.*
239 *The Musical Times* August 1947

Harris's erstwhile assistants (Surplice and Dakers) make particular mention of his sensitive psalm accompaniment.

For the centenary concert programme in 1983 Lionel Dakers wrote:

'In company with those who worked with him over the years, one recalls so vividly his superb accompanying of, for example, the choruses from Brahms' *Requiem* ("it's not what you play so much as what you leave out"), or the miniature score of Haydn's *Seven Last Words from the Cross* which had a permanent home on the organ console and from which he never tired of playing. Not least was his love of finding a partner who would improvise with him on the two consoles which were such a unique feature of the St George's organ in those days. ... As a musician. he was a fine and demanding choir trainer with an uncanny sense of what was needed whatever the occasion, be it at Windsor or for the 1937 and 1953 Coronations, for which he composed miniature anthems of considerable distinction.'[240]

In his memoirs *Places where they sing*, Dakers comments further on the Haydn *Seven Last Words*:

'[He] would delight in playing one of the movements for the voluntary after Evensong. Here, as in Brahms' *Requiem* he would "orchestrate" in a colourful way, even to the extent of including soft sustained chords for the horn parts, so well did he know the full score'

Dakers also observes that Harris's psalm accompaniment was on a par (almost) [Dakers' brackets] with Bairstow's. Alwyn Surplice, who went on to be appointed Organist at Bristol then Winchester Cathedrals, also refers to Harris's artistic treatment of the psalms. In common with what seems to have been standard practice at most cathedrals, Harris accompanied the choir on the organ most of the time 'It became something of an event when WHH conducted an accompanied anthem.'[241] It has been noted that Harris's conducting style, both from the piano at rehearsal, and on the rare occasions when he conducted in the service, was also economic in gestures. "Very small hand movements" one former chorister recalled. 'Doc H was (rightly) of the opinion that conducting in church should never be ostentatious, nor too vigorous, and he made only the minimum amount of movement with his hands.'[242] The last thing that he would have wanted would be to draw attention to himself. It had become a long-standing custom for chapel services during Lent to be unaccompanied. Thus the organ was not used from Ash Wednesday until Easter Day, giving Harris ample scope to put his beloved Tudor music on the music list.

As regards his organ playing, Dakers goes on to make the comment that the fashionable and relatively new pursuit of Baroque interpretation was anathema to Harris, who described it as 'tinkle, tinkle' or 'bubble and squeak' sounds. Harris was an advocate of authentic registration, as well as absolute clarity, and tended not to approve of the use of stops which would have been unknown at the time of Bach. Performing his beloved Bach, Harris would invariably start the fugue using an 8' Diapason. 'Feeling skittish one day he suddenly pulled out the 4' Principal as well and chucklingly proclaimed "Aha – Baroque!" as he set off.'[243] Martin How, member of the RSCM's Headquarters staff, also remembers the same anecdote.

This was contrasted somewhat to the more flamboyant style of Dr Henry Ley[244], Precentor [Director of Music] at Eton College, and a close personal friend of Harris. One chorister at St

---

240 Dakers 1983 *Op. cit.*
241 Dakers 1995 *Op. cit.*
242 Hodgson *Op. cit.*
243 Dakers 1995 *Op. cit.*
244 Henry G Ley (1887-1962), a former chorister of St George's, Windsor, received organ lessons from Walter Parratt. He was a music scholar at Uppingham School and then, aged 15 went to the RCM. He won an organ

George's, Alastair Sampson, comments that, during his five years in the choir, he heard Harris use the tuba stop on average once a year, whereas Etonians were hearing theirs probably five times a week. In many ways, Ley's playing was in a complete contrast to Harris's. His playing in Eton College Chapel has been described as being:

> '...fiery, warm-hearted and always vividly-coloured. The school had a sense of this in his choice of voluntaries. The trumpet tunes of Purcell and Jeremiah Clarke were great favourites, Ley playing them, all guns blazing [...] He also revelled in transcriptions of popular orchestral pieces.'[245]

Ley had had most of the trumpet stops at Eton re-voiced in the 1930's to produce a more powerful sound, and had added (in 1939) a 32' reed on the pedal. Little wonder that the repertoire was chosen to show off the solo reeds. At Eton Ley certainly enjoyed a reputation as a "window rattler."

By contrast, Harris had commented that, with reference to the playing of Bach fugues:

> 'only when reeds are made more beautiful in tone, and there is less desire for fire and brilliance, together with better blending qualities, will Bach fare better. But a prelude and fugue played on modern instruments is often a distressing experience unless the player will cunningly avoid using stops provided by a skilful, but ill-advised builder for the performance of music not originally written for the organ.'[246]

It is hardly surprising then that the St George's chorister, referred to above, would hear the Windsor tuba stop so infrequently. In the same article, Harris also makes the comment; 'Our swell organs are too often ill-designed for clear part-playing, and the unveiling of the contrapuntal texture of fugues.' One is reminded of the quote in Gordon Reynolds' humorous book *Organo Pleno*:

> 'An infallible way of detracting attention from the architecture of the last two pages of any Bach fugue is to allow Full Swell to creep in and blur the edges. This will thrill the listener and also save a great deal of practice time.'[247]

Harris was very fond of improvising after a service, rather than playing a set piece. Indeed there was, on his insistence, no printed list of organ voluntaries on any music list. If asked what he was intending to play as a closing voluntary, his reply would be along the lines of "I'll see what the mood of the service is and then decide what to play". His improvisations 'showed keen imagination and great harmonic resource.'[248] Was Harris's penchant for improvising a result of the Saturdays spent at the console of the Temple Church in his student days, when Walford Davies would give a master-class on improvisation?

The Very Revd Henry Julian White (1859-1934), Dean of Christ Church from 1920 until his death, had made a colourful comparison of the two organists thus:

> 'when Ley plays, it's like Liszt extemporising on the piano: when Harris plays, it's like Bach playing his own fugues.'[249]

Ley and Harris had been students together at the RCM and were appointed professors there within two years of each other. Ley had been a chorister at St George's under Parratt. Thorndike, who was a senior chorister when Ley joined the choir as a small boy, described

---

scholarship to Keble College, and then was appointed Organist at Christ Church Cathedral whilst still an Oxford undergraduate. In 1926 Ley moved to Eton College as Precentor [Director of Music].

[245] Osborne, Richard E., *Music & Musicians of Eton College: From 1440 to the present*, London, Cygnet Press, 2012.
[246] Harris 1935 *Op. cit.*
[247] Reynolds, Gordon, *Organo Pleno*, London, Novello & Co, 1970.
[248] Surplice *Op.cit.*
[249] Personal reminiscence from Sir Thomas Armstrong.

him as '...that rare creature, a natural genius.'[250] Ley would have an intimate knowledge of the chapel and its services from that time. They had subsequently enjoyed a long association, especially as Ley was "just down the road" at Eton College. They, together with their wives, also spent some time together during holiday periods.

Even after Ley had retired from Eton, and moved to Devon, Harris would still call upon him to help out at Windsor. One such occasion was when Harris spent three months examining for the Associated Board in the West Indies[251], and asked Ley to "hold the fort" at St George's. Dakers recalls one occasion when Ley played a piece by Basil Harwood for the outgoing voluntary, which he admitted he had not played for 40 years. Predictably, there were many mistakes. Not in the least disconcerted, Ley turned to Dakers and said "They gathered up the wrong notes – five baskets of them."[252] One is tempted to speculate that, in his heyday, Harris would hardly have filled one basket.

Right:
This photograph is annotated:

**'Sir William & Lady Harris, Dr Henry Ley,
Norwich [IAO] Congress 1954
Taken at Blickling Hall (Anne Boleyn's house)'**

WHH was IAO President 1954/55

Left: Parry Centenary 1948

1948, the centenary of Sir Hubert Parry's birth, occasioned numerous concerts and celebrations. The authors believe that the above photograph was taken during the Oxford Festival of Music in May 1948. Vaughan Williams takes centre stage in his doctoral robes with Harris in his doctoral robes second from the right and Dr Thomas Armstrong far right.

---

[250] Thorndike *Op.cit.*
[251] As well as examining for the ABRSM in the West Indies, Harris also made examining visits elsewhere, including three trips to Canada.
[252] Dakers 1995 *Op. cit.*

Chapter 12: Conclusion

On 15th October 1913, whilst assistant at Lichfield, Harris married Kathleen Doris Carter[253] at St John's Church in Clifton, Bristol. They had met in the early 1900's and had a very long engagement. In order to allay any nervousness before the 2.30pm wedding, his best man (Harold Darke) suggested that they go for a cycle ride during the morning. They ended up at the church of St Mary Redcliffe and played the organ there for such a long time that Harris was very nearly late for his wedding.

Over their fifty-five year marriage, William and "Dora" (as she was known) had two daughters, Anne Patricia[254] and Margaret Mary[255]. According to the family, he was not at all practical about the house, the domestic routine being maintained by his wife.

As early as 1925, Doris had all but lost her hearing, though experts advised that hers was a condition that advancing techniques might well someday remedy. Amazingly, in 1961, after an operation, her hearing was partially restored after a long period of profound deafness. While the surgery was a huge success, Harris' wife could not cope with the "sudden inrush of sound, which was all too much for her". She died in 1968.

Harris was extremely critical of his own work, a kind of perfectionism that possibly ventured into the realm of self-deprecation. His daughter Margaret Brockway commented: 'He certainly didn't shun publicity but he didn't like it […] He didn't in any way want to blow his own trumpet.' He was fiercely self-critical, as his own manuscript comments bare witness: 'this needs a broader, fuller orchestration—it's all too thin and fussy; too much unnecessary detail – v. ineffective; needs drastic overhauling.'"[256] Armstrong, too, writes along similar lines: 'His profound humility could at times manifest itself as self-deprecation, and perhaps even sheepishness.'[257] His daughter also makes the following observation: 'He was a very difficult person, you see. He didn't always know what was happening [...] in his dreamy way, [he] didn't have a clue.'[258]

That he lived and breathed music, through the testimony of the many who knew and worked with him, is self-evident. He always strove for the highest possible performance standard. Margaret Brockway, quoted in Parker,

'[Harris] always said "You must sing just as well on the darkest day in February with no congregation at all as when the whole chapel is full on a great occasion." This was how he worked the choir.'

Furthermore, Harris did not go out of his way to offer his services as a composer to others, a primary means by which to promote his own music. In this light, Harris' strongest positive personality trait– humility—was likely a significant impediment to his own professional success as a well-known composer. In all probability, Harris regarded himself as an organist, choir trainer and composer – in that order, hence the title of this book.

---

253 Kathleen Doris Carter was born in 1889 at Carmarthen to James Perrins Carter (b. 1843, Islington; d. 1928, Bristol) and Helen Amelia Carter (née Jenkins, b. 1848, Haverford West; d. 1904, Carmarthen). Doris's father, a grocer and wine merchant by profession and a widower, was living in retirement in Bristol at the time of her marriage hence the marriage in that city.

254 Anne was known to family and friends as "Squibbs". This was a nickname suggested by Sydney Watson on account of the fact that she was born on 5th November. Watson was organ scholar at Keble College in Oxford at the time of her birth in 1923 and also deputised for Harris at New College once a week whilst Harris was in London teaching at the RCM.

255 Margaret Brockway (b. 1918, Croydon; d. 2007, Burford).

256 Carwood Op. cit.

257 Parker Op. cit.

258 Brockway Op. cit.

In retirement, he spent a portion of his time, when not composing, listening to music - mainly on the radio rather than gramophone recordings. He seems to have had a dislike of recorded music. Was this a dissatisfaction with recordings he had made in the past, or was it that he considered music was only for one moment in time?

He was a smoker for most of his life and would often be discovered with cigarette ash down his waist-coat and a neglected lit cigarette between his fingers. Martin How at Addington also recalls this as well as his grandsons and it clearly did not affect his longevity. A former student at Addington recalls that he used to smoke cigarettes as he taught them paperwork, and would forget to knock the ash off. 'I remember sitting waiting for it to fall on his suit.'[259]

Dakers wrote:

> 'Then there were his mannerisms – hands on forehead or clutching the lapels of his jacket, his consultation with his pocket watch which became the more frequent when he was slightly nervous or agitated.'[260]

He had a life-long love of reading; his favourite authors were Wilkie Collins (especially *The Moonstone*) and Charles Dickens, (especially *David Copperfield*), Hardy, Thackeray, Mendelssohn's Letters and Boswell. 'Of the poets, Browning was an early enthusiasm and, of course, always Shakespeare.'[261] His love for literature is manifest in his choice of texts. It would be safe to say that it was the words which inspired the music. Perhaps this is why his service settings are, by and large, less inspiring.

In an article written for *The World of Church Music* and published ten years after Harris's death, Thomas Armstrong posed the following question:

> '...we may ask what the verdict will be when his [Harris's] work comes to be examined dispassionately by critics who never experienced his practical skills, or enjoyed his genial companionship.'

The authors of this book being mindful of this, have been prompted to set in print an account of Harris's life and achievements whilst living memory is still obtainable.

Eric Routley, in his book *Twentieth Century Church Music*, gives a succinct, albeit brief, summary of Harris's standing as a church music composer:

> 'The most prolific composer in the traditional style born between 1880 and 1900 is undoubtedly Sir William Harris, who first appears in English church music as one of those who contributed harmonisations to the *English Hymnal* (1906) but who in the second quarter of the [twentieth] century sent a steady stream of music into the Church's libraries.'[262]

Music libraries in most cathedrals – and in many parish churches too, contain sets of anthems and services by Harris, still in current use, although it is to be regretted that a number of his compositions are sadly out of print. This surely bears testimony to his standing amongst composers for the church and he would be happy with this. That he did not break into the mainstream of music and become a celebrity would not have bothered him at all.

---

[259] Ian Barber quoted in Henderson/Jarvis Addington *Op. cit.*
[260] Dakers 1983 *Op. cit.*
[261] Brockway *Op. cit.*
[262] Routley *Op. cit.*

Bibliography:

A Gift Book, London, SECM, 1935,

Armstrong, Sir Thomas, 'William H Harris (born 28 March 1883)' *The World of Church Music 1983*, RSCM, 1983

Bailey, Cyril, *Hugh Percy Allen*, London, Oxford University Press, 1948

Beechey, Gwilym. "The Church Music of Sir William Harris." *English Church Music 1974: A Collection of Essays*. Croydon, England: The Royal School of Church Music, 1974. 43-50.

Beechey, Gwilym.. "William Harris (1883-1973) – His Church Music and Organ Music." *Musical Opinion*, 106, no. 1265 (March 1983): 178-80.

Blom, Eric [ed.], *Grove's Dictionary of Music and Musicians*. 5th edition, London, Macmillan & Co, 1975, 10 Vols.

Brockway, Margaret, Unpublished hand-written notes from Harris's daughter.

Budd, Vincent, http://www.musicweb-international.com/bantock/buddint.htm retrieved Sep 2017

Carwood, Andrew, CD Notes for *Harris: Faire is the Heaven*, ASV CD DCA 1015, ASV, 1997

Colles, Hugh Clendon, *Walford Davies: A Biography*, London, Oxford University Press, 1942

Dakers, Lionel, *Places where they sing: Memoirs of a Church Musician*, Norwich, Canterbury Press, 1995

Dakers, Lionel, St George's Chapel Centenary Concert Programme 19th March 1983

Edmunds, Jonathan, *New College Brats: a History of the Life and Education of the Choristers of New College, Oxford*, Oxford, New College School, 1996

Ellison, Randall, Letter from Randall Ellison to Paul Hale June 1977, by courtesy of Paul Hale.

English Church Music, Croydon, RSCM, May 1956

Erpelding, Matthew William, *The danger of the disappearance of things: William Henry Harris' The hound of heaven* (DMA Thesis), Iowa City, University of Iowa, 2014

Fellowes, Edmund Horace, *Organists and Master of the Choristers of St George's Chapel in Windsor Castle*, London, SPCK, 1939

Graves, Charles L, *Hubert Parry: His life and works*, London, Macmillan & Co, 1926, 2 Vols.

Hackett, Maria, *A Brief Account of Cathedral and Collegiate Schools*, London, J B Nichols and Son, 1827

Hale, Paul, in *Music and Musicians, in New College Oxford 1379-1979* ed. Buxton, John & Williams, Penry, Oxford, New College, 1979

Harris, William Henry, RCO January Presidential Address, *The Musical Times* February 1947

Harris, William Henry, RCO July Presidential Address, *The Musical Times* August 1947

Harris, William Henry, RCO January Presidential Address, *The Musical Times* February 1948

Harris, William Henry, RCO July Presidential Address, *The Musical Times* August 1948

Harris, William Henry, 'The Organ Works of Bach and Handel', *Music & Letters*, 1935, Vol. 16

Henderson, John; Jarvis, Trevor, *The Addington Years*, Salisbury, RSCM, 2015

Henderson, John; Jarvis, Trevor, *Sydney Nicholson and his Musings of a Musician*, Salisbury, RSCM, 2013

Hesford, Bryan, "The Contemporary Cathedral Organist as Composer for the Church," *Musical Opinion*, September 1976

Hodgson, Frederic, *Choirs and Cloisters: Sixty years of music in Church, College, Cathedral and Chapels Royal* London, Thames Publishing, 1988

Hollis, Howard, *The best of both worlds: A life of Sir William McKie*, Melbourne, Sir William McKie Memorial Trust, 1991

Horton, Peter, "Edward John Hopkins: an organist and choirmaster re-examined (II)", *RCO Journal 2010*, p.34

Howells, Herbert, N., in *English Church Music* Croydon, RSCM, 1973

Howells, Herbert, N., Radio broadcast 28th March 1973, BBC Radio 3, *A tribute to Sir William Harris (he being ninety)*, also quoted in full in Palmer, Christopher. *Herbert Howells: A Celebration*, 2nd. Edition, London, Thames, 1995

Humphreys, Maggie, Evans, Robert, *Dictionary of Composers for the Church in Great Britain and Ireland*, London, Mansell, 1997

Jebb, John, *The Choral Service of the United Church of England and Ireland: Being an enquiry into the liturgical system of the cathedral and collegiate foundations of the Anglican Communion*, London, John W Parker, 1843

Jenkinson, Matthew, *New College School, Oxford – A History*, London, Bloomsbury Publishing, 2013

Judd, Roger, *The Organs in Windsor Castle: Their History and Development*, Oxford, Positif Press, 2015

Lewer, David, *A Spiritual Song: The Story of the Temple Choir London*, The Templars' Union, 1961

Nightingale, Bruce, *Seven Rivers to Cross: A Mostly British Council Life*, London, Radcliffe Press 1996

Osborne, Richard E., *Music & Musicians of Eton College: From 1440 to the present*, London, Cygnet Press, 2012

Parker, Timothy James, *Sir William Henry Harris (1883-1973) His life and work with particular reference to his anthems.* (MMus Thesis), Sheffield, University of Sheffield, 1997

Pound, Reginald, *Sir Henry Wood: A Biography*, London, Cassell & Co, 1969

Rennert, Jonathan, *George Thalben-Ball*, Newton Abbott, David & Charles 1979

Reynolds, Gordon, *Organo Pleno*, London, Novello & Co, 1970

Riley, Malcolm, *Percy Whitlock: Organist and Composer*, London, Thames Publishing, 1998

Routley, Erik, *Twentieth Century Church Music*, London, Herbert Jenkins, 1964

Sampson, Alastair, CD Notes by Alastair Sampson for *Sir William Harris: Anthems* Naxos 8.570148, 2006

Sampson, Alastair and Eggar, Anne, Correspondence between Alistair Sampson and Anne Eggar 2006

Shaw, Harold Watkins, *The Succession of Organists*, Oxford, Clarendon Press, 1991

Spicer, Paul, *Sir George Dyson: His Life and Music* Martlesham, The Boydell Press, 2014

Statham, Michael, 'Sir William Harris: A choirboy's memories', *Musical Opinion,* October 1983

Surplice, Alwyn, 'Sir William Harris: A personal appreciation', *Organists' Review*, October 1973

The Cathedral Quarterly 1913-1916

The Present State of Cathedral Music, Church Music Society, 1934

Thorndike, Russell, *Children of the Garter: Being the Memoirs of a Windsor Choir-boy, during the Last Years of Queen Victoria*, London, Rich & Cowan, 1937

Tovey, Donald F. and Parratt, Geoffrey, *Walter Parratt: Master of the Music*, London, Oxford University Press, 1941

Tuckwell, Revd William, *Reminiscences of Oxford* , London: Cassell, 1901

Vaughan Williams, Ursula, *RVW: A Biography of Ralph Vaughan Williams*, London, Oxford University Press, 1964

Wallin, Peter, 'A Lifetime of Singing', in *New College Choir Association Newsletter – July 2012*, Oxford, New College Choir Association, 2012

Wridgway, Neville, *The Choristers of St George's Chapel*, Slough, Chas. Luff, 1980

Appendix 1: 20C Assistant Organists at St George's Chapel

Dates	Name
Nov 1900–April 1924	R F Martin Akerman
April 1924–Jan 1925	Geoffrey S Kitchingman
Jan 1925–April 1932	Malcolm Boyle
1927–1932	Alwyn Surplice
1932–1945	Alwyn Surplice (as Sub-Organist)
Jan 1941–Dec 1945	John Forster
1946–1949	Philip Moore
1950–1954	Lionel Dakers
1955–1959	Richard Greening
1959–1967	Clement McWilliam
1968–1972	John Morehen (as Sub-Organist)
1972–1985	John Porter
1985–2008	Roger Judd

Richard Frank Martin Akerman

Martin Akerman (1871-1938) studied at the RCM. He was assistant organist from November 1900 until April 1924, when he resigned because of ill health. He also taught at Eton College from 1908 to 1934. He became chief editor for The Year Book Press in London and was responsible for their catalogue of church music and secular songs.

Geoffrey S Kitchingman

Geoffrey Kitchingman was briefly assistant organist from April 1924 to January 1925, replacing Martin Akerman. Edmund Fellowes, who was acting as interim choirmaster, engaged his services. Kitchingman remained in charge of music at the school, before departing for New Zealand during the summer term of 1925. He was a former chorister of the Chapel.

Malcolm Courtenay Boyle

Malcolm Boyle (1902-1976) was a chorister at Eton College (and organ pupil of Sir Walter Parratt at St George's) before winning the Goss Scholarship to the RAM in 1918. He became assistant organist from January 1925 and his father had previously been a lay clerk at the Chapel. In April 1932 he became organist of Chester Cathedral serving until 1949 when, as a divorcee wishing to remarry, he was dismissed by the Dean and Chapter. He was appointed an examiner for the Associated Board of the Royal Schools of Music, travelling widely in this role, and was Director of Music at King's School in Canterbury from 1951 to 1954. In retirement he was organist and choirmaster at his local parish church in Sandiway, Cheshire.

Reginald Alwyn Surplice

Alwyn Surplice (1906-1977) was assistant organist (1927-1932) and then sub-organist (1932-1945) with a break for war service. He was also organist of Holy Trinity Garrison Church in Windsor. Appointed organist of Bristol Cathedral in 1946 and subsequently organist of Winchester Cathedral (1949-1971), he was concurrently a professor at the RAM and tutor at King Alfred's College, Winchester. Channel 4 television newsreader Jon Snow was a chorister at Winchester under Surplice and recounts the following: [263]

---

[263] Jon Snow in *Speaking of Faith* Canterbury Press, 2016

'...he was a mythical figure because not only did he train us absolutely beautifully, he was a wonderfully caring and brilliant musician. He had been at Bletchley during the war, code breaking, and in some way the code breaking involved him tapping a lot, and every time there was a duff note in an organ voluntary, people would say "Bletchley"! Because, apparently, his fingers were slightly clustered together as a result of constantly tapping – whether it's true or not, that's the sort of myth one grew up with'

John Charles Stirling Forster

John Forster (1915-19xx) was assistant organist from January 1941 until December 1945, covering Alwyn Surplice's absence for war service. A graduate of Durham University gaining his FRCO in 1936, he was concurrently organist at the Royal Chapel in Windsor Park. He then moved to Salisbury Cathedral as sub-organist (1947-1950), after which he held a number of school appointments.

Philip Harold Moore

Philip Moore (1921-2010), a native of Shrewsbury, studied at the RCM and was organist of St Thomas in Regent Street prior to assisting Harris in Windsor. On leaving Windsor, he was organist of St Augustine's in Edgbaston (where Harris had served) from 1949-1960 and also worked for the BBC in Birmingham. From 1960 he became head of music for the BBC South and West in Bristol until retirement. He conducted the BBC West of England Singers.

Lionel Frederick Dakers

Lionel Dakers (1924-2003) attended Rochester Cathedral Choir School and then studied under Sir Edward Bairstow at York. He was appointed assistant organist from 1950, moving to Ripon Cathedral as organist in 1954 and then Exeter Cathedral in 1972 before appointment as Director of the RSCM. He retired in 1989.

Richard George Greening

Richard Greening (1927-1979) was a chorister at New College in Oxford and was for a time organist of St Giles, Oxford, before becoming assistant organist in Windsor from 1955 to 1959. He moved to Lichfield as organist from 1959-1977. He played his part in maintaining the links between Lichfield, Windsor and New College, which had been established by William Harris.

Clement Charles McWilliam

Clement McWilliam (1934-2007) was a chorister at Winchester Cathedral, and a classics scholar at Charterhouse before training at the RCM. He became assistant organist in 1959, was DOM at St George's School and (for one year) organist of the Royal Chapel in Windsor Great Park. In 1967 he was appointed Director of Music at the Pilgrims' School (the choir school of Winchester Cathedral) and sub-organist of the Cathedral. When Alwyn Surplice retired in 1971, a disappointed McWilliam (he had hoped to be offered the post of organist) moved away to teach at Hawtrey's School in Wiltshire, before moving back to Winchester in retirement.

McWilliam had a considerable reputation at improvisation. '...anyone who heard them will remember their ingenious streams of musical invention, often uplifting, sometimes witty and irreverent, occasionally startlingly modern.'[264]

Clement McWilliam was asked by Harris's daughter, Anne Eggar, to catalogue her husband's manuscripts and papers. After completing this task and dividing the material into 16 packets,

---

[264] Gerard McBurney in McWilliam's obituary in *The Independent* 3rd Oct 2007.

he wrote to her on 4th May 1995[265] suggesting what she might like to do with them – some perhaps to be destroyed and others to be given to Winchester and Lichfield cathedrals, some to the RCM or RSCM and others to St George's. In the end she kept most of the *mss*.

John Manley Morehen

John Morehen (b. 1941) was educated at Clifton College in Bristol and was a Hymns A&M Scholar at Addington Palace before going to Oxford as organ scholar of New College, followed by a doctorate at Cambridge. He was sub-organist at St George's from 1968-1972 and organ tutor at the RSCM from 1969-1972. Thereafter he taught at Nottingham University becoming Professor of Music there in 1989. His scholarly editions of 16/17C church music are widely used.

John Porter

John Porter was assistant organist from 1972 until his sudden death in 1985. He was concurrently a music master at St George's School.

Roger Langley Judd

Roger Judd (b.1944) was a chorister at Winchester Cathedral and was assistant organist at Ely Cathedral, before moving to St Michael's College, Tenbury, as Master of the Music in 1973. He remained there until the College's closure in 1985. He was assistant organist at St George's Chapel from 1985-2008, and Acting Organist and Master of the Choristers from September 2002 to Christmas 2003. Now sub-organist at St Laurence's Church in Ludlow, he is the author of *The Organs in Windsor Castle: Their History and Development*, Oxford, Positif Press, 2015.

---

[265] McWilliam also thanks her in the letter for the gift of some, if not all, of WHH's piano duet music.

Appendix 2: Catalogue of Compositions

With musical examples of the organ and sacred choral works.

Very few of the published works bear a date of composition – the dates given are that of publication unless otherwise stated.

The compositions are in alphabetical order within each section and the era of his life when the work was first known is shown in code.

HTT	Holy Trinity, Tulse Hill (chorister)	OXC	Christ Church, Oxford
STD	St Davids (pupil)	SGW	St George's, Windsor
RCM	RCM (student)	SGW/ADD	Windsor and RSCM
LCH	Lichfield (assistant)	RET	Retirement
OXN	New College Oxford		

Unless indicated, the location of original *mss.* are unknown. Harris's personal *mss.* passed to his daughter Anne Eggar and the EGG references given here indicate in which folder or package within this collection the various *mss.* can be found.

The authors can only apologise for the poor reproduction of some *mss.*, many of which are dark and dirty. Even some of the printed editions are of rather poor quality.

1: Anthems

1) **All creatures of our God and King**

Voicing	SATB	Publ No	A222	Pages	6	Date	1959	Era	SGW
Publisher	RSCM	Text	St Francis of Assisi tr. W H Draper					ms.	RSCM
Note	WHH also composed an organ voluntary based on this anthem – see p. 268								

2) Almighty and most merciful Father

Voicing	SATB (div)	Date	1983	ms.	Lichfield Cathedral	Era	RET	Pages	4
Publisher	Novello		Text	Samuel Johnson's last prayer					
Dedication	To R G Greening[266] and the choir of Lichfield Cathedral								
Note	Published posthumously, date of composition unknown.								

---

[266] Richard Greening had been Harris's assistant at SGW from 1955 to 1959.

3) And the disciples came to Jesus

Voicing	T, B Soli, SATB, organ	Pages	10	ms.	EGG A	Date	1916
Note	Uses the Coverdale Bible text of Matthew 24: 1-14 "Swanage and Lichfield 1916" (revised Oxford 1928) "Written when I was organist of St Augustine's, Edgbaston, in 1916 for Robert Davies (Baritone) a fine singer, sensitive and expressive. Too much influenced by Walford Davies and some Elgar I had just heard. Modulates too freely, too restless"						

4) Antiphon: I believe verily

Voicing	SSAATTBB	Pages	3	Text	Ps 27: 15	Date	1911	Era	LCH
Note	Privately printed by Dinham Blyth & Co in London								
Dedication	Composed for the unveiling of a memorial window to Herbert Mortimer Lucock (1833-1909), Dean of Lichfield Cathedral from 1892 until 1909.								

ANTIPHON

Slow and very sustained.

William H. Harris.

5) Ascribe unto the Lord

Voicing	SATB	Pages	14	Publ No	OA1270	Date	1948	Era	SGW
Publisher	Novello	Series		Octavo Anthems		Text	Psalm 96: 7-13		

Dedication Composed for the six hundredth anniversary of the foundation of the Order of the Garter 1948.

Ascribe unto the Lord: Organ introduction

Ascribe unto the Lord: Choral entry

6) Be merciful unto me, O God

Voicing	Bass solo, SATB, organ		Pages	12	Date	May/June 1899
Note	Composed at the RCM with the comment "sent in for 1st term composition exam"				ms.	EGG G

7) Beatus vir: Three Psalms. (1, 15, 121)

Voicing	S Solo, SSA, piano	Pages	18	Date	1965
Text	Psalms. 1, 15, 121			ms.	EGG A
Note	Dated January 1965, some later pencilled amendments.				

Psalm 15

Psalm 1

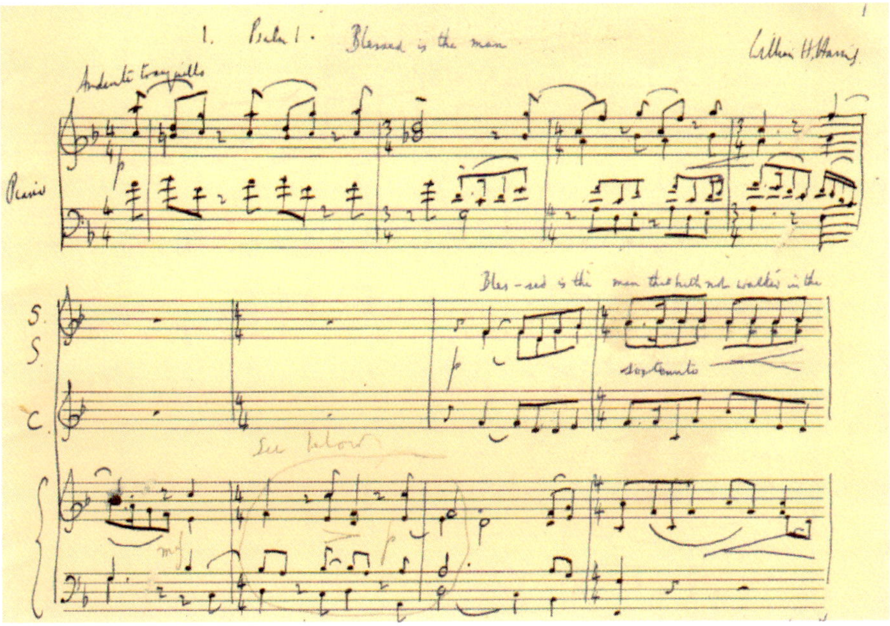

Psalm 121

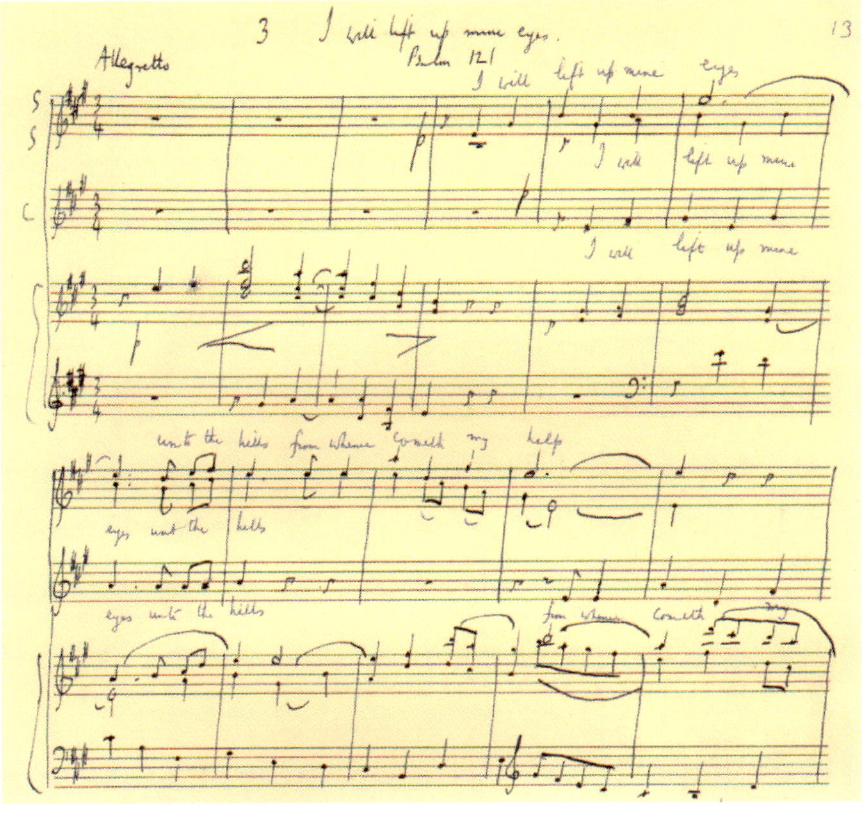

8) Be strong in the Lord

Voicing	B solo, SATB, organ	Publ No	YBP98	Pages	12	Era	SGW
Date	1948	Text		Ephesians 6; I, Timothy 6 and the Collect for St George's Day			
Publisher	A&C Black, The Year Book Press						

Dedication	Composed for the six-hundredth anniversary of the foundation of the Most Noble Order of the Garter and sung in St George's Chapel, Windsor, 23 April 1948 .
WHH Note	Alternative section for when sung on Saints' days other than St George.

9a) Behold now, praise the Lord (SS)

Voicing	SS, organ	Publ No	CS87	Pages	4	Date	1949	Era	SGW
Publisher	Novello	Series	Chorister Series			Text	Psalm 134		
Dedication Composed for Julian Lambart[267] and the Eton College Lower Chapel Choir.									

---

[267] Julian Harold Legge Lambart (1893-1982) was consecutively Housemaster, Lower Master and Vice-Provost of Eton College. He married Walford-Davies' widow Margaret in 1948.

9b) Behold now, praise the Lord (ATB)

Voicing	ATB, organ	Publ No	MV144	Date	1961	Pages		6	Era	SGW
Publisher	Novello	Series	Services and Anthems for Men's Voices				Text		Psalm 134	

Dedication The original version was written for Julian Lambart and the Eton College Lower Chapel Choir .

Note Arrangement probably by WHH.

10) Behold, the tabernacle of God is with man

Voicing	SATB Organ		Publ No	208	Pages	4	Date	1954	Era	SGW
Publisher	RSCM	Text	Sarum Antiphon for the Dedication of a Church						ms.	RSCM
Note	ms. 'Windsor March 1954'		Dedication For Gerald Knight, and composed for the Official Opening of the new Headquarters of the Royal School of Church Music at Addington Palace, Croydon. 10th July 1954.							

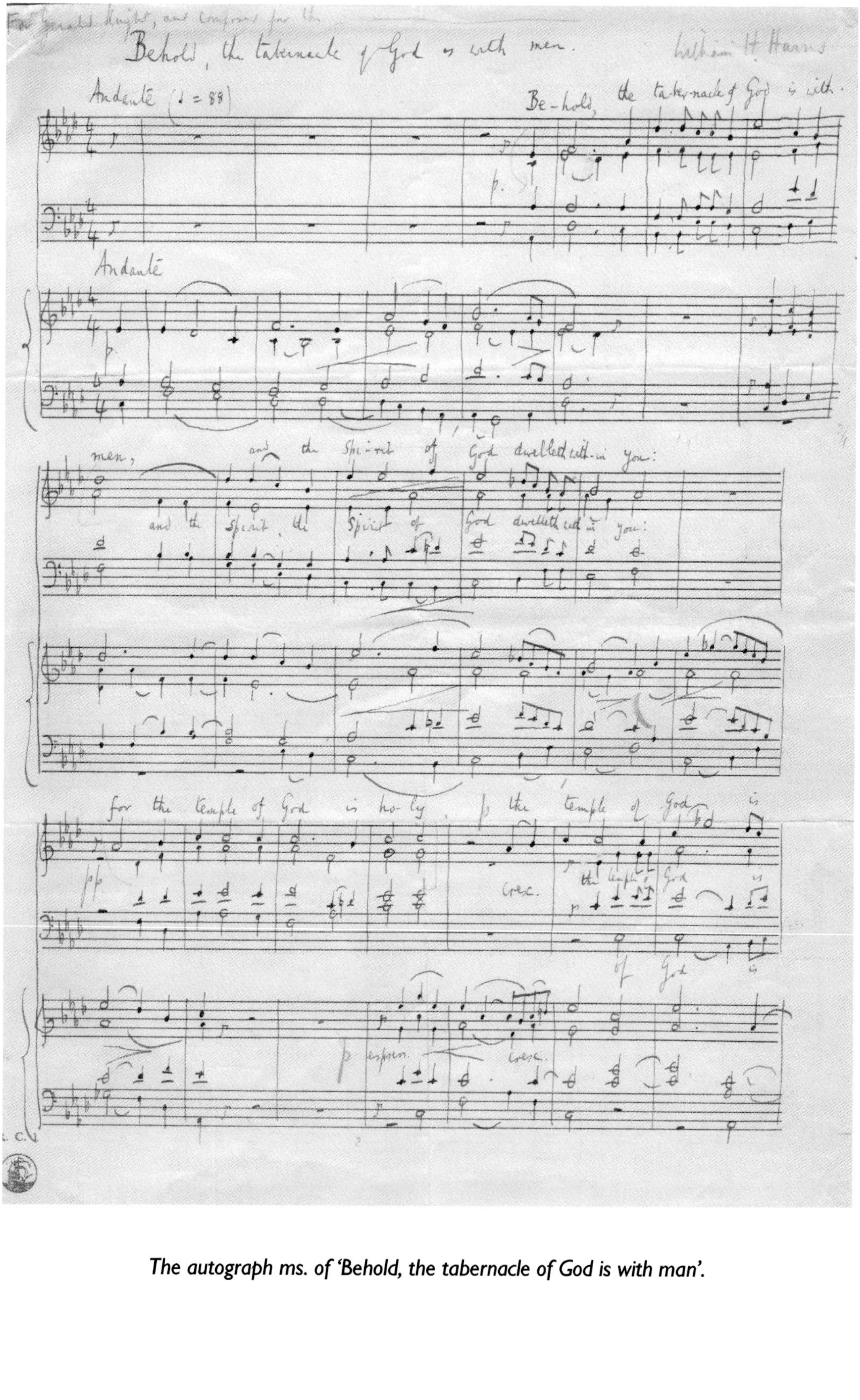

The autograph ms. of 'Behold, the tabernacle of God is with man'.

11) Benedic anima mea (Psalm 104)

Voicing	S solo, choir, orchestra	Pages	ms. A 28pp ms. B 37pp	Era	SGW
Date	1952	Text	Psalm 104	ms.	EGG A

Note
One ms. vocal score, 28pp, is dated April 30th 1952, Eastington, Northleach, Glos. A second score is dated January 1954. This copy dedicated "To Thomas Armstrong and the Oxford Bach Choir" and contains a letter from TA to WHH saying that he would recommend the piece to the Bach Choir committee. However it was never published or performed. No orchestral score located.

107

12) Bring us, O Lord God (Motet for double choir)

Voicing	SATBSATB	Publ No	Pages	8	OA1368	Era	SGW/ADD
Publisher	Novello	Text	John Donne (1572-1631)			Date	1959
Series	Octavo Anthems						

13a) Collect for St George (April 23rd): Short Anthem for Full Choir

Voicing	SATB	Publ No	A95	Pages	2	Date	1947	Era	SGW
Publisher	A&C Black, The Year Book Press					Text	Collect for April 23rd		
Note	The SATB and TTBB versions are published together in the same edition. Annotated for tonic sol-fa.								

13b) Collect for St George (April 23rd): arr. for Mens' Choir

Voicing	(A)TTBB	Publ No	A95	Pages	2	Date	1947	Era	SGW
Publisher	A&C Black, The Year Book Press			Text	Collect for Apr 23rd				
Note	The SATB and TTBB versions are published together in the same edition. Annotated for tonic sol-fa.								
WHH Note	The altos should sing in unison with the First Tenors.								

14) Come down, O Love divine: Hymn-anthem on the tune "North Petherton"

Voicing	SATB Organ	Publ No	OA1449	Date	1965	Era	RET
Publisher	Novello	Pages	6	Series	Octavo Anthems		
Text	Bianco da Siena tr. by R F Littledale (1833-1890)						

15a) Come, my Way, my Truth, my Life! (The Call)

Voicing	SATB, organ ad lib.	Publ No	OA1224	Era	SGW
Publisher	Novello	Pages	4	Date	1937
Series	Octavo Anthems	Text	The Call: George Herbert (1593-1633)		
Note	Also included in *The Sydney Nicholson Commemoration Book* published in 1948 by the RSCM.				
WHH Note	"This anthem may be sung unaccompanied"				

15b) Come, my Way, my Truth, my Life! (The Call) for SSA and Piano

Voicing	SSA, piano	Publ No	Trios664	Pages	4	Date	1937	Era	SGW
Publisher	Novello	Text	The Call; George Herbert (1593-1633)						
Series	Trios and Quartets for Female or Boys' Voices								

16) Eternal God!: Motet for SATB (unaccompanied)

Voicing	SATB	Publ No	SA 346	Pages	4	Date	1965	Era	RET
Publisher	Novello	Series		Short Anthems		Dedication	To Derek Holman		
Text	Francis Quarles (1592-1644)								

17) Eternal ruler of the ceaseless round

Voicing	SATB, organ	Publ No	A39	Pages	5	Date	1930	Era	OXC
Publisher	OUP	Series	The Oxford Series of Modern Anthems						
Text	J W Chadwick (1841-1882)								
Note	The final section of *The Heavens declare the Glory of God (Anthem founded on Gibbons' Song I)* with a new organ introduction – see **71**).								

18) Evening Hymn: The night is come

Voicing	SATB(div), solo Ba, organ	Publ No	A141	Pages	11	Era	SGW/ADD
Date	1961	Text	Words by Sir Thomas Browne (1605-1682)				
Publisher	Ascherberg, Hopwood and Crew: The Year Book Press	Dedication "For Richard Latham and his St Paul's Festival Choir"					
Series	The New "Canterbury" Series of Anthems and Church Music						
Note	Also scored for an accompaniment of strings and organ [EGG F]. WHH notes "Scored at Petersfield August 1961" with pencil note (composed at Windsor). He also notes "The last section must not drag, but keep _moving_; quietly happy."						

19) Faire is the Heaven: Motet for double choir

Voicing	SATBSATB	Publ No	UPS261	Pages	12		Era	OXN
Date	1925/1948	Publisher	Ascherberg, Hopwood and Crew					
Series	The Year Book Press Series of Unison and Part-Songs		Dedication Affectionately dedicated to Sir Hugh Allen. Revised Version 1948.					

Faire is the Heaven:

Differences between the original and revised versions.

1925 Edition		1948 Revised version	
Bar 1	No metronome mark	Bar 1	Metronome mark (minim = 60)
Bars 63/64	No dynamic markings	Bars 63/64	*mf* markings added
Bar 72	*accel.*	Bar 72	No *accel.*
Bar 77	(minim = one in a bar)	Bar 77	(crotchet = crochet)
Bars 77-83 are all 3/4 bars.		Bars 77-79 77/78 are 2/2, 79 is 3/2.	
		This re-barring reduces the the piece by four bars. The four chords for the text "God's owne per – son" are effectively reduced in duration by one third.	
		Bar 78	No *accel.* And a longer **>**
Bar 80	*accel.* **>**	Bar 80	No "(minim = dotted minim)" – it is not needed.
Bar 84	(minim = dotted minim)	Bar 84	No *Più mosso* or *mf*
		Bar 86	*allargando* (starts earlier than 1925)
Bar 88	*Più mosso mf*		
Bar 91	*allarg.*	Bar 110	Choir 1 bass starts F# on beat one.
Bar 114	Choir 1 bass has a rest or beat one.		
Total 127 bars		**Total 123 bars**	

Few people would disagree with Peter Parfitt, director of the Aberdeen Bach Choir, who wrote:

> '*Faire is the Heaven*, perhaps his most enduring and best-loved piece, is a spacious and expansive piece for double choir, which exploits and challenges the pitch range of the human voice. The words are taken from a much longer poem by Edmund Spenser (1552–1599), *A Hymne of Heavenly Beautie*. The setting of Spenser's glorious words is sublime – managing to be colourful, calm, deeply reflective, reverent and hugely exciting all at once. Harris's management of tonality, the frequent but subtle changes from major to minor and back, the skilful modulations and the slow harmonic pulse, allowing each new tonality to establish itself, all serve to encapsulate the joyous yet profound meaning of the text.'[268]

---

[268] Courtesy of The Aberdeen Bach Choir.

20) Fear not, O Land: Anthem for Harvest

Voicing	SATB, organ	Publ No	E73	Pages	8	Date	1955	Era	SGW
Publisher	OUP	Series	Oxford Easy Anthems			Text	Joel 2		

21) Forth in thy name

Voicing	SATB organ	Pages	3	Date	1967	ms.	RSCM	Era	RET
Unpublished		Text	Charles Wesley (1707-1788)						
Note	Based on Gibbons' "Song 34" (Angels' Song). The original ms. at the RSCM is dated June 1967 with a fair copy in the hand of Gerald Knight.								

22) From a heart made whole (Motet)

Voicing	SSAATTBB	Publ No	A66	Pages	4	Date	1935	Era	SGW
Publisher	OUP	Dedication		"for Canon A Nairne"[269]		ms.		EGG R (partial)	
Text	A C Swinburne (1837-1909) by permission of Messrs Heinemann Ltd.								
Series	The Oxford Series of Modern Anthems								

---

[269] Alexander Nairne, D.D. (1863-1936) was Dean of Jesus College, Cambridge and became Regius Professor of Divinity at the Cambridge University in 1922. He was also a Canon of St George's, Windsor, and combined the two roles until he resigned his professorship in 1932, remaining a Canon at Windsor until his death.

23) Glory, Love, and Praise and Honour: Anthem for Harvest

Voicing	SATB, organ	Publ No	236	Pages	9	Date	1963	Era	RET
Publisher	RSCM	Text	Charles Wesley (1707-88)						

24) He hath understanding of righteousness

Voicing	T solo, SATB	Pages		2	Date	n.d.	ms.	EGG R
Note	"Anthem for a Saint's Day or a Martyr" Text from the Salisbury Antiphoner Probably composed between 1967 and 1971.							

25) He that is down needs fear no fall

Voicing	SSA, S solo, organ		Publ No	E132	Pages	3	ms.		EGG E	Era	RET
Publisher	OUP	Series			Oxford Easy Anthems				Date	1973	
Text	John Bunyan (1628-1688): The Shepherd Boy's Song in the Valley of Humiliation (The Pilgrim's Progress)										
WHH Note	Composed May 1967, revised 1972.										

26a) Holy is the true light: Short Anthem for Saints' Days

Voicing	SATB	Publ No	MT1259	Pages	4	Date	1948	Era	SGW
Publisher	Novello	Series	The Musical Times						
Text	Words from the Salisbury Diurnal by Dr G H Palmer (1846-1926)								
Dedication	"To the memory of Evelyn Mary Ley" (wife of organist Henry G Ley).								

26b) Holy is the true light: Short Anthem for Saints' Days

Voicing	ATTB	Publ No	MV142	Pages	4	Date	1959	Era	SGW/ADD
Publisher	Novello	Series	Services and Anthems for Men's Voices						
Text	Words from the Salisbury Diurnal by Dr G H Palmer (1846-1926)								
Note	Arranged by WHH		Dedication To the memory of Evelyn Mary Ley.						
WHH Note	Baritones might perhaps sing with Tenor II when the notes are within their compass.								

27) How bright these glorious spirits shine

Voicing	SATB, organ	Unpublished	Pages	7	Date	1971	Era	PET
Text	Isaac Watts (1674-1748)						ms.	EGG R

Note The tune 'Sennen Cove' was written for Hymns A&M Revised 1950 for the text How bright these glorious spirits shine. There are several draft versions of the anthem, one (not the final version) dated Sep 1971.

28) Hymn to God the Father: Motet for SATB

Voicing	SATB	Pages	12	Date	1967
Text	Samuel Wesley (1691-1739)			ms.	EGG E

29) I have set God always before me: Anthem for Boys' voices

Voicing	SS, organ	Pages	4		Date	1969	ms.	EGG R	Era	RET
Unpublished		Text	Psalm 16: 9-16							
Dedication		For John Bradley[270] and the Choir of St George's Church, Toronto.								
Note		First draft dated 22nd Aug 1969, final version dated 15th October 1969.								

---

[270] Toronto teacher and organist John Bradley (d. 2010) was co-founder, with Healey Willan, of St George's College in Toronto 1964, it had a men & boys choir.

30) I heard a voice from heaven

Voicing	SATB	Publ No	A117	Pages	3	Date	1947	Era	SGW
Publisher	OUP	Series	The Oxford Series of Modern Anthems						
Text	Revelation 14:13, as rendered in the 1549 BCP								
Dedication Composed for the Funeral Service of HRH Prince Arthur of Connaught, St George's Chapel, Windsor, September 16, 1938.									

31) I said to the Man who stood at the Gate of the Year

Voicing	TTBB	Publ No	A277	Pages	2	Date	1970	Era	RET
Publisher	OUP	Text	M Louise Haskins (1875-1957)					ms.	EGG R
Series	The Oxford Series of Modern Anthems								
Dedication	"Dedicated by gracious permission to Her Majesty Queen Elizabeth, the Queen Mother"								

WHH Note
"These words were broadcast to his people by King George VI on the first Christmas Day of the Second World War, in 1939. They are from *God Knows* and are used by kind permission of the author and Hodder and Stoughton Ltd."

Also an unpublished *ms.* version for tenor solo and organ, and two variant draft copies. The version used for publishing is dated May 1969.

32) In Christ Jesu

Voicing	SATB, organ	Unpublished		ms.	EGG F	Date	1973	Era	RET
Text	From Ephesians 2								
Dedication	Composed for the 1300th anniversary of the Foundation of Hexham Abbey by St Wilfred [in June 1974].								

Note

The letter from Terence Atkinson, organist of the Abbey, requesting the commission is dated 20th Feb 1973. The text was suggested by the Rector of Hexham and Harris was agreeable to this. The anthem was completed and sent to Hexham in June 1973 and Harris charged the Abbey £20. Never satisfied with his efforts, when he replied on 25th July 1973 to acknowledge the payment, he enclosed an amended *ms.* with a new introduction.

33) In the heavenly kingdom: Short Anthem for Saints' Days

Voicing	SATB	Publ No	MT1262	Pages	4	Date	1948	Era	SGW
Publisher	Novello	Series	The Musical Times						
Text	Words from the Salisbury Diurnal by Dr G H Palmer (1846-1926)								

34) It is a good thing to give thanks

Voicing	SATB, organ	Unpublished		Pages	5	Era	RET
Date	1971	Text	Psalm 92		ms.		EGG R
Note							

Note
Many drafts, one dated February 1971, enough material to complete the work. At one time this was intended to be the first of a "Medley of Psalms" with Psalm 108 intended to be the next in the sequence.

35) Jesus, these eyes have never seen

Voicing	SATB (div), organ	Unpublished	Pages	3 "A4" pages	Era	SGW
Note	ms. in the Archives at Windsor : M185		Text	Ray Palmer (1808-1887)		
Dedication For Canon Duncan Armytage[271], written at his request.						
WHH Note	Melody [Gräfenberg] from Praxis Pietatis Melica 1653.					

[271] Canon Duncan Armytage (1889-1954) was Canon of the Ninth Stall at St George's from 1947 until his death in 1954 and so presumably this anthem dates from that period. He was also Precentor.

36) King of Glory, King of Peace: Anthem for Boys' Voices

Voicing	SSA, organ	Publ No	A2	Pages	7	Date	1925	Era	OXN
Publisher	OUP	Text		George Herbert (1593-1633)					
Series	The Oxford Series of Modern Anthems								
Dedication	To Cullis, Gooderson, and all the other New College Choristers.								

37) King of glory, King of peace (Short Anthem, or Introit) for general use

Voicing	SATB, T solo, organ	Publ No	CC193		Date	1914		Era	LCH
Publisher	Stainer & Bell		Pages	6	Text	George Herbert (1593-1633)			
Series	Church Choir Library								
Dedication	"Dedicated to the Very Revd The Dean of Lichfield"[272]								

[272] The Very Revd Henry Edwin Savage (1854-1939), Dean of Lichfield from 1909-1939.

38) Laudamus (Anthem for Victory)

Voicing	SATB, organ	Publ No	A112	Pages	7	Date	1945	Era	SGW
Publisher	OUP		Series	The Oxford Series of Modern Anthems					
Text	Anthony C Deane[273]								
WHH Note	Words by kind permission of the author.								

[273] See p. 178

39) Lead, kindly light (Tune: Alberta)

Voicing	U + Descant (or SATB), organ	Publ No	E92	Era	SGW/ADD
Publisher	OUP	Pages	4	Date	1961
Series	Oxford Easy Anthems	Text	Cardinal J H Newman		
Note	Arranged with descant by Eric Gritton[274] (presumably with the approval of WHH).				

---

[274] Eric William Gritton (1889-1981), a former chorister of King's College in Cambridge was a pupil of Sir Hubert Parry, Sir Frederick Bridge, Charles Wood and Sir Charles Stanford. A professor at the RCM and well known piano accompanist, he succeeded his father as organist of Reigate Church in 1929.

40) Let my prayer: Anthem for SATB

Voicing	SATB (div), organ	Publ No	SA313	Date	1953	Era	SGW
Publisher	Novello	Pages	3	Text	Psalm 141 v.2		
Dedication	Composed as the Gradual for the Coronation of Queen Elizabeth II in 1953.						
Series	Novello's Short Anthems		Note	Text source not stated on the music			

41) Lord of the worlds above: Anthem for S.A.T.B. and Organ

Voicing	SATB, organ	Publ No	OA1411	Pages		8	Era	SGW/ADD
Publisher	Novello	Series	Octavo Anthems				Date	1961
Text	Isaac Watts (1674-1748)							

Dedication. Composed for the Centenary Festival, Christ Church, Wanstead, July 19th 1961.

42) Lord, who shall dwell in thy Tabernacle

Voicing	T solo, SSA chorus, organ	Date		1928 rev.1958		Era	OXN
Text	from Psalm 15 with a verse from a hymn of John Keble (1792-1866) [Bless'd are the pure in heart]						
Note	Unpublished		ms.		EGG A		

43) Love of Love and Light of Light (Motet for double Choir)

Voicing	SATBSATB		Publ No	A62	Date		1934	Era	SGW
Publisher	OUP	Series	The Oxford Series of Modern Anthems				Pages	8	
Text	Robert Seymour Bridges (1844-1930)								
Dedication	"For MMB (in memoriam Robert Bridges)"								
Note	MMB was Mary Monica Bridges (née Waterhouse) wife of the poet Robert Seymour Bridges. The printed score is dated March 28 1934.								

44) Most glorious Lord of life (Anthem for general use)

Voicing	SBarB choir, organ	Publ No	E12	Pages	4	Date	1932	Era	OXC
Publisher	OUP	Series		The Oxford Series of Easy Anthems					
Text	Edmund Spenser (c.1522-99)								

45) My spirit longeth for Thee (SATB unaccompanied)

Voicing	SATB (Dec and Can)		Publ No	A85	Date	1933	Era	SGW
Publisher	H F W Deane & Sons				ms.	Early draft in EGG E		
Series	The Year Book Press		Text	John Byrom (1691-1763)				
Dedication	To the Reverend Canon Watson, DD, Christ Church, Oxford[275].							
Note	Part I. **The Wish** [My spirit longeth for thee]. Part II. **The Answer** [Cheer up desponding Soul].							
WHH Note	The phrasing and accentuation of the words must be preserved in the singing. Occasional suggestions have been made by grouping together rhythms of twos and threes. The anthem may be sung full throughout.							

Part I: The Wish

Part II: The Answer

---

275 The Revd Edward William Watson (1859–1936) was a Canon of Christ Church, Oxford, and Regius Professor of Ecclesiastical History at Oxford University.

46) O come hither

Voicing	SATB, organ	ms.	EGG F	Date	1968	Era	RET
Note	Dated September 17th 1968			Text	Psalm 66: 6-18		

47) O God, the Protector: Anthem for SATB (unaccompanied)

Voicing	SATB	Publ No	OA1479	Pages	4	Date	1969	Era	RET
Publisher	Novello	Series	Octavo Anthems					ms.	EGG R
Text	Collect for Trinity IV								
Dedication	In memoriam KDH July 26th 1968 [the date of his wife's death]								
Note	Annotated for tonic sol-fa, divisi in the first line only Harris signed it " + 4th October 1968" This may reflect the date he finished it, or possibly the date her ashes were interred in St George's Chapel. There are two versions, the earlier one is dated July 18th 1968, i.e. composition was begun before his wife died. Intended to be No. 4 of "An Evening Benediction" see p. 306.								

48) O joyful light of the heavenly glory: Evening Anthem

Voicing	SATBSATB, Bass solo	Publ No	A88	Date	1939	Era	SGW
Publisher	OUP	Series	The Oxford Series of Modern Anthems			Pages	7
Text	Words from the Greek (7th century)						

49) O love divine, how sweet

Voicing	SATB, organ		ms.	EGG E	Date	1970	Era	RET
Pages	3	Text	Charles Wesley (1707-1788) Hymns A&M Rev 195 vv.1/2/4					
Note	Dated January 19th 1970. WHH sketched a new ending but otherwise complete.							

50) O praise the Lord of heaven: Anthem for Treble voices

Voicing	SS, organ	Publ No	CS94	Pages	8	Date	1955	Era	SGW
Publisher	Novello	Series	Chorister Series		Text	Psalm 148: 1-12			
WHH Note		"Written in 18th-century Siciliano style"							

150

51) O Saviour of the world: Anthem or Introit

Voicing	SATB (div)	ms.	EGG R	Date	1972	Era	RET
Key	G-minor	Text	Collect for the visitation of the sick (BCP)				

Note
Dated March 8 1972. The 'organ part' only doubles the voices and Harris probably intended this to be sung without accompaniment.

52) O sing unto the Lord with thanksgiving: Anthem for S.A.T.B.
Suitable for Harvest

Voicing	SATB, organ	Publ No	OA1317	Pages	7	Date	1954	Era	SGW
Publisher	Novello	Series	Octavo Anthems						
Text	Ps. 147: vv.7-9,12-14 and Ps.145 vv.17-19								
Dedication To James Gordon[276] and the choir of Windsor Parish Church.									

[276] James Gordon was a chorister at St George's Chapeland went on to be a Choral Scholar at King's College, Cambridge. He taught at Eton College and was organist of Winsor Parish Church before teaching in Africa at the Duke of York School in Kenya. He was RSCM Special Representative in South Africa and was made FRSCM in 2012.

53) O valiant hearts

Voicing	SATB, organ	Pages	3	ms.	EGG E		Era	RET
Note	Dated November 1970			Text	Sir John S Arkwright (1872-1954)			

O valiant hearts

Sir John S. Arkwright (1872–1954)

Sir William H. Harris (1883-1973)

54a) O what their joy and their glory must be: Anthem for full choir

Voicing	SATB (div), organ (or orchestra)		Publ No	A48	Pages	10	Era	OXC
Publisher	OUP	Series	The Oxford Series of Modern Anthems				Date	1931
Text	Translated from the Latin of Abelard by J M Neale (1818-1866)							
Note	Orchestral parts and score are available on hire. Performed with orchestra at the Three Choirs' Festival in Gloucester in 1934.							
WHH Note	Founded on a French Melody [O Quanta Qualia, Paris Antiphoner 1681].							

54b) O what their joy and their glory must be: Anthem founded on a French melody

Voicing	SSA, piano	Publ No	A207	Pages	14	Date	1964	Era	RET
Publisher	OUP	Series		The Oxford Series of Modern Anthems					
Text	Translated from the Latin of Abelard by J M Neale (1818-1866)								
Note	This arrangement for female voices by WHH. The melody is *O Quanta Qualia*, Paris Antiphoner 1681.								

55) Offertorium: O hearken Thou

Voicing	SATBSATB, organ	Publ No	SA278	Date		1937	Era	SGW
Publisher	Novello	Series		Novello's Short Anthems			Pages	3
Text	Psalm 5 v.2							
Note	Composed for the communion section of the 1937 Coronation liturgy, though sung on that occasion with an accompaniment of both organ and orchestra. [Orchestral score in EGG F]							

56) Our day of praise is done

Voicing	S(S)ATB, T or S solo, organ		Publ No	E133	Pages	4		Era	RET
Publisher	OUP	Series	The Oxford Series of Easy Anthems					ms.	EGG E
Text	J Ellerton and part of a bidding prayer by E Milner-White					Date			1968/1973
Dedication The early (1968) versions of this anthem were dedicated to C F Simkins[277].									

---

[277] Cyril Frank (k/a Simmie) Simkins (b. 1902) studied at St Michael's College in Tenbury, and served as an alto lay clerk first in Gloucester Cathedral and then at St George's Chapel in Windsor for nearly forty years until retirement in 1967. Co-author (with Sir. Walford Davies) of a book about the organs of St George's Chapel, he made many editions of 17th C and 18th C choral music, and, noted for his penmanship, he compiled chant books for several cathedrals.

57) Peace I leave with you: Short Meditation, or Anthem

Voicing	SATB, TB soli, SAT verse, organ	Publ No	MT1229	Era	SGW
Publisher	Novello	Pages	4	Date	1945
Series	The Musical Times	Text	John 14		
WHH Note	If practicable the organ is only to be used in the introduction, recitatives (where indicated) and final chorus; a quiet background.				

58) Peace: A Mystery Carol for Christmastide

Voicing	SATB T&B soli, organ	Pages	6	Date	1905	Era	RCM
Publisher	Houghton	Text	A C Benson (1862-1925) from "Peace, and Other Poems.")				

59) Praise the Lord, O my Soul (Psalm 103) Set to Music for Double Choir

Voicing	SATBSATB	Publ No		none	Pages	47	Date	1938	Era	SGW
Publisher	Novello	Series	Novello's Original Octavo Edition				Text	Psalm 103		

Dedication To the memory of Sydney Charles Scott[278]

Note 1st performance was in the Sheldonian Theatre in Oxford on 27th November 1938 by the Oxford Bach Choir under Thomas Armstrong. WHH was unable to be present as it was his daughter Anne's confirmation that day at her school in Calne, Wiltshire.

---

278 Sydney Charles Scott (1849-1936) was a solicitor, gifted pianist and member of the Society for Psychical Research.

60) Praised be the God of Love: Antiphon

Voicing	SATB, organ ad lib.	Publ No	OA1225	Pages	4	Era	SGW
Publisher	Novello	Series	Novello's Octavo Anthems			Date	1937
Text	George Herbert (1593-1633)						
WHH Note	"Herbert's division: Chorus, Men and Angels must be observed Chorus - Full; Men - Dec.; Angels -Can."						

61) Prelude to a Solemn Music

Voicing	T solo, SATB, organ	Publ No	OA1283	Pages	14	Era	SGW
Publisher	Novello	Series	Octavo Anthems			Date	1950
Text	Canon Adam Fox[279]						

Dedication The words and music specially written for the Festival Service of St Ceciia at St Sepulchre's Church, Holborn, on November 22nd 1950.

---

[279] Adam Fox (1883-1977) was the Dean of Divinity at Magdalen College, Oxford, and a canon at Westminster Abbey from 1941 until retirement in 1963. He is buried at The Abbey in "Poet's Corner".

62) Prevent us, O Lord

Voicing	SATB	Publ No	MT1567	Pages	4	Date	1973	Era	RET
Publisher	Novello	Series	The Musical Times				ms.	EGG R
Text	Book of Common Prayer		Note		Annotated for tonic sol-fa		

Dedication To Petersfield Choral Society, and its Conductor, T Warden Lane[280]

[280] For information on Tim Lane see p. 267

63) Requests: Motet for SATB (unaccompanied)

Voicing	SATB	Pages	6		Era	RET
Date	1966	ms.	EGG E	Text	Digby Mackworth-Dolben[281]	

---

[281] Digby Mackworth-Dolben (1848-1867), a cousin of poet Robert Bridges who later edited his works, was educated at Eton and tragically died young by drowning before going up to Oxford University.

64) Sing a song of joy

Voicing	SATB	Publ No	MT1236	Pages	4	Date	1946	Era	SGW
Publisher	Novello	Series	The Musical Times						
Text	Thomas Campion (1567-1620)								

65) Strengthen ye the weak hands (Suitable for St Luke's Day)

Voicing	T solo, SATB, organ, some divisi			Publ No	OA1275	Era	SGW
Publisher	Novello	Pages	12	Date	1950	ms.	RSCM
Series	Octavo Anthems	Text		Bible and Book of Common Prayer			
Dedication Composed and sung in Canterbury Cathedral for the opening service in commemoration of the Science and Art of Healing - Canterbury Festival. June 25, 1949.							
Note	ms. dated Windsor May 23 1949						

Page 1 of the original ms. of 'Strengthen ye the weak hands'.
The red ink and pencil markings were added by the publisher before typesetting.

66) The Ascension opus 1 (1891) [EGG G] See Chapter 10

67) The Ascension: Introit or Anthem

Voicing	SATB, organ	Pages	5	ms.	EGG R	Era	RET
Date	1971	Text	Joseph Beaumont (1628-1699)				
Unpublished	Note Early draft is dated Jan 1971, two later versions undated.						

68) The Beatitudes (Set to music for double choir)

Voicing	SATBSATB	Publ No	OA1258	Pages	10	Date	1942	Era	SGW
Publisher	Novello	Series	Octavo Anthems		Text	Matthew 5: 3-12			
Dedication	"In affectionate memory of HWD" [Henry Walford Davies]								
Note	First performed in 1941 at the July Windsor Festival.								

69) The beauty of heaven

Voicing	SATBSATB	Unpublished	ms.	EGG R	Date	1970	Era	RET
Pages.	14	Text		Selected from Ecclesiaticus Ch 43				
Note	Final draft dated 4th June 1970. Many drafts exist and WHH initially composed this for SATB with organ before deciding to make it double choir.							

70) The eyes of all wait upon Thee, O Lord

Voicing	SATB, organ	Publ No	A142	Pages	4	Date	1956	Era	SGW/ADD
Publisher	OUP	Series		Oxford Anthems		Text	Psalm 145: 15-20		

Dedication For Harold Darke and the Choir of St Michael's, Cornhill. June 1956. [Darke's 40th anniversary at Cornhill]

71) The Heavens declare the Glory of God (Anthem founded on Gibbons' Song I)

Voicing	SATBSATB, T solo, organ	Publ No	A37	Date	1930	Era	OXC
Publisher	OUP	Series	The Oxford Series of Modern Anthems			Pages	16
Text	Psalm 19 with two verses from 'Eternal Ruler' by J W Chadwick (1840-1904)						
Note	The final section *Eternal Ruler* uses Gibbons' Song 1 and was issued separately as OUP A39 see **17)** The first section was published separately as *Psalm XIX* OUP A38						

Dedication For the 276th Anniversary of the Festival of the Sons of the Clergy in St Paul's Cathedral, May 21 1930.

72) The Holy Eucharist: Introit

Voicing	SATB	Publ No	Pages		2	ms.	EGG A	A233	Era	RET
Publisher	OUP	Series	Oxford Anthems				Date	1959 publ. 1966		
Dedication "for St George's Chapel, Windsor"							Text	Douglas J L Bean[282]		

Note
Original (dated Ascension Day 1959) has music for only one verse. It was revised in an extended form before publication in 1966.

---

[282] Douglas Jeyes Lendrum Bean (b.1925) was a minor canon at St George's from 1954 to 1959 when this piece was written. He was subsequently vicar of St Pancras Church, retiring in 1993, and a canon at St Paul's Cathedral.

73) The King, O God, his Heart to Thee upraiseth (Hymn-anthem for National Thanksgiving)

Voicing	SATB (divisi ad lib.), organ	Publ No	MT1219	Pages	4	Era	SGW
Publisher	Novello	Series	The Musical Times			Date	1944
Text	From the Yattendon Hymnal based on F R Tailour (1615)						

74) The Lord is my Shepherd (Trio for equal voices)

Voicing	SSC, piano	Publ No	574		Date	1939	Era	LCH/SGW
Publisher	Novello	Series	Novello's Octavo Edition of Trios etc. for Female Voices					
Text	Psalm 23	Pages	11					
Dedication	Dedicated to Miss Mary Ray, and the Choir of Penrhos College, Colwyn Bay							
WHH Note		"First version 1912 (Lichfield), Revised 1939 (Windsor)"						

175

75) The Lord my Pasture shall prepare (Suitable for a Wedding)

Voicing	SATB, organ	Publ No	MT1222	Pages	3	Date	1944	Era	SGW
Publisher	Novello	Series	The Musical Times		Text	J Addison (1672-1719)			
Dedication	For Margaret and Michael, March 17th, 1944 [his daughter's wedding]								
Notes	Only verse 1 is the same as **76)**								

76) The Lord my Pasture shall prepare: Anthem for boys' voices
(Suitable for a Wedding)

Voicing	SS, organ	Publ No	CS116	Pages	4	Era	SGW/ADD
Publisher	Novello	Series	Chorister Series			Date	1961
Text	J Addison	Dedication For Margaret and Michael, March 17th, 1944 [his daughter's wedding]					
Note	Only verse 1 is the same as **75)**						

End of v.1 and start of v.2

77a) The Shepherd-men were keeping a little flock from ill

Voicing	SATB, organ	Publ No	CC423	Pages	2	Date	1933	Era	SGW
Publisher	Stainer & Bell	Series	Church Choir Library			Text	Anthony C Deane[283]		
Note	also SSA arrangement see **77b)**								

No scan available

77b) The Shepherd-men were keeping a little flock from ill

Voicing	SSA, organ	Publ No	CC600	Pages	2		Era	SGW/ADD
Publisher	Stainer & Bell	Series	Church Choir Library			Date	1960	
Text	Anthony C Deane							
Note	also SATB arrangement see **77a)**							

---

283 The Revd. Anthony Charles Deane (1870–1946) was Vicar of Great Malvern and a canon of Worcester Cathedral. From 1929 until his death he was Canon of the Ninth Stall at St George's Chapel.

78) Think good Jesu

Voicing	SATB, organ	Unpublished		Date	1948	Era	SGW
ms.	SGW ms. M.144-XIII-2 and EGG A (slightly different versions)						
Text	Verses from the Dies Irae	Dedication		"for Canon Crawley's Funeral in George's Chapel"[284]			
WHH Note	May be sung after Walford Davies' setting to Psalm 23.						
Note	The ms. is undated but Canon Crawley's died on the 8th October 1948 suggesting that this piece was composed around that time.						

ms. M.144-XIII-2

ms. EGG A

---

[284] Arthur Stafford Crawley (1876-1948) was Canon of the Sixth Stall at St George's from 1934 until his death.

79) This joyful Eastertide: Dutch Carol arranged as an anthem

Voicing	SATB, organ	Publ No	OA1367	Pages		7	Era	SGW/ADD
Publisher	Novello	Series	Novello's Octavo Anthems				Date	1958
Text	The words are taken from *The Cowley Carol Book* by permission of A R Mowbray.							
WHH Note	The unaccompanied sections may be lightly accompanied.							

80) Thou hast made me (Motet for Double Choir)

Voicing	SATBSATB	Publ No	OA1268	Pages	16	Date	1947	Era	SGW
Publisher	Novello	Series		Novello's Octavo Anthems					
Text	John Donne (1572-1631) (from the Holy Sonnets)								

81) Thou whose birth on earth: Christmas Carol

Voicing	SATB (div)	Pages	2	Date	1962	Era	SGW/ADD & RET
Text	Algernon C Swinburne (1837-1909)				ms.	EGG E	
Note							

Version 1 in E-minor, subtitled "Christmas Antiphon", is dated Windsor, December 1960.
Version 2 in E-flat minor, subtitled "Christmas Carol", is dated Petersfield, 1964.

82) Through the day thy love hath spared us

Voicing	SATB, organ	Unpublished	ms.	EGG E	Era	RET
Text	Thomas Kelly (1769-1855)				Pages	20

Note: Originally composed as a unison hymn tune see p. 225
An earlier anthem version was in D-flat.
Final version dated February 24th 1962.

WHH Notes "The first verse may be sung by a semi-chorus; the second by the full choir".
Also notated "For RSCM ?"

83) Thus saith the Lord God

Voicing	SATB, organ	Publ No	OA1324	Pages	20	Date	1955	Era	SGW
Publisher	Novello	Series	Novello's Octavo Anthems						
Text	Isaiah (various) and a hymn by Isaac Watts (1674-1748)								
Dedication	"Composed for a service of the Most Noble Order of the Garter in St George's Chapel, Windsor, 13 June 1955"								

84) Vox ultima crucis (Tarry no longer toward thine heritage)

Voicing	U (div), organ	Publ No	E31	Pages	2	Date	1937	Era	SGW
Publisher	OUP		Series	The Oxford Series of Easy Anthems					
Text	John Lydgate (1370?-1447)								
Note	Reissued as edition No.241 by the RSCM in 1971								
WHH Note	The old English has been modernized, but 'bigg'd above the starres clear' and 'most entere' (entire) have been retained.								

85) Ye that do your master's will: Hymn-Anthem

Voicing	SATB, organ	Pages	2	ms.	EGG R	Date	n/d		Era	RET
Note	"This anthem may be sung unaccompanied, omitting the organ Note (in small type)"						Text		Charles Wesley	

2: Liturgical Music

1) A Simple Communion Service in F

Voicing	SATB, organ	Publ No	16	Pages	7	Date	c.1939	Era	SGW
Publisher	SECM/RSCM	Series	Choir Book Reprints Reissued 1950 as RSCM 111						
Note	Kyrie has both English and Latin texts.								

KYRIE ELEISON

RESPONSES TO THE COMMANDMENTS

Lord, have mer-cy up-on___ us, and in-cline our hearts to keep this law.

Lord, have mer-cy up-on___ us, and write all these thy laws in our hearts, we be-seech thee.

SANCTUS

Slowly

PRIEST

ev-er-more prais-ing thee and say-ing:

Ho - ly, ho-ly, ho - ly, Lord___

BENEDICTUS

Slightly faster

Ho -

Bless-ed is he that com- eth in the Name of the Lord.

AGNUS DEI

Unaccompanied if possible, or⁽¹⁾*Boys only,*⁽²⁾*Men only, then*⁽³⁾*Full.*

Slowly

O Lamb of God, that tak-est a-way the sins of the world, have

GLORIA IN EXCELSIS

Slow

Faster

and in earth peace, good will to-wards men. We

PRIEST

Glo-ry be to God on high,

Slow

Faster

praise thee, we bless thee, we__ wor-ship thee, we glo-ri-fy__ thee, we give

2) Benedicite, Omnia Opera in A. (Shortened form)

Voicing	SATB, organ	Publ No	PCB1303	Pages	12	Date	1951	Era	SGW
Publisher	Novello	Series		Parish Choir Book		Note		Shortened form	

3) Communion Service in B-minor

Voicing	SATB, organ	Pages	25	ms.	EGG F	Date	1964/1968	Era	RET
Unpublished	Note	Kyrie; Responses to the Commandments; Creed, Sanctus; Benedictus, Agnus Dei, Gloria. Dated March 28th 1964 (revised February 1968)							
		In renumbering the pages 1-26, WHH accidently omitted the number 20.							

Creed
4
Tempo moderato
The Father Almighty Maker of Heaven and earth
I believe in one God.
Tempo moderato
and of all things visible and in-vi-si-ble
And in one Lord

Andante maestoso
Sanctus and Benedictus
12
Ho-ly, Ho-ly, Ho-ly, Lord God of
cresc.
Andante maestoso
hosts. Heaven and earth are full of thy glory
Heaven and earth

Agnus Dei

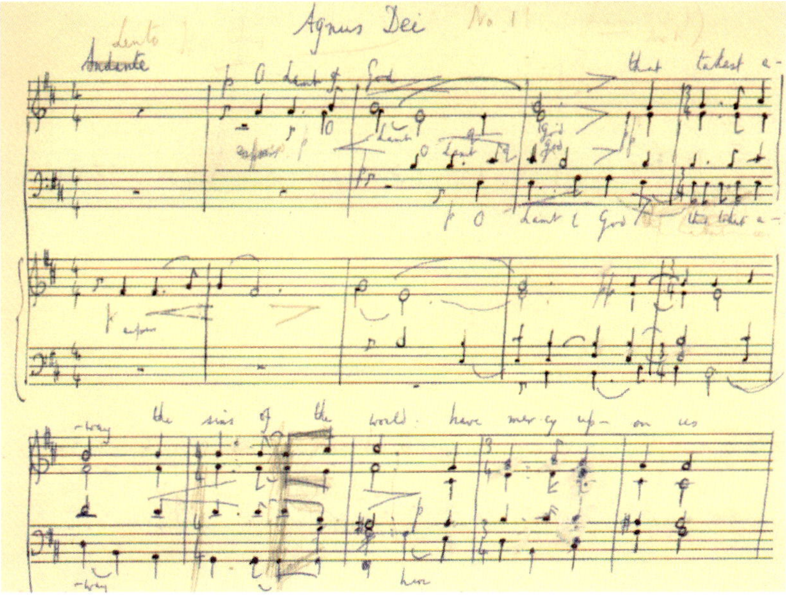

Gloria

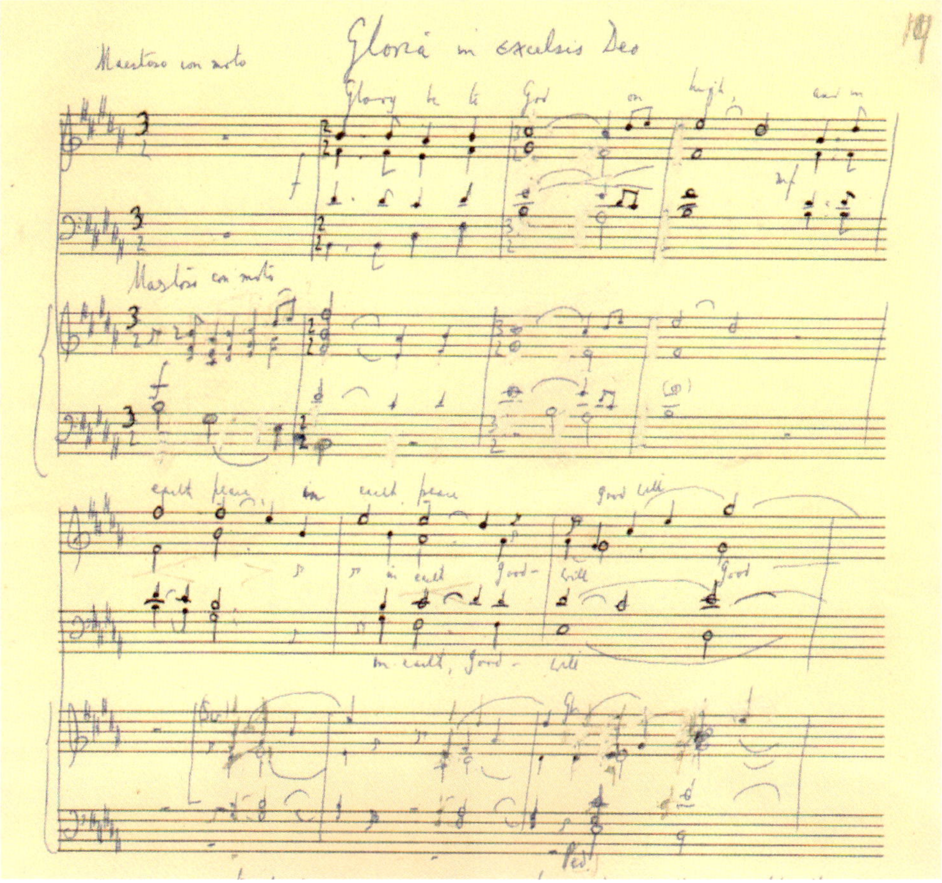

4) Communion in C

Voicing	SATB	Publ No	OCS523	Pages	8	Date	1951	Era	SGW
Publisher	OUP	Series	Oxford Church Music		Dedication		"In memoriam T J B."		
Note	A family copy has a pencil annotation (probably by Clement McWilliam) "T J B may have been Tim Burrage, Old Chorister 1933-1938, killed in Palestine."								

KYRIE ELEISON

RESPONSES TO THE COMMANDMENTS

SANCTUS AND BENEDICTUS

AGNUS DEI

GLORIA IN EXCELSIS DEO

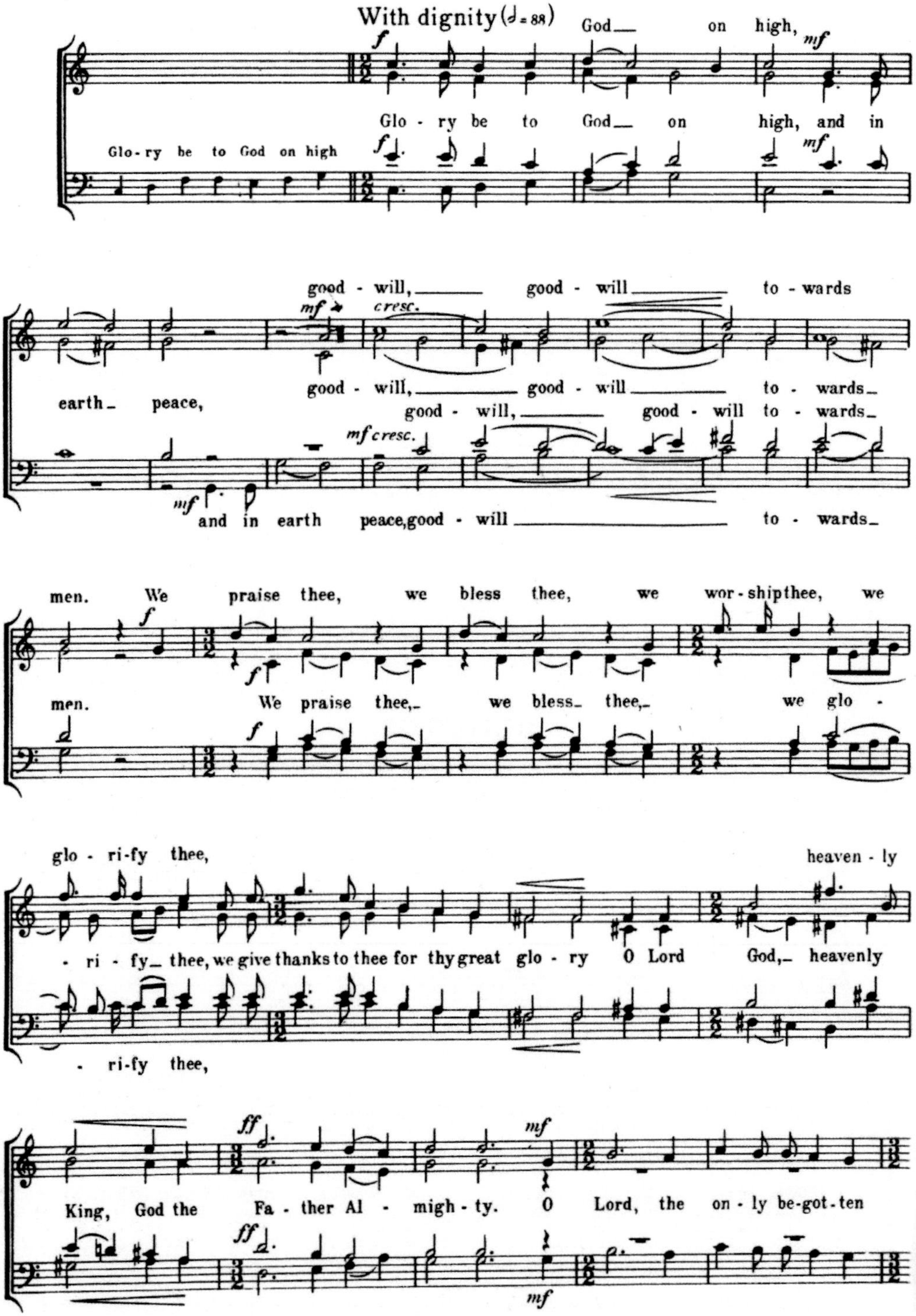

5) Descant and harmonisation for "Gopsal"

Voicing	U + descant, organ	Pages	I	Date	c.1933	Era	OXC
Publisher	Manchester Diocesan Church Music Society printed by Novello						
Note	Printed in Manchester Diocesan Church Music Society Service Book 1933 "By permission of Dr W H Harris".						

DESCANT for last verse.   W. H. Harris.

ORGAN.

6) Descant and harmonisation for "Nun Danket"

Voicing	U + descant, organ	Publ No	FSB3	Date	1969		Era	RET
Publisher	RSCM	Pages	I	ms.	RSCM and EGG E			
Series	Festival Service Book Three							

7) Kyrie [in E-minor]

Voicing	SATB		Unpublished	Date	n.d.	Era	SGW
Note	ms.	SGW Windsor Archives M.144-XIII-4					

8) Magnificat and Nunc Dimittis in A (Evening Service in A) [1897]

Voicing	SATB, organ	Pages	8	Date	1897	Era	HTT
Publisher	Weekes & Co	Note	His earliest published composition. See p. 72				

MAGNIFICAT.

W. 3447.

NUNC DIMITTIS.

Slowly.

Lord, Lord, Lord, now lettest Thou Thy ser——vant de—part in peace: ac——cording to Thy word. For mine eyes have seen, have seen: Thy sal——vation. Which

9) Magnificat and Nunc Dimittis in A [1947]

Voicing	SATB, organ	Publ No	514	Pages	10	Date	1947	Era	SGW
Publisher	OUP		Series	Oxford Church Services					
Note	A unison part for congregation was arranged by A W Bunney, presumably with WHH's approval, and published by OUP as 514A in 1961.[285]								

MAGNIFICAT

NUNC DIMITTIS

---

[285] Organist Allan Walter Bunney (1905-1980) studied at the RCM (possibly with WHH) and was director of music at Tonbridge School from 1941. He presumably made the arrangement to enable the piece to be sung at the school. He also directed the Tonbridge Philharmonic Society.

10) Magnificat and Nunc Dimittis in A-Minor

Voicing	SATB, organ	Publ No	A94	Pages	8	Date	1947	Era	SGW
Publisher	A&C Black	Series	The Year Book Press						

MAGNIFICAT

NUNC DIMITTIS

11) Magnificat and Nunc Dimittis in B-flat

Voicing	SATB, organ	Pages	13	Publisher	Riordan	Date	1907	Era	RCM
Note	Composed for the 34th Annual Festival of the London Church Choir Association 1907.								

MAGNIFICAT

NUNC DIMITTIS

12) Magnificat and Nunc Dimittis in D (for equal voices)

Voicing	SSS or SSA, organ	Publ No	CS105	Pages	12	Era	SGW/ADD
Publisher	Novello		Series	Chorister Series		Date	1958
Dedication	"For the choir of Whiteland's College, Putney"[286]						
WHH Note	The third soprano part is optional						

MAGNIFICAT

---

[286] Whitelands College was founded in 1841 as a Church of England Teacher Training College for Women.

NUNC DIMITTIS

13) Magnificat and Nunc Dimittis in E

Voicing	SATBSATB	Unpublished	Pages	11	Date	1908	Era	RCM
Dedication	"To Dr Walford Davies & the Temple Church Choir for whom it was written in 1908"					ms.		EGG A
Note	WHH made a revised version in 1967.							

14) Preces and Responses (ATTB)

Voicing	ATTB	Publ No	CM366	Pages	4	Date	1969	Era	SGW
Publisher	Cathedral Music	ms.	EGG E						
Dedication	"For Roy Massey and the Choir of Birmingham Cathedral"								
Note	Annotated by WHH "Sent to Roy Massey September 25th 1969. Published in 1991, Harris did not set "And with thy spirit" or provide an Amen for the Creed. These were added in the published edition by Barry Rose (b. 1934).								

15a) Te Deum in A

Voicing	SATB, organ	Publ No	513	Pages	11	Date	1946	Era	SGW
Publisher	OUP			Series	Oxford Church Music				
Note	Published 1948	WHH Note		This Te Deum may be sung unaccompanied					

This Te Deum may be sung unaccompanied.

15b) Te Deum Laudamus: Set to music in the key of A flat for A.T.B.

Voicing	ATB, organ	Publ No	MV140	Date		1958	Era	SGW/ADD	
Publisher	Novello	Series	Novello's Services and Anthems for Men's Voices					Pages	8
Note	"Adapted from the Service in A for SATB published by the Oxford University Press" (see previous page). The arrangement is probably by Harris himself.								

16) Te Deum in B flat (founded on the Second Tone)

Voicing	SATB (div), organ	Publ No	PCB1215	Date	1938	Era	SGW
Publisher	Novello		Series	Novello's Parish Choir Book		Pages	12
Dedication	Composed for a Service of the Most Noble Order of the Garter in St George's Chapel, Windsor, on June 14, 1937.						

17) Te Deum in G for Congregational Use (with Descant for Choir)

Voicing	U + SATB, organ		Publ No	435		Date	1930	Era	OXC
Publisher	OUP	Series	Oxford Church Music			Pages	6		

PRAISE TO THE HOLY TRINITY

3: Hymn Tunes

A) Published Tunes

1) Alberta: Metre 10 4 10 4 10 10

Voicing	Unison	Was composed for the words "Lead, kindly light" whilst travelling through Alberta from Calgary to Edmonton by train in 1924. He was in Canada examining. It was published in a leaflet in March 1925 and first appeared in *Songs of Praise* in 1931 in D-flat.
Date	1925	
Publisher	Novello then OUP	
Hymn Book	Songs of Praise 1931	By coincidence, the text by Cardinal John Henry Newman (1801-1890) was also written whilst travelling. He was becalmed for a week on board a ship travelling from Palermo to Marseilles when he wrote these words.
Hymn No.	554	
Era	OXN	

ALBERTA. (10 4. 10 4. 10 10.)
In moderate time. Unison.

There is also an hymn-anthem arrangement – see p. 139

2) Ewell: Metre 7 6 7 6 D

Voicing	SATB	
Date	1912	
Publisher	A S Barnes Co., New York.	Written specifically for the text "Divine, Majestic Maker" by Marion M Scott. See p. 18.
Hymn Book	Hymns of the Church: New and Old	
Hymn No.	495	
Era	RCM	

3) Kybald Twychen: Metre 7 7 7 7 5 7 7 7

Voicing	SATB
Date	c.1948
Publisher	Hymns A&M
Hymn Book	Hymns A&M (Revised) 1950
Hymn No.	614
Era	SGW

Written specifically for Hymns A&M Revised 1950 for the text "Holy Spirit, gently come" by William Hammond (1719-1783).

Kybald Twychen is a 17C house in Oxford, the residence of the Harrises whilst he was at New College and now owned by Corpus Christi College.

4) North Petherton: Metre 6 6 11 6 6 11

Voicing	SATB	Written specifically for Hymns A&M Revised 1950 for the text "Come down, O love divine". It was reworked in 1965 into the anthem with the same title.
Date	c. 1948	
Publisher	Hymns A&M	
Hymn Book	Hymns A&M (Revised) 1950	North Petherton, near Bridgwater in Somerset, was the birthplace of both Harris's mother and grandmother
Hymn No.	235	
Era	SGW	NB WHH used this name for another hymn tune in 1938[287].

[287] See p.222

5) Petersfield: Metre 7 7 7 7

| Voicing | SATB | Written specifically for *Hymns for Church and School* 1964 for the text " Hark, my soul, it is the Lord " by William Cowper (1731-1800).

Petersfield in Sussex was his home in retirement. |
|---------|------|---|
| Date | c.1964 | |
| Publisher | Novello | |
| Hymn Book | Hymns for Church and School 1964 | |
| Hymn No. | 132 | |
| Era | RET | |

6) Sennen Cove: Metre CM

| Voicing | SATB | Written specifically for *Hymns A&M Revised* 1950 for the text "How bright these glorious spirits shine" by Isaac Watts (1674-1748).

Sennen Cove is near Penzance in Cornwall.

This tune exists in three versions. Two are below, the third is an unpublished hymn-anthem with an independent organ part dated September 1971. See Anthem **27)** |
|---------|------|---|
| Date | c.1948 | |
| Publisher | Hymns A&M | |
| Hymn Book | Hymns A&M (Revised) 1950 | |
| Hymn No. | 528 | |
| Era | SGW | |

A) Sennen Cove Original Version

VERSES 3 AND 4 SHOULD BEGIN THUS

B) Later Version

7) Stoner Hill: Metre 10 10 10 10

Voicing	SATB
Date	c.1964
Publisher	Novello
Hymn Book	Hymns for Church and School 1964
Hymn No.	195
Era	RET

Written specifically for *Hymns for Church and School* 1964 for the text " Come, risen Lord, and deign to be our guest " by George Wallace Briggs (1875-1959).

Stoner Hill is near Harris's home in Petersfield.

B) Unpublished Tunes

8) Ledsam / Addington: Metre 8 8 8 8 8 8

Voicing	SATB	ms.	EGG R	Era	RET
Text William Dalrymple Maclagan (1826-1910) "The Saints of God! their conflict past." "For FCAL[288] on his 70th Birthday from his old friend WHH"					
The tune (with the same text) was renamed 'Addington' and sent to Gerald Knight, Director of the RSCM on June 8th 1972, but was not published by the RSCM.					

THE SAINTS OF GOD

LEDSAM   William H. Harris

---

[288] See p. 25 regarding Fred Ledsam.

9) North Petherton: Metre LM

Voicing	SATB	For the text "Fight the good fight", A&M (1916) No 540 Annotated 'Like a mighty army'. A decade later he used the same name for a different tune to be published in *Hymns A&M (Revised)*. See p.217
ms.	EGG R	
Date	Jan 1938	
Era	SGW	

10) Unnamed Tune A: Metre 7 5 7 5 7 5 7 5

Voicing	SATB	Dated Jan 1938 for the text A&M 74 (1916 edition) "Father let me dedicate all this year to Thee" (for New Year's Day). Text: Lawrence Tuttiett (1825-1897)
ms.	EGG R	
Date	1938	
Era	SGW	

Tune A

11) Unnamed Tune B: Metre CM

Voicing	SATB	Dated June 1st 1968 No text suggested
ms.	EGG R	
Date	1968	
Era	RET	

Tune B

12) Unnamed Tune C "Love divine, all loves excelling": Metre CM

Voicing	SATB	Dated August 7th 1973, possibly the last thing he wrote.
ms.	EGG R	
Date	1973	Text: Charles Wesley (17087-1788)
Era	RET	

Tune C

13) Unnamed Tune D "Through the day thy love hath spared us"
Metre 8 7 8 7 7 7

Voicing	SATB, organ	4 lines unison, 2 lines harmony
ms.	EGG R	Text: Thomas Kelly (1769-1855)
Date	1962	Version 1 Hymn tune in D-flat [EGG F]
		Version 2 Hymn-anthem in D-flat
Era	RET	Version 3 Hymn-anthem in C see p. 183

Tune D

4: Psalm Chants

The dates of composition of these chants are unknown.
No manuscript sources are known apart from the two chants noted.

Single in G for Psalm 18 vv.16-19

From *St George's Windsor Chantbook* ed. Harris No. 27

Double in A-minor for Psalm 70

From *Lichfield Chant Book* 1959 No.104

Double in B-flat for ATB

From *Lichfield Chant Book* 1960 ATB Psalter No.21

Double in C for Psalm 18 vv.20-end

From *St George's Windsor Chant Book* ed. Harris No. 26

Double in C for Psalm 29

From *St George's Windsor Chant Book* ed. Harris No. 46

The small note in the last quarter are for vv. 4 and 10. [*ms. EGG E*]

Double in D ATTB

From *St George's Windsor Chant Book* ed. Boyle No. 47

Double in D for Psalm 29

From *Ripon Psalter* 1960 No.37

Double in D for Psalm 67

From *Eton Chant Book* 1939 No. 67

Double in D for Psalm 78 vv. 66-73

From *St George's Windsor Chant Book* ed. C. Robinson c.1980

Psalm 78 vv.66-73

Double in D for Psalm 78 vv.66 to end

From *St George's Windsor Chant Book* ed. Harris No. 130

Psalm 78 vv. 66 to end   Sir WH Harris

Double in D for Psalm 84

From *Lichfield Chant Book* 1959 No.137

Psalm 84   Sir WH Harris

Double in D-flat for Psalm 122

From *Lichfield Cathedral*

Psalm 122   Sir WH Harris

Double in E-flat for Psalm 119 vv.33-56

From *Oxford Chant-Book 2* 1934 No. 296

Psalm 119 vv. 33-56   Sir WH Harris

Double in G for Psalm 27 vv.1-7/15-end

From *St George's Windsor Chant Book* ed. Harris No. 42 [*ms. EGG E*]

Psalm 27 vv. 1-7 & 15 to end   Sir WH Harris

Quadruple in F for Ps.78 vv.1-17

From *Lichfield Chant Book* 1959 No.124

Psalm 78 vv. 1-17

Quad.

Sir WH Harris

5: Works for organ solo

1) A Fancy

Voicing	Organ 3 mans/ped			Pages	8	Date		Publ. 1947	Era	SGW
Publisher	Novello	Series		Original Compositions for Organ (New Series)				Pub. No.		204
Dedication	To the memory of Percy Whitlock, for whom it was written									

2) A Little Organ Book in memory of Henry Ley

In 1963 WHH composed 'Four Short Introductory Voluntaries'

1. **Meditation** [in E-flat]

2. **Elegy** [in C-minor]

3. **Allegretto** [in B-flat], renamed **Interlude**

4. **Adagio** [in B-major]), renamed **Reverie (in the style of Schumann)**

At an unknown date Harris decided to create 'A Little Organ Book in memory of Henry Ley'. He renumbered these pieces 2 to 5 and presumably intended to compose a new first piece for the set. No trace has been found of such a piece, but the other four are complete and the Elegy is marked "revised 1969".

1. **Meditation** [in E-flat]

2. **Elegy** [in C-minor]

3. **Allegretto** [in B-flat], this version renamed **Interlude**

4. **Adagio** [in B-major]), renamed **Reverie (in the style of Schumann)**

3) Allegretto in F#-minor

Voicing	Organ: 3 mans/ped		Pages	6	Date	1900	Era	RCM
Publisher	Vincent	Series	The Anglican Organist		Pub. No.	Vol. 19 No.233		

4) Andante in D

Voicing	Organ: 2 mans/ped	Pages		5	Date		1899	Era	RCM
Publisher	Vincent	Series	The Anglican Organist			Pub. No.		Vol. 17 No.217	
Dedication		W M Brooke Esq[289].							

To W. M. BROOKE Esq.

63

Nº 217.

Andante in D.

WILLIAM H. HARRIS.

Prepare Organ. { Gt soft 8 ft. with Sw. coupled. / Sw. 8 ft. with soft reed. / Ped. soft 16 ft. with Gt coupled.

Con espressione. M. M. ♩ = 88.

Manual.

Gt p

Pedal.

cresc.

dim.

pp

William H. Harris. F.R.C.O. Born in London 1883.

561

---

[289] William Montagu Brooke (1861-1939) was acting organist of St Davids Cathedral briefly before the appointment of Herbert Morris and arrival of WHH. He was organist of Pembury Parish Church in Kent, from 1899, when this piece was published.

5) Cadenza for Handel Organ Concerto in B-flat

Voicing	Organ with pedals	Unpublished	Pages	2	Date	n.d.
Note	The *ms.* appears to be from the 1920's				*ms.*	EGG F

6) Cadenza for Handel Organ Concerto in G

Voicing	Organ with pedals	Pages	3	Unpublished	
Date	Dec 1st 1921			*ms.*	EGG F

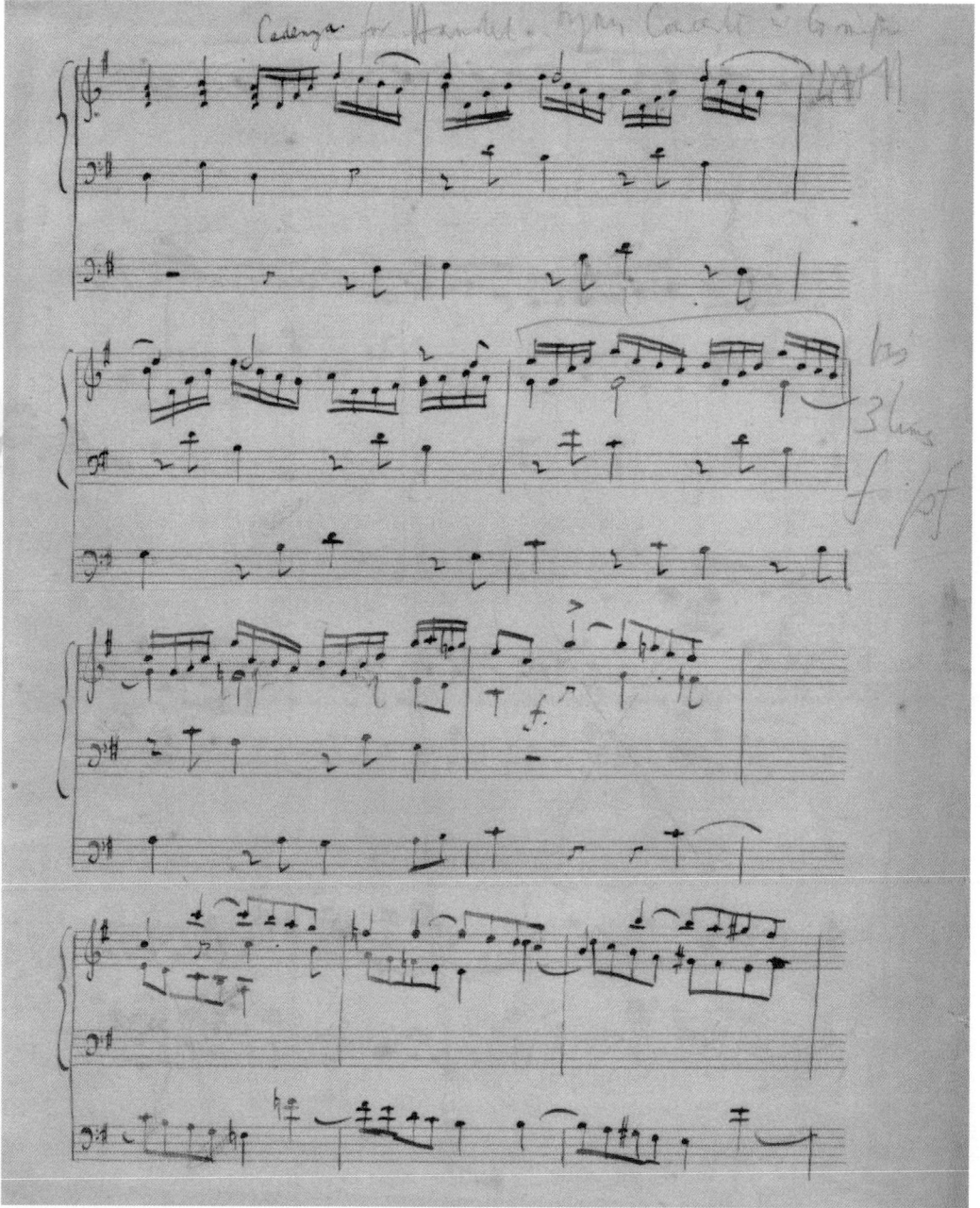

7) Elegy

Voicing	Organ 2 mans/ped ad lib.		Pages	2	Date	1959	Era	SGW/ADD
Publisher	Novello	Pub. No.	"Second Set"					
Series	Two-Stave Voluntaries by Modern Composers							

8) Epilogue on "Dix"

Voicing	Organ 2 mans/ped		Pages	4	Date	1956	Era	SGW
Publisher	Novello	Pub. No.	Festal Voluntaries: Christmas and Epiphany (album)					
Note	Also issued separately as Original Compositions for Organ (New Series) No. 270.							

9) Fantasia on an English folk tune ["Monk's Gate"]

Voicing	Organ 4 mans/ped	Pages	12	Date	1930	Era	OXC
Publisher	Oxford University Press	Dedication		Dedicated to Dr W G Alcock[290]			

---

[290] Sir Walter Alcock (1861-1947) was a professor at the RCM, assistant organist of Westminster Abbey from 1896, and then organist of Salisbury Cathedral from 1916 until his death.

10) Fantasy on "Easter Hymn"

Voicing	Organ 4 mans/ped	Pages	5	Date	1956	Era	SGW
Publisher	Novello		Series		Festal Voluntaries: Easter (album)		
Note	Also issued separately as Original Compositions for Organ (New Series) No. 249.						

11) Fantasy on the tune "Babylon's Streams"

Voicing	Organ 4 mans/ped	Pages	12	Date	1922	Era	OXN
Publisher	Stainer & Bell	Dedication		"To Harold Darke"			
Series	Organ Solos edited and arranged by Henry G Ley				Pub. No.		No.10
Note	The first version is dated Lichfield Jan 1916 [EGG F]. It bears a sub-title not printed in the published version — "How shall we sing the Lord's song in a strange land" [Psalm 137: 4] and the work is substantially different to and shorter than the final published version.						

241

12) Fantasy-Prelude

Voicing	Organ 3 mans/ped		Pages	5	Date	1959	Era	SGW/ADD
Publisher	Novello	Series	In Retrospection (album)			ms.		EGG A

Note:

This piece was commissioned around 1959 by H W Gray of New York (a subsidiary of Novello) for inclusion in a project to publish a companion volume to *The Modern Anthology* of 1949 edited by David McKinley Williams (1887-1978). This second volume was never published, but some of the commissioned works were issued separately by Gray. A letter from Novello & Co. dated 30th September 1969 indicates that they had sent the proofs to Harris for proof-reading.

Gray never published this piece but in 1982 Novello decided to include the work in their 1983 anthology *Retrospection*. Harris's daughter and executor Anne was delighted that this new publication would coincide with Sir Williams' centenary in the following year.

13) [Sonata No.2 in A-major]

EGG A contains a folder marked "Sonata No.2 in A-major Petersfield 1963." The pieces are numbered; suggesting that this unpublished sonata was planned to have four movements:

1. **Festal Voluntary** [in A]

2. **Retrospect (Meditation)** [in F]

3. **A Frolic (Scherzetto)** [in G-minor]

4. **Animato** [in A, only a few bars sketched]

From amendments on the cover, it would appear that Harris later decided to abandon his sonata and rework these movements into a set of "Three Pieces". It is likely that these final titles may not have been those that he would have used had the work become a formal sonata.

13a) Festal Voluntary

Voicing	Organ 3 mans/ped	Pages	10/11	Era	RET
Unpublished		Date	1963	ms.	EGG A

The latest version (of three) for the Festal Voluntary has a sub-title added: "Inservi Deo, et Laetare" – Serve God, and be cheerful – the motto of John Hackett, a 17th Century Bishop of Lichfield.

243

13b) Retrospect (Meditation)

Voicing	Organ 3 mans/ped	Pages	7	Era	RET
Unpublished		Date	1963	ms.	EGG A

Harris was clearly unhappy with this second movement - he annotated p.1 with "Many unnecessary long bars - needs speeding up (shortening)" and on p.5 he wrote "Rhythmically dull & too leisurely". No further revision was found among his mss.

13c) A Frolic (Scherzetto)

Voicing	Organ 3 mans/ped	Pages	7	Era	RET
Unpublished		Date	1963	ms.	EGG A

This piece exists in three *ms.* versions and Harris notes on all three "To be played lightly, on clear, bright stops."

14 Flourish for an Occasion

Voicing	Organ 3 mans/ped	Pub. No.	203	Pages	8	Date	1948	Era	SGW
Publisher	Novello	Series		Original Compositions for Organ (New Series)					

15a) Four Short Pieces: No.1 Prelude

Voicing	Organ: 2 mans/ped.	Pages		2	Date	1931/1935		Era	OXC
Publisher	School of English Church Music				Series	The Gift Book (see below)			
WHH Note	Composed in the Thomaskirche, Leipzig, August, 1931						ms.	EGG G & RSCM	
Note	Reissued as No.1 of *Four Short Pieces* in the Original Compositions for Organ (New Series) No.170 by Novello in 1938.								

In August 1941 WHH arranged this piece for the Jacques String Orchestra [EGG G] who performed it in St George's Chapel on 27th September 1941 (along with the following *Reverie*) under the baton of Reginald Jacques.

H C Colles wrote in the SECM *Gift Book* 1935:

'The delicate choral prelude for organ which is here published is all the more interesting because it was not written for that purpose. When on holiday in Germany not long since he visited that church, never to be approached by musicians without a sense of peculiar awe, Bach's church of St Thomas in Leipzig. There, where the greatest masterpieces of organ music still seem to linger on the air, Dr Harris wrote the prelude [written in 1931] which he now gives us.'

The original ms. of Harris's E-flat Prelude for organ. The red and blue markings were added by the printer before typesetting. A later autograph ms. for Novello's "Four Pieces" edition is in EGG G.

15b) Four Short Pieces: No.2 Reverie

Voicing	Organ: 2 mans/ped.	Pages	3	ms.	EGG G	Date	1938	Era	SGW
Publisher	Novello	Series	Original Compositions for Organ (New Series) 170 No.2						

In August 1941 WHH arranged this piece for the Jacques String Orchestra who performed it in St George's Chapel on September 27th 1941 (along with the preceding *Prelude*) under the baton of Reginald Jacques. [EGG G]

In October 1941 WHH also arranged it for piano [both *mss.* EGG G] and for oboe and piano [*ms.* EGG E].

15c) Four Short Pieces: No.3 Interlude in the form of a canon

Voicing	Organ: 3 mans/ped.	Pages	3	ms.	EGG G	Date	1938	Era	SGW
Publisher	Novello	Series	Original Compositions for Organ (New Series)170 No. 3						

15d) Four Short Pieces: No.4 Scherzetto

Voicing	Organ: 3 mans/ped.	Pages	5	ms.	EGG G	Date	1938	Era	SGW
Publisher	Novello	Series	Original Compositions for Organ (New Series)170 No. 4						

16) Improvisation on the Old 124th, Genevan Psalter

Voicing	Organ: 3 mans/ped	Pages	6	Date	1925	Era	OXN
Publisher	Stainer & Bell	Dedication		Dr Henry G Ley			
Series	Organ Solos edited and arranged by Henry G Ley No.15						

17a) Miniature Suite: Introduction and Fugue

Voicing	Organ 2 mans/ped	Pages	6	Date		1957	Era	SGW/ADD
Publisher	Novello	Series		Novello's Organ Music Club No. 9 No.1				
Dedication	"To Fred Ledsam"[291]							

[291] See p.25

17b) Miniature Suite: Pastorale

Voicing	Organ 3 mans/ped	Pages	3	Date		1957	Era	SGW/ADD
Publisher	Novello		Series		Novello's Organ Music Club No. 9 No.2			
Dedication	"To Fred Ledsam"							

17c) Miniature Suite: Romance and Scherzetto (Variation)

Voicing	Organ 3 mans/ped	Pages	7	Date	1957	Era	SGW/ADD
Publisher	Novello	Series		Novello's Organ Music Club No. 9 No.3			
Dedication "To Fred Ledsam"				ms.	EGG A		

18) Opening Voluntary in Memoriam HWD

Voicing	Organ with pedals	Pages	1	Date	1969	ms.	EGG R	Era	RET
Unpublished	Annotated "In memoriam HWD" and "for Sept. 6th" (which would have been Walford Davies' 100th birthday). Although on two staves, pedals are clearly to be used. Although the notes have been inked over, the pencil markings and dynamics have not. A playable piece but not fully completed for publication.								

19) Postlude

Voicing	Organ 2 mans/ped ad lib.	Pages	2	Date	1959	Era	SGW/ADD
Publisher	Novello	Series	Two-Stave Voluntaries by Modern Composers Second Set				

20) Prelude in G

Voicing	Organ 1 Man/Ped		Pages	2	Date		1973/1975	Era	RET
Publisher	OUP	Series	A Second Easy Album for Organ				ms.	EGG F	

On 26 April 1973 Christopher Morris of OUP wrote to Harris saying that they wished to publish a second 'Easy Album' for 'real beginners' and asking if he would contribute, and offering his own choice of composing something in the style of either a prelude or a postlude for 1 or 2 manuals.

Harris set straight to work, initially giving his piece the title 'Quiet Interlude' but ultimately changing this to 'Prelude'. He also added at the bottom "From Six Short & Easy Organ Pieces"" suggesting that he was minded to compose additional pieces.

On 1st May he sent his offering to OUP receiving a swift acknowledgment to say that 'there will be some delay before you see proofs because I am convinced that the other contributors will not be so prompt!' WHH was paid £15 for his work.

This piece was played by Martin Baker before the funeral of Princess Diana at Westminster Abbey in 1997. The RSCM, and probably other music retailers, have often been asked since then to locate the music for purchase. Customers sometimes seem disappointed because what they receive is just two pages lasting a couple of minutes rather than the much longer piece of music heard on recordings of the service. The reason is very simple for, as the cortege move through the Abbey, it was necessary for Martin Baker to improvise and extend the piece until the start of The National Anthem. So seamlessly and 'in style' was this improvisation, that few people realised that the whole was not by Harris.

21) Processional March

Voicing	Organ 3 mans/ped	Pages	4	Date	1960	Era	SGW/ADD
Publisher	Novello	Series		Original Compositions for Organ (New Series) No. 312			

WHH Note
For the Queen's Procession; and played by the composer at the Marriage of HRH Princess Margaret in Westminster Abbey, May 6 1960.

There are two further versions of this piece arranged by WHH [*mss*. EGG A]:

1) Arranged for full orchestra - double woodwind, 4 horns, 2 trumpets, 3 trombones, tuba (ad lib.), timpani, side drum (ad lib.), strings and organ (ad lib.)

2) Arranged for piano.

22) Reverie in A-flat

Voicing	Organ 3 mans/ped	Unpublished	Pages	6	Era	Possibly SGW
Note	From a *ms.* in the Archives of St George's Windsor.				Date	n/a

23 Saraband Processional

Voicing	Organ 3/4 mans/ped		Pages	6	Date	1949 publ. 1954	Era	SGW
Publisher	Novello	Series	Original Compositions for Organ (New Series) No.238					
Dedication	Composed for the St Cecilia's Day Festival Service at St Sepulchre's Church, Holborn November 22nd 1949.							
Note Original title was *Sarabande for St Cecilia's Day,* WHH's copy annotated "4 minutes". The Musical Times critic at the Festival Service described it as " tranquilly lovely"								

An undated version for orchestra and organ [ms. EGG A] is marked by WHH "First performance Birmingham Town Hall conducted by Julius Harrison.

This performance was on 8th December 1954 at the centenary concert of the Birmingham and Midland Institute. The reviewer commented "In Sir William Harris's Serenade [sic] Processional, a little ceremonial piece originally written for St Cecilia and now scored for organ and orchestra, the organist interpreted ad libitum to mean that he could leave his part out – which he mistakenly did."

In a further 'Note after performance' WHH writes "This needs a broader & fuller orchestration. It's all too thin & fussy. Too much unnecessary detail & ineffective."

24) Sonata in A-minor

Voicing	Organ: 4 mans/ped.	Date	1938	Era		SGW
Publisher	Novello	Pages	I: Moderato con moto (10) II: Adagio espressivo (6) III Maestoso (8)			
Series	Original Compositions for Organ (New Series) No.173					

Movement I

Movement II

Movement III

25a) Three Opening Voluntaries: No.1 Pastoral Prelude

Voicing	Organ 2 mans/ped		Pages	4	Date	1957	Era	SGW/ADD
Publisher	Novello	Series	Original Compositions for Organ (New Series) No. 284					
WHH note: Finished Mar 28th 1956							ms.	EGG A
Dedication: "To Frank Netherwood and the members of the Incorporated Association of Organists"								
Note: Composed for the 1956 Glasgow conference of the Incorporated Association of Organists.								

Harris subsequently arranged this for cello and piano (ms. EGG E) and the cello part is sub-titled "Pastorale Prelude on English Themes".

25b) Three Opening Voluntaries: No.2 Meditation on the Tune "Cheshire"

Voicing	Organ 2 mans/ped		Pages	3	Date	1957	Era		SGW/ADD
Publisher	Novello	Series	Original Compositions for Organ (New Series) No. 284						
Dedication "To Frank Netherwood and the members of the Incorporated Association of Organists"									
Note Composed for the 1956 Glasgow conference of the Incorporated Association of Organists.									

25c) Three Opening Voluntaries: No.3 Evening Melody

Voicing	Organ 2 mans/ped	Pages	3	Date	1957	Era		SGW/ADD
Publisher	Novello	Series	Original Compositions for Organ (New Series) No. 284					
Dedication "To Frank Netherwood and the members of the Incorporated Association of Organists"								
Note Composed for the 1956 Glasgow conference of the Incorporated Association of Organists.								

26a) Three Organ Voluntaries No. 1: In-Voluntary

Voicing	Organ 3 mans/ped	Unpublished		Date	1971	Era	RET
Pages	2	Dedication	To T Warden Lane[292]			ms.	EGG E

---

[292] Tim Lane was director of music at Churcher's College near Petersfield, organist of St Peter's Church, MD of the Petersfield Operatic Society and conductor of the Petersfield Choral Society from 1945-1981. He served on the Petersfield Festival Committee during the same period becoming its President in 1983 but died in the following year. Harris's anthem *Prevent us, O Lord* was also written for him.

26b) Three Organ Voluntaries No. 2: Interlude

Voicing	Organ 3 mans/ped		Unpublished		Date	1971	Era	RET
Pages	4	Dedication		To T Warden Lane			ms.	EGG E

26c) Three Organ Voluntaries No. 3: Out-Voluntary

Voicing	Organ 3 mans/ped		Unpublished		Date	1971	Era	RET
Pages	2	Dedication	To T Warden Lane				ms.	EGG E
Notes	"Founded on the composer's anthem 'All creatures of our God and King' published by the RSCM" Early versions of this piece were titled 'Paean'.							

27a) Three Preludes: No.1 Pastorale

Voicing	Organ 3 mans/ped		Pages	4	Date	1952	Era	SGW
Publisher	Novello	Series	Original Compositions for Organ (New Series) No.213					

27b) Three Preludes: No.2 Lament

Voicing	Organ 3 mans/ped		Pages	4	Date	1952	Era	SGW
Publisher	Novello	Series	Original Compositions for Organ (New Series) No.213					
Note	This piece is dedicated "In memory of Hubert Hunt[293]" . As Hunt died in 1945, it may have been composed some time earlier prior to publication in 1952.							

---

[293] Hubert Walter Hunt (1865-1945) was a former chorister of St George's Chapel in Windsor where his father was a lay-clerk. A graduate of Trinity College in Cambridge, he was an articled pupil of Sir George Elvey and Sir Walter Parratt. Organist of Bristol Cathedral from 1901 until his death, he was also a violinist.

27c) Three Preludes: No.3 Combewater

Voicing	Organ 3 mans/ped			Pages	3	Date	1952	Era	SGW
Publisher	Novello	Series		Original Compositions for Organ (New Series) No.213					
Note	Combewater Cottage in Metcombe, Devon, was a cottage owned by Henry Ley and used as a holiday retreat by WHH. Evelyn Ley died there in 1946.								

6: Vocal and Secular Choral Music

1) Ancient Hunting Song [The hunt is up!]

Voicing	Unison, Piano		Pages	4	Date	1921	Era	OXN
Publisher	H F W Deane & Sons		Publ No	UPS190		Text	Anon	
Series	The Year Book Press Series of Unison and Part-Songs							

2) Awake, my heart, to be loved

Voicing	SATB	Pages	4	Date	1946	Era	SGW
Publisher	Novello	Publ No	MT1239	Text	Robert Bridges		
Series	The Musical Times						

3) Dame Flora. Part-Song for three voices

Voicing	SSC, piano ad lib.	Pages	5	Date	1922	Era	OXN
Publisher	H F W Deane & Sons		Publ No	UPS198	Text	16th C	
Series	The Year Book Press Series of Unison and Part-Songs						
Dedicatee "To Miss Anne Thackeray and Miss Mary Venables[294]"							

4) Dirge

Voicing	SSCC	Pages	n/a	Date	Publ. 1923	Era		LCH
Publisher	Boosey & Co		Text	Emily Jenkinson		Publ No	88	
Series	Boosey's Choral Miscellany		Note	Performed in Birmingham in 1917.				

5) Epitaph [Here lies a most beautiful lady]

Voicing	High Voice, piano	Pages	2	ms.		EGG R	Era	RET
Unpublished		Text	Walter de la Mare		Date		1966	
Note	A setting, dated 15th November 1966, of "Here lies a most beautiful lady"							

6) Everyone sang[295]

Voicing	T Solo, SA, orchestra	Publisher	Novello	Date	1938	Era	SGW
Pages Vocal score 6pp Chorus part 2pp					Text	Siegfried Sassoon	
Dedication "Specially composed for the Royal Command Concert, Royal Albert Hall, Empire Day 1938"							

---

[294] Violinist Mary Venables, a pupil of Hungarian virtuoso violinist Joseph Joachim, lived on Cumnor Hill in Oxford and was leader (and principle organiser) of the Oxford Orchestral Society, an orchestra founded in 1902 by Hugh Allen primarily to accompany the Oxford Bach Choir. She later became the orchestra's Vice-President.

[295] See also p. 62

7) Fairy flight. Unison Song

Voicing	U, piano	Pages	5	Date	1922	Era	OXN
Publisher	H F W Deane & Sons	Publ No	UPS193	Text	"M" (a small child)		
Series	The Year Book Press Series of Unison and Part-Songs						

8) I know a baby

Voicing	Voice, Piano	Pages	2	Date	1925	Era	OXN
Publisher	H F W Deane & Sons		Text	Christina Rossetti			
Series	The Year Book Press		Dedicatee	To "Squibbs" (A P H)			
Note In the anthology *Kikirikee*[296]: words by Christina Rossetti; music by various composers							

9) I love the Jocund dance: Unison Song

Voicing	U, Piano	Pages	3	ms.	EGG E	Date	1966	Era	RET
Publisher	Novello	Publ No	907	Series	Singing Class Music	Text	William Blake		

10) If the sun could tell us half

Voicing	Voice, Piano	Pages	2	Date	1925	Era	OXN
Publisher	H F W Deane & Sons		Text	Christina Rossetti			
Series	The Year Book Press		Dedicatee	"To Margaret (M M H)"			
Note In the anthology *Kikirikee*: words by Christina Rossetti; music by various composers							

11) May

Voicing	3-part song	Pages	8	Publ No	SCM221	Date	1949	Era	SGW
Publisher	Edward Arnold	Series		Singing Class Music		Text	E Thurlow (1781-1829)		
Dedicatee "For Owen[297], who sent me this poem from somewhere in the East"									

12) Owls: Two-part song

Voicing	SS, Piano	Publ No	UPS246	Date	1925	Pages	6	Era	OXN
Publisher	H F W Deane & Sons		Text			Will H Ogilvie			
Series	The Year Book Press Series of Unison and Part-Songs								

---

[296] This and No. 10, also from *Kikirikee*, were dedicated to his two daughters, then aged 7 and 2.
[297] Re Owen Morshead see p. 62

13) Piskies

Voicing	Baritone, piano		Date	1927	Pages	7		Era	OXN
Publisher	OUP	Text	T P Cameron Wilson						

14) Slumber song: Unison Song

Voicing	U (div)	Pages	6	Publ No	SCM866	Date	1956	Era	SGW
Publisher	Edward Arnold		Series	Singing Class Music		Text Alfred Noyes (1880-1958)			

The accompaniment of SCM866 was arranged for strings by WHH for a Reading Education Committee festival in July 1957 [*ms.* EGG A]

15) Someone: Unison Song

Voicing	Voice, piano	Pages	3	Publ No	UPS239	Date	1924	Era	OXN
Publisher	H F W Deane & Sons					Text	Walter de la Mare		
Series	The Year Book Press Series of Unison and Part-Songs								

16a) Song of May-Day: Choral Song

Voicing	SATB, Orchestra or Piano		Pages	25	Date	1940	Era	SGW
Publisher	Novello	Series	Novello's Octavo Edition		Text	Beaumont & Fletcher		

16b) Song of May-Day: Choral Song (accompaniment)

Voicing	Two pianos	Pages	Primo 15, secundo 11			Era	SGW
Date	1941	Text	Beaumont & Fletcher		*ms.*	EGG G	

Note Unpublished, annotated by WHH: "Time of performance 7-10 minutes"
First performance: Windsor & Eton Choral Society, Centenary Concert in Eton School Hall. June 14th 1941. Two Pianos Dr H G Ley & Mr Philip Moore Conductor Dr W H Harris Second Performance with orchestra (Leslie Woodgate) BBC May 7th 1942

17a) Spring, the sweet Spring

Voicing	U, piano	Pages	6	Publ No	MS90	Date	1914	Era	LCH
Publisher	Stainer & Bell		Series	Modern Songs		Text	T Nashe		

17b) Spring, the sweet Spring

Voicing	SATB	Pages		6	Date		1948	Era	SGW
Publisher	Edward Arnold		Publ No		ACM520		Text	T Nashe	
Series	Arnold Choral Music			Dedicatee	"For DD June 12th 1946"[298]				

---

[298] 12th June was his wife's birthday and DD stands for 'Dear Doris'

17c) Spring, the sweet Spring

Voicing	SS, piano	Pages		6	Date		1948		Era	SGW
Publisher	Edward Arnold		Publ No			SCM641		Text		T Nashe
Series	Singing Class Music				Dedicatee "For DD June 12th 1946"					

18) The Bey of Bamra

Voicing	Soli. SSA choruses (boys and girls), piano		Ms.	EGG E	Era	SGW/ADD
Unpublished	Date	1958	Text	A W S Bridge and F M Bridge		
Note: For December 1958 [for St George's School] Autograph ms. plus typewritten libretto.						

19) The despairing lover. Part-Song for vocal quartet or chorus

Voicing	SATB	Date		1956		Pages	8	Era	SGW/ADD
Publisher	J Curwen & Sons		Text	Anon.	Publ No	61476			

20) The Encore Song

Voicing	U, piano	Date		1935	Pages	n/a	Era	SGW
Publisher	H F W Deane & Sons		Publ No	UPS400	Text	F M Bridge		
Series	The Year Book Press Series of Unison and Part-Songs							

21) The Heather

Voicing	SATB	Date	1920	Publ No	CL159	Pages	7	Era	OXN
Publisher	Stainer & Bell	Series	Choral Library		Text	Neil Munro (1864-1930)			
Note "To be sung just so fast as clearness of words and good enunciation will allow"									

22) The Huntsman's song "Up, up, ye dames"

Voicing	SS, piano	Pages	5	Publ No	A226	Date	1924	Era	OXN
Publisher	H F W Deane & Sons: The Year Book Press						Text	Samuel T Coleridge	

23) The Moor

Voicing	Baritone, piano	ms.	EGG G	Date	1923	Era	OXN
Text	Ralph Hodgson	Unpublished	Dedicatee	Sumner Austin[299]			
Notes	Autograph ms. signed Weston-sub-Edge [Gloucestershire] August 14 1923						

24) The Song of the Mermaid

Voicing	2-part, piano	Pages	6	Date	1934	Era	SGW
Publisher	H F W Deane & Sons	Publ No	UPS390	Text			Anon.
Series	The Year Book Press Series of Unison and Part-Songs						

25a) There sits a Bird on yonder Tree

Voicing	SSA, piano	Pages	n/a	Date	1950	Publ No	Trios589	Era	SGW
Publisher	Novello	Text		From the Ingoldsby legends					
Series	Novello's Trios and Quartets for Female or Boys' Voices								

25b) There sits a Bird on yonder Tree

Voicing	SATB, piano ad lib.	Pages	6	Date	1950	Era	SGW
Publisher	Novello	Publ No	PSB1549	Text	From the Ingoldsby legends		
Series	Novello's Part Song Book						

26) The witches' steeds: Part-Song for three voices

Voicing	SSS or SSA, organ	Pages	8	Date	1922	Era	OXN
Publisher	H F W Deane & Sons	Publ No	UPS197	Text	Will H Ogilvie		
Series	The Year Book Press Series of Unison and Part-Songs						

---

[299] Baritone Sumner Francis Austin (1888-1981) subsequently produced operas at both Sadlers Wells, The Old Vic and Covent Garden.

7: Cantatas and Opera

1) Michael Angelo's Confession of Faith (Vocal Score)

Voicing	Ba Solo, Chorus, Orchestra	Pages	24	Date	1935	Era	SGW
Text	The poem by Morna Stuart (1905-1972) is a free adaptation of Wordsworth's lines "From the Italian of Michael Angelo".						
Publisher	Novello	Dedicatee For Gloucester Three Choirs Festival 1935					
Note The *ms.* vocal score [EGG A], dated October 15th 1934, indicates that the original title was to have been 'Heaven's Exile: Peregrinando' [Pilgrimage].							

2) Fantasy: The Hound of Heaven

Voicing	Baritone solo, chorus, orchestra		Pages	n/a	Era	LCH
Date	1918 publ. 1920	Text	Francis Thompson (1859–1907)			
Publisher	Stainer & Bell on behalf of the Carnegie United Kingdom Trust					
Notes	See also p. 75 et seq.					

3) Nativity Ode: Some stanzas from 'On the morning of Christ's Nativity'

Voicing	T solo, 8-part chorus & orchestra		ms.	EGG H	Era	RCM
Note See also p. 11		Date	1909	Pages	171	Text	John Dryden (1631-1700)

4) Veni creator spiritus

Voicing	Soli, SATTB & strings	Pages	53	Date	1903	Era	RCM
Note See also p. 11		Text		John Dryden (1631-1700)			
ms.	Bodleian Library Mus. Sch. Ex. c.182						

5) Marsyas (Opera in one act)

Voicing	Soloists, chorus and orchestra	Pages	69	Era	OXN
Date	1927	Text	J Roland Evans		
Note The autograph vocal score is annotated "Time of performance 40 minutes"			ms.	EGG H	

8: Instrumental and Orchestral music

1) A Hunting Tune

Voicing	Horn, piano	Pages	6 + 2	Era	RET
Date	1967, publ. 1984	Publisher	Oliver Brockway Music		
Note: Composed for (the 21st birthday) and published by his grandson Oliver. A piano version also exists, dated by WHH April 1972					

2) Heroic Prelude

Voicing	Orchestra and chorus	Date	1943	Era	SGW
Publisher	Novello [The score and parts are still available for hire from Novello.]				
Note Performed in the Royal Albert Hall at the Promenade Concert on 4th August 1942 by the BBC Symphony Orchestra and Chorus, conducted by WHH. See also p. 55					

2a) Heroic Prelude

Voicing	Two Pianos	Pages	Primo 7, Secundo 4		Era	SGW
Unpublished		Date	1943	ms.	EGG G	
Note Arranged for two pianos "Windsor Castle (July/August 1943)"						

3) Sonata for Violin and Piano

Voicing	Violin, piano	Unpublished	Pages	37	ms.	EGG A	Era	LCH
Note								

Two copies dated Lichfield Autumn 1915 and January 1917. The 1915 copy has pasted revisions and is marked by WHH "Revised October 1935"
A romantic and virtuoso piece in three movements:
  I) Allegro moderato ma maestoso [in D]
  II) Lento espressivo (quasi fantasia) [in D-minor]
  III) Allegretto quasi Andante [in D]

The score contains a letter from Sybil Eaton to WHH when she returned the score to him in 1957, apologising for the delay (over 20 years) and recalling that she had played it rather badly.

Despite this comment, she was a gifted violinist and dedicatee and first performer of the *Violin Sonata* by Howells, the *Violin Concerto* by Finzi and the *Irish Rhapsody No.5* by Stanford.

SONATA in D MAJOR

1

Ist Movement

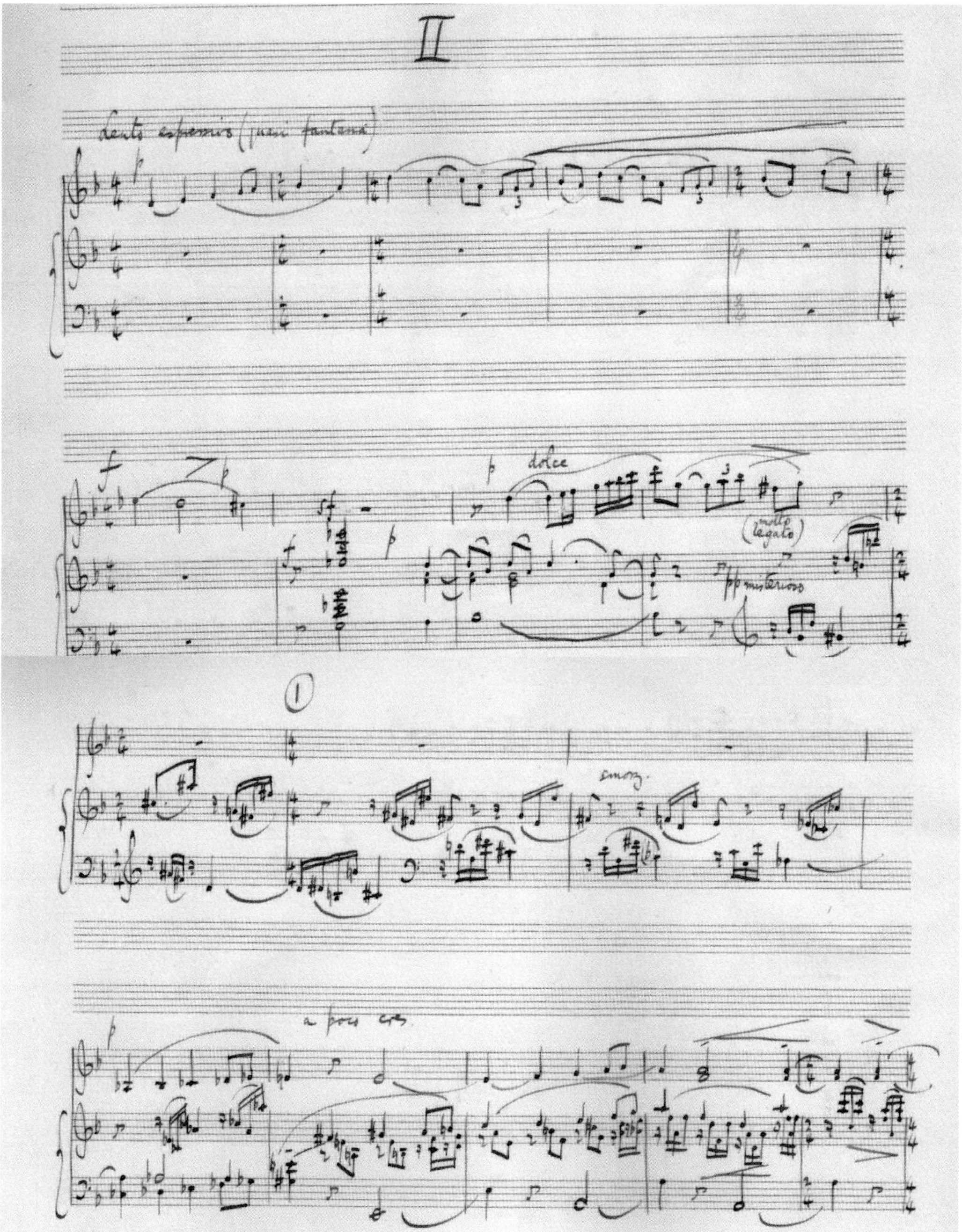

2nd Movement

3rd Movement

4) Three Pieces for Oboe and Piano

Voicing	Oboe, piano		Unpublished	Pages		4 / 4 / 4	Era	RET
No. 1 Unquiet, No. 2 Spring Song, No. 3 Reverie				Date	1967	ms.	EGG E	
Note Originally intended as 'Two pieces for Oboe (or Flute) and Piano', WHH changed the title to 'Three pieces' and deleted "or flute". No. 1 Marked " Arranged from the original piano piece[300] June 1967" No. 3 Marked " An arrangement of No. 2 of Four Short Pieces for the organ"								

5) Theme with Variations (Variations on an original theme in E-minor)

Voicing	Piano	Unpublished		Pages	1st ms. 15, 2nd ms. 21		Era	RCM
WHH Note Written when a scholar at the RCM with Walford Davies.				Date	1901	ms.	EGG H	
Note There are two ms. copies. The original has some pencil changes which are incorporated into the second, presumably later, copy which is not in WHH's hand. The second copy is entitled *Variations on an original theme in E-minor*.								

6a) Northleach Church Bells

Voicing	Piano solo	Pages	3		Date	1956	Era	SGW
Publisher	Curwen	ms.	EGG C	Dedicatee "For Oliver and Roger"				
Publ No	8980	Note For his two grandsons by Margaret Brockway.						

6b) Northleach Church Bells

Voicing	Piano duet	Pages	4	Date	1951	ms.	EGG G	Era	SGW
Note Unpublished A piano duet version of 6a) dated Eastington Manor, Northleach, New Years' Day 1951									

7) Overture 'Once upon a time' (Full Score)

Voicing	Orchestra	Pages	45		Date	1940	Era	SGW
Publisher	Unpublished	ms.			EGG G			
Note WHH has annotated "8½- 9 minutes". First performance (conducted by WHH) Queen's Hall Promenade Concert September 5th 1940. Also a two-piano arrangement dated September/October 1940								

8) Suite for viola and pianoforte

Voicing	Viola, piano	Pages	12 + 5	Date	1953	Era	SGW
Publisher	OUP	Note Viola part edited by Watson Forbes					

---

[300] Also dated June 1967

9a) The Windsor Dances

Voicing	Piano duet	Pages	16	Date	1939	Era	SGW
Publisher	Novello	1. Castle Walls, 2. Down by the River, 3. At a Canter					

Note Dedicatee Dedicated, by gracious permission, to Their Royal Highnesses The Princess Elizabeth and The Princess Margaret

9b) The Windsor Dances

Voicing	Arranged for small orchestra (in two different instrumentations) 1. Flute, oboe, clarinet, bassoon, horn and strings. 2. Flute, oboe, 2 clarinets, 2 bassoons, 2horns, strings and double-bass.				
Date	1939	Unpublished	*ms.*	EGG G	*Era*	SGW
1. Castle Walls, 2. Down by the River, 3. At a Canter				*Note* Scored August 1939	

10) King John: Incidental music (Full Score)

Voicing	Orchestra	Pages	112	Date	1933	Era	OXC
Unpublished	*Dedication* OUDS (New Theatre Oxford) Feb.21-25 1933				*ms.*	EGG A	
Note ms. dated 31st Jan 1933. See also p. 33							

11) Prelude

Voicing	Horn, organ	Key	E-flat	Date	Publ. 1984	Pages	4	Era	SGW
Publisher	Oliver Brockway	*ms.*	EGG A						

Note Published together with an arrangement by Harris of Schumann's *Abendlied* as *Two Pieces for Horn and Organ (or piano)*

12) Prelude, Fugue and Minuet on EHF

Voicing	Keyboard	Pages	4	Date	1949	*ms.*	EGG A	Era	SGW
Unpublished	*Dedicatee* Dedicated to Dr and Mrs Fellowes on their Golden Wedding January 12th 1949								

Note Subtitled " in the style (as HGL puts it) of the olde Fellowes"
It quotes Gibbons' *Hosanna to the Son of David* and the *ms.* is signed "Windsor and Combewater Cottage, Metcombe, Devon, January 1-7 1949.

9: Editions and Arrangements of music by others composers

A) Published Organ Arrangements

1) A Bax: Funeral March

Voicing	Organ: 3 Mans/Ped.	Pages	6	*ms.*	EGG E		Era	SGW
Publisher	Chappell & Co	Publ. No.	1729	Date	1942, published 1945			
Note	See also p. 58 for the genesis of this piece.							

2) E Elgar: Nimrod Op. 36/9

Voicing	Organ: 4 Mans/Ped		Pages	3	Date	1932	Era	OXC
Publisher	Novello	Series	Modern Transcriptions for Organ			Publ. No.		I

3) F Mendelssohn: String Quartet in F Op.80: Adagio

Voicing	Organ: 3 Mans/Ped	Pages	6	Publ. No.	19	Date	1927	Era	OXN
Publisher	Stainer & Bell	Series		Organ Solos edited and arranged by Henry G Ley					

From String Quartet in F minor. Op.80

MENDELSSOHN
Arranged by WILLIAM H. HARRIS

4) H Purcell: Chaconne. The Grand Dance (King Arthur)

Voicing	Organ: 3 Mans/Ped	Pages	6	Date	1933	Era	OXC
Publisher	Cramer	Publ. No.		Set 3 No.8			
Series	Cramer's Library of Organ Music by British Composers						

B) Unpublished Organ Arrangements

1) L van Beethoven

Harris left four unpublished Beethoven arrangements [EGG E]. A note contained within them suggests that he was intending to offer them for publication and it reads like the preface to a printed edition:

'There are no doubt many organists who (like myself) wish to play some of the slow movements of the later string quartets of Beethoven. Although the profundity of this music cannot adequately be revealed through any medium but that for which it was written, much may be done by sympathetic handling & a <u>simple</u> registration. WHH' [underlining by WHH]

The four movements (all undated) are:

- Adagio ma non troppo from the String Quartet in E-flat Op. 127
- Cavatina from the String Quartet in B-flat Op. 130 (extract below)
- Adagio from the String Quartet in C-sharp minor Op. 131
- Lento assai from the String Quartet in F Op. 135

2) J Brah*ms*. Organ Fugue in A-flat minor

Voicing	Piano	Pages	5	Era	SGW	ms.		EGG E
Note	Autograph *ms.* dated April 29 1938							

3) J Brahms. Symphony No.3: Andante

Voicing	organ	Pages	8	Era	LCH	ms.	EGG E
Note	Autograph *ms.* dated March 19th/20th 1913						

4) J Brahms. Symphony No.4: Andante moderato

Voicing	organ	Pages	9	Era	LCH	ms.	EGG E

5) G F Handel: Dead March in Saul

Voicing	Organ 3 Mans/Ped	Pages	2	Date	28th January 1936	Era	SGW
Note	For the funeral of King George V					ms.	EGG E
WHH Note	"Play very simply without any filling in of chords" "4 minutes and 20 seconds"						

(The final bars)

6) F. Mendelssohn: Octet: Slow movement

Voicing	Organ Two Consoles	Pages	5 + 5	ms.	EGG F	Era	SGW
Note arranged for the two Rothwell consoles in St George's Chapel.				*WHH Note*		Use no 16ft pedal	

7) C H H Parry: Entre'acte from the "Birds of Aristophanes"

Voicing	Organ 2 Mans/Ped	Pages	2	ms.	EGG E	Era	SGW/ADD

C) Published Choral Arrangements

1) J S Bach: Bist du bei Mir (If Thou art near) BWV 508

Voicing	SATB	Pages	8	Publ No	MT1277	Date	1949	Era	SGW
Publisher	Novello	Series	The Musical Times						
Text	Tr. and an additional verse added by Mary Venables[301]								
Note	Notenbuch der Anna Magdalena Bach No. 25								

2) J S Bach: King of Glory, King of Peace

Voicing	SATB, organ, (2nd Choir - Verse)		Pages	3	Date	1933	Era	OXC
Publisher	OUP	Text	George Herbert (1593-1633)					
Note	J R Ahle harmonised by J S Bach. Arranged for *The Church Anthem Book* (No. 48) ed. Walford Davies and Henry G Ley. Also published separately. WHH *Note* "May be sung full throughout"							

3) L Bourgeois: O strength and stay

Voicing	SATB, organ	Pages	3	Publ No	MT1277	Date	1937	Era	SGW
Publisher	Novello	Series	The Musical Times		Text	St Ambrose tr. J Ellerton			
Note	For 1937 Coronation, though not used in the service.								

4) C Gesualdo: O vos omnes

Voicing	SATTB	Pages	6	Publ No	OA1271	Date	1948	Era	SGW
Publisher	Novello	Series	Novello's Octavo Anthems			Text	Latin text only		

5) C Monteverdi: Orpheus (Continuo realised by W H Harris)

Voicing	Various	Publisher	OUP	Pages	180	Date	1925	Era	OXN
Note	"Newly edited from the 1615 edition by Jack Allan Westrup; the realisation of the continuo by William H Harris; the English translation by Robert Louis Stuart" See also pp. 31/32								

6) C H H Parry: Prevent us, O Lord

Voicing	SATB, organ ad lib.	Pages	5	Text	BCP	Date	1944	Era	SGW
Publisher	Church Music Society	Series	Church Music Society Reprints No.27						
Note	"Edited for Church Music Society by Dr W H Harris by special permission of Lady Ponsonby"								

---

[301] See p. 271.

7) F Schubert: Litany (for All Souls' Day, Funerals, and Memorial Services)

Voicing	SATB, organ or piano	Pages	3	Date	1966		Era	RET
Publisher	OUP	Series		Oxford Easy Anthems		Publ No		E107
Text	tr. AH Fox Strangways and Steuart Wilson							
Note	*Litanei auf das Fest aller Seelen* D 343							

8) H Schütz Praise to Thee, Lord Jesus (Anthem for Passiontide)

Voicing	SATB	Pages	4	Publ No	OA1202	Date	1935	Era	SGW
Publisher	Novello		Series		Novello's Octavo Anthems				
Note	The conclusion of *St Matthew Passion* SWV 479, tr. Lucy E Broadwood Also a Tonic Sol-fa edition Novello's Tonic Sol-fa Series 2700								

9) T Tallis: Come, Holy Ghost

Voicing	SATB	Pages	3	Publ No	21	Date	1924	Era	OXN
Publisher	SPCK	Series	SPCK Church Music	Text		Matthew Parker (1504-1575)			

10) M Wise: Abide with me

Voicing	SATB	Pages	6	Publ No	A29	Date	1924	Era	OXN
Publisher	H F W Deane & Sons: The Year Book Press					Text	H F Lyte (1793-1847)		
Note	Using the modern text with descant and with added harmonies by WHH, this anthem contains more Harris than Wise.								

11) M Wise: Thy Beauty, O Israel

Voicing	SATB, TTB verse, organ	Pages	9	Publ No		OA1245	Era	SGW
Publisher	Novello	Series	Novello's Octavo Anthems		Date		1941	
Text	Samuel: 1							
Note	Composed to be sung at morning prayer on 30th January, the anniversary of the execution of King Charles I. Harris probably encountered the *ms.* at Christ Church, Oxford.							

D) Unpublished Choral Arrangements

1) W Crotch: Blessed is he whose righteousness is forgiven

Voicing	T solo, SATB, organ	Pages	10	ms.	EGG F
Date	Unknown			Text	From Psalm 32

WHH Note
"The Editor is responsible for the organ accompaniment (the original has 'continuo' only) & the marks of expression.
Crotch's bass takes the form of a quaver 'moto perpetuo'; this has been divided between the manuals & pedals"

2) W Crotch: My God, my God, look upon me

Voicing	SA soli, SATB, organ	Pages	7	ms.	EGG F
Date	Unknown			Text	From Psalm 22
WHH Note	"The Editor is responsible for the organ accompaniment (the original has 'continuo' only) & the marks of expression."				

298

3) H Purcell: Behold, I bring you glad tidings

Voicing	SATB, verse, organ	Date	1959	ms.		EGG A	Era	SGW
WHH Note	Edited and the organ part added by WHH From Vol.3 Boyce's Cathedral Music 1788 Pencil note: For Christmas 1959 (Robert Davies solo)					Text		Luke 2

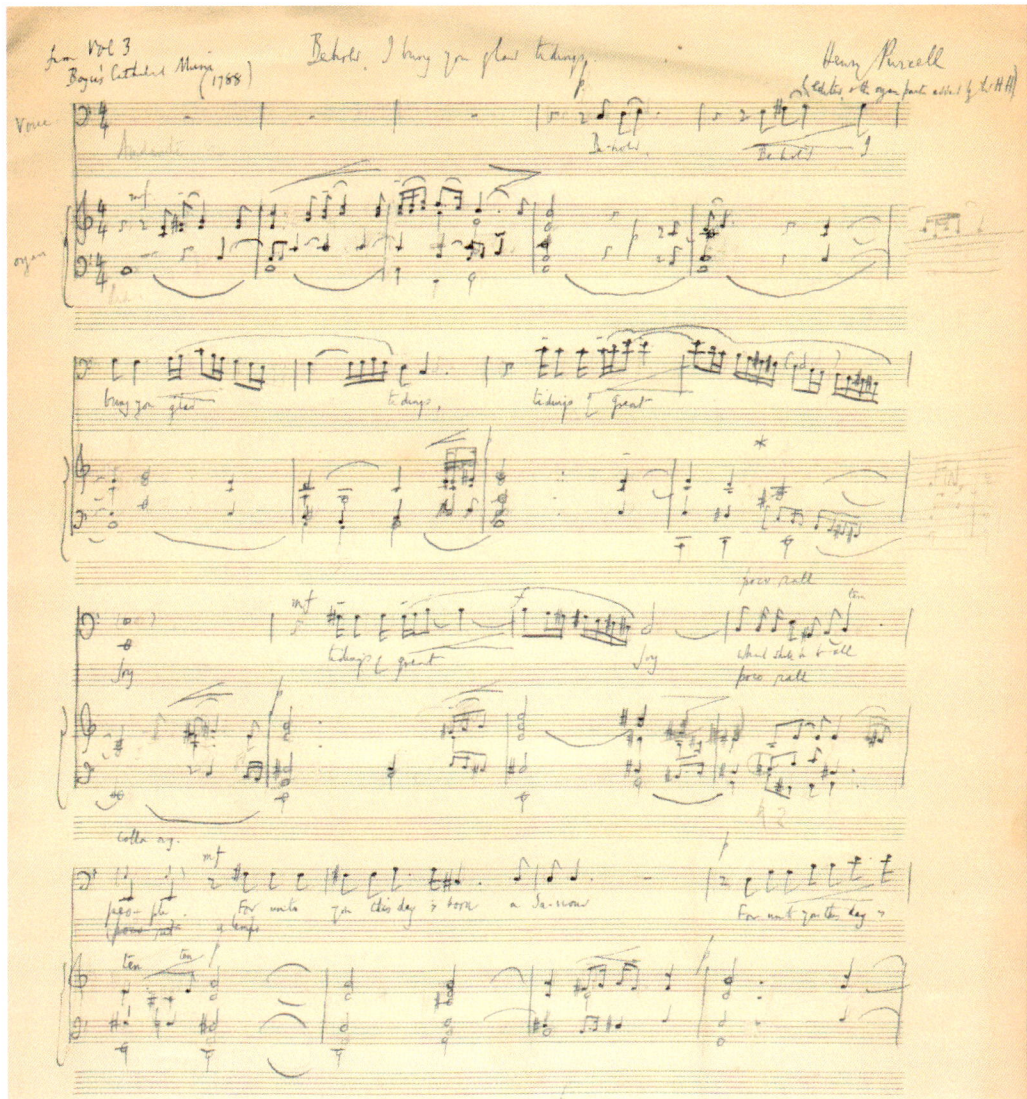

4) R Vaughan Williams.: O God of earth and altar

Voicing	Unison voices, Orchestra	Date	1924	Era		OXN
Text	G K Chesterton (1874-1936)	ms.	EGG F			
Note	An orchestral arrangement of Vaughan Williams' tune Kings Lynn Dated Dec 1924 to the above text.					

E) Published Instrumental Arrangements

1) J S Bach: An Wasserflüssen Babylon BWV 653

Voicing	Two pianos	Date	1945	Era	SGW
Publisher	Novello	Pages	5	ms.	EGG G (pf.2 only)

2) J S Bach: In dir ist Freude BWV 615

Voicing	Two pianos	Date	1945	Era	SGW
Publisher	Novello	Pages	7	ms.	EGG G (pf.2 only)

3) J S Bach: Toccata in the Dorian Mode BWV 538

Voicing	Two pianos	Date	1945	Era	SGW
Publisher	Novello	Pages	16	ms.	EGG G (pf.2 only)

4) J S Bach: Wir glauben all' an einem Gott, Vater BWV 740

Voicing	Two pianos	Date	1945	Era	SGW
Publisher	Novello	Pages	4	ms.	EGG G (pf.2 only)

5) J S Bach: Herr Jesu Christ, dich zu uns wend BWV 655

Voicing	Two pianos	Date	1947	Era	SGW
Publisher	Novello	Pages	9	ms.	EGG G (pf.1 only)

6) D Buxtehude: Ciacona in E minor BuxWV 160

Voicing	Two pianos	Date	1947	Pages	12	Publisher	Novello	Era	SGW

F) Unpublished Instrumental Arrangements

1) C W Gluck: Ballet from 'Orpheus'

Voicing	Piano	Pages	3	ms.	EGG F	Date	n.d.	Era	unknown
Note	Nos. 29 and 30 from *Orfeo ed Euridice* 1762								

10: Miscellaneous unpublished works

Unpublished music is also listed in sections 1, 2, 3, 5 and 9

During his retirement years WHH would compose every day, jotting down ideas and revising them frequently. Unfortunately he was a messy writer. It is sometimes hard to distinguish between sharps, flats and naturals; he rarely wrote out the key signature except at the beginning and sometimes merely wrote 'C-minor' or similar when the key changed. Moreover his hand-writing of text was often illegible. Money was always tight in the family and he would use manuscript paper more than once by deleting the pencil drafts of previous music in order to reuse the paper. Sometimes it is hard to tell what was old and what was new. He usually wrote in pencil and when satisfied he would ink over the pencil music rather than making a fair copy on new paper giving a rather blurred and ambiguous effect. Whether in his haste or due to eyesight, he latterly even missed the correct line or space so that some notes are clearly misplaced! Fortunately he wrote in a tonal style which allows correction of these misplaced notes with some confidence.

It has been possible to identify a number of further works that appear to be complete. Musical examples from the sacred pieces are provided here.

1) A Holiday Tune

Voicing	Piano	Pages	2	ms.	EGG R	Date	April 1972

2) A rouse for Prince Charles

Voicing	SATB, piano	Pages	4	ms.	EGG R	Date	July 1969
Note	Although HRH Prince Charles was created Prince of Wales in 1958, his investiture was not held until 1st July 1969, an event which triggered WHH to compose this chorus. Beginning "O Land of our Fathers", and with both text and music by WHH, this song is in a somewhat dated language and nationalistic style!						

3) An Evening Benediction

The cover of this unpublished project shows that WHH initially planned *Two short anthems: 1) Our day of praise is done*[302] *2) As now the sun's declining rays* with the instruction "These two anthems are intended to be follow each other, possibly at the close of an Evening Service". He then added a third anthem, *The day is gently drawing to its close*, setting a tune by William Monk, and he changed the subtitle to 'Three Short anthems". He subsequently added *O God, the Protector*, already published in 1969[303], to the collection.

The sentiment of this project and the fact of his own life drawing to a close is perhaps understandable. He spent much time on *Our day of praise* and there are many drafts developing what initially seemed like a simple hymn tune into something more elaborate. Harris was notable for his skilful use of modulation but this assemblage of pieces (F-minor, F-major, D-major, B-minor) has no overall plan.

The remaining two unpublished pieces are reflective hymns. *As now the sun's declining rays* is a setting of an 18C Latin hymn translated into English by John Chandler (1806-1876) in his

---

[302] See also p. 157
[303] See also p. 147

Hymns of the Primitive Church 1837. Harris sets the verses slightly differently to reflect the text and with a more extended doxology.

As now the sun's declining rays

Each verse uses his trademark modulation to the major key of the mediant that he used so effectively in "Holy is the true light". The first version of the piece is dated February 1968, but he returned to the piece a few months after the death of his wife and the second *ms.* is annotated "Finished September 30th 1968". This was just a few days before he also finished *O God, the Protector* on October 4th, dedicated to the memory of his wife.

"The day is gently drawing to its close" is the cover title for the final piece, though on the *ms.* the title is *Evening Hymn: arranged as a short anthem by William H. Harris*. The cover titles was a typographical error on Harris's part, for the text he actually used is "The day is gently sinking to a close" by Christopher Wordsworth (1807-1885). Harris uses a melody by William Henry Monk (1823-1889) which the authors have been unable to identify. *The Musical Times* of 1st August, 1866 mentions that "A well written hymn by Mr W H Monk, 'The day is gently sinking to a close' concluded the afternoon service." Monk did not however use this tune for *Hymns Ancient & Modern* and so far we have not found a hymn book containing this tune. Harris notes that:

'Monk's melody & harmony are unaltered. Some liberty has been taken with the barring, and in shortening some of the chords at the cadences which serves to give more flexibility & freedom to the words. Two verses of the original four are used here'

He also notes that he sent a copy to Gerald Knight, Director of the RSCM, on 14th June 1971. It does not appear to have been used by the RSCM, possibly because of the somewhat dated style of both music and text.

Evening Hymn: W. H. Monk

4) Fanfare

Voicing	Four trumpets		Pages	I	Date	N.D.
Note	For Andy's Wedding				ms.	EGG R

5) Four Pieces for Piano Solo

Voicing	Piano	ms.	EGG E	Date	June 1967
1. **Unquiet**	Andante In B-flat, 3/8 time, 2 pages. At the end WHH wrote 'They are all gone unto the world of light' (Vaughan) This piece was also arranged for oboe and piano as No. 1 of *Three Pieces for Oboe and Piano* See also p. 282				
2. **Interlude (Retrospect)**	Andante espressivo in A-minor, 4/4 time, 1 page. "To be played quite freely (tempo rubato). It ends on a dominant 7th chord and marked 'attacca No. 3' and was intended to be a pair with the following piece.				
3. **Birthday Greeting**	Allegretto in A-major, 4/4 time, 2 pages. "For KDC June 12th 1967" [KDC were his wife's maiden initials and 12th June was her birthday]				

4. **Quodlibet (What you will) for a boys' play**	Allegretto in E-flat, 2/4 time, 2 pages. Dated July 1971 The folio originally had the title 'Three Pieces for Piano Solo'. This was changed to 'Four' with the addition of this Quodlibet, presumably in 1971. This quodlibet is not the usual musical combination of different melodies, but "whatever pleases you" – the meaning of the Latin word.

6) Improvisation (Romance) in B-major

Voicing	Piano (or organ)	Pages	2	Date	1972	ms.	EGG R
Note	WHH does not specify an instrument. Despite the lack of piano pedalling marks and some long-held Note more suited to the organ, a bottom B-flat grace note beyond the compass of the organ suggests that this piece was intended for the piano. First draft dated April 17th 1972						

7) Introduction-Theme and Gigue on "Cruel Barbara Allen"

Voicing	Toy orchestra	Pages	13	ms.	EGG A	Date	1919	Era	LCH
Note	Harris' movement for the RCM Toy Dance Suite – see pp. 12/13								

8) Invictus

Voicing	Baritone, piano	Pages	4	Date	c.1912	Era	LCH
Text	William Ernest Henley (1849–1903)			ms.	EGG F		
Note: Dedicated to Herbert Parker, a Lay-Clerk in Lichfield Cathedral Choir							

9) Lines on the Massacre at Piedmont

Voicing	Bar, piano	Pages.	2	Date	1901	Era	RCM
ms.	EGG G	Text	John Milton (1608-1674)				
Note	ms. includes sketches for alternative endings						

10) Reverie [in B-major]

Voicing	Piano		Pages	1	Date	1972
Note	dated February 15th 1972 Ash Wednesday				ms.	EGG R

11) Sextet

Voicing	String quartet, flute, clarinet	Date	1901	Era	RCM
Note	ms. full score and parts			ms.	EGG F

12) The Boy and the Angel

Voicing	Vocal quartet, string quartet, piano		Date	1905	Era	RCM
Text	Robert Browning	Pages	39	ms.	EGG G	
Note	Dated Feb-June 1905, Full score and parts, composed for the Folk-Song Quartet. 'The Folk-Song Quartet' consisted of Beatrice Spencer (soprano), Florence Christie (mezzo-soprano), Louis Godfrey (tenor) and founder Foxton Ferguson (bass). They were active under this name from 1905 until Ferguson's death in 1920.					

13) The Empty Cottage

Voicing	Piano	Date	1949	ms.	EGG G	Pages	4	Era	SGW
Dedicatee For Baba Speyer and Maria Donska*[304]									
WHH Note * "on leaving The Old Cottage, Dedsworth, Windsor, in 1949."									
Note Below Harris's note is a musical code in numbers: 975...824...6529									

14) The Student's Song of the Sun (from "The Spook Sonata")

Voicing	Voice, harp	ms.	EGG F	Date	1920's	Era	OXN
Note	Composed between 1923 and 1926. WHH has annotated "Performed at the play in Oxford and London" The 'Spook Sonata' was a play by Arnold Strindberg (1883-1946) "For J B Fagan". James Bernard Fagan (1873-1933) was an actor, playwright and the first manager of the Oxford Playhouse from 1923.						

15) Theme with Variations

Voicing	String quartet		Date	1900	Era	RCM
Note	Full score and parts, dated Dec 1899/Jan 1900				ms.	EGG F

16) Three George Herbert (1593-1633) Songs
1. The Flower, 2. Bitter Sweet, 3. The Temper

Voicing	Tenor, Piano	ms.	EGG E	Date	1962	Era	RET
Pages	No. 1: 5pp, No.2: 2pp, No.3: 5pp						
Text	George Herbert (1593-1633)		Dedication		Wilfrid Brown		
Note	Autograph ms. signed July/August 1962. First performance was on BBC Home Service 29th May 1964, Wilfred Brown accompanied by Edna Blackwell						

---

[304] Maria Donska (1912–1996) was a Polish-born British pianist and piano teacher who first became popular with the public during World War II as a performer at the National Gallery lunchtime concerts. She lived with Leonora Speyer (1905-1987), a daughter of American violinist and poet Leonora Speyer (1872-1956).

17) Three Shakespeare Songs:
1. O Mistress Mine, 2. Come away, death, 3. When that I was

Voicing	Voice, piano	Date	1908	ms.	EGG F	Era	RCM
Note	Originally composed in September 1908 for tenor voice and piano. A newspaper review also mentions a version for "Vocal quartet, string quartet and piano, but this has not been located. Only the *ms.* of No. 1 is extant, dated September 1908.						

17a) Three Shakespeare Songs:
1. O Mistress Mine, 2. Come away, death, 3. When that I was

Voicing	Voice, piano	Date	unknown	ms.	EGG E	Era	SGW
Note	Three songs for counter-tenor and inscribed to Perceval Bridger (1919-1970) is extant. Bridger was an alto lay clerk at Exeter Cathedral and then for 14 years at St George's Chapel until his death suggesting a date of composition between 1956 and 1970. No.1 is different to the 1908 song above. Nos. 2 and 3 may also be new compositions rather than revisions of the 1908 songs.						

18) Westward

Voicing	Piano	Pages	4	Date	1930	ms.	EGG F	ERA	OXC
Note	Finished 8th August 1930. two copies. WHH has noted that there is a revised 2nd version. This seems. to be lost. "For Jean Cotton". Jean Cotton (1906-1984) was a Canadian-born pianist who studied at the RCM in the 1920's before returning to Calgary around 1930. Perhaps the title hints at her return home.								

19) You spotted snakes (Midsummer Night's Dream)

Voicing	SS, piano	Pages	4	ms.	EGG G		Date	1926	Era	OXN
Dedicatee	To Jean Forbes Robertson (Titania) & her Fairies. O.U.D.S. Summer Play 1926						Text	Shakespeare		
Note	"Written for O.U.D.S. Summer Play in Magdalen Grove"									

11: Lost and unfinished works

1) Kyrie Eleison [in A-minor]

Voicing	SATB, organ	Pages	I	Date	1972
Note	Dated Nov 1st 1972			ms.	EGG R

2 Jubilate in B-flat

Voicing	Organ	Pages	I	Date	1970?
Note	In a *ms.* book with unfinished organ Variations on the Tune 'Laus Deo'			ms.	EGG R

3) Lament

Voicing	Oboe, organ	Pages	3	Era	RET
Note	No date, but certainly composed in retirement			ms.	EGG R

4) Meditation: Andante espressivo in E-minor

Voicing	Organ	Pages	I	Date	n.d. RET
Note	unfinished			ms.	EGG R

5 Organ Voluntary in B-flat

Voicing	Organ	Pages	I	Date	1970
Note	dated 25th May 1970 but unfinished			ms.	EGG R

6) Short Voluntary in G-minor

Voicing	Organ	Pages	I	Date	1970
Note	dated June 18th 1970 but unfinished			ms.	EGG R

7) Variations on a Country Tune

Voicing	Organ or piano?	Pages	2	Date	n.d./RET
Note	Sketches for two movements			ms.	EGG R

8) Variations on "Regent's Square" (Henry Smart)

Voicing	Organ	Pages	I	Date	n.d. RET
Note	A complete harmonisation suitable for use as a 'last verse' setting is complete. Sketches for a prelude and some variations are incomplete.			ms.	EGG R

9) Variations on the Tune 'Laus Deo' (Richard Redhead)

Voicing	Organ	Pages	I	Date	1970
Note	The ms. book also contains a sketch for a (sung) Jubilate in B-flat			ms.	EGG R

10) Variations on the Tune 'Ledsam'

Voicing	Organ	Pages	I	Date	n.d.
Note	Two slightly different versions, both unfinished.			ms.	EGG R

11) The King shall Rejoice

Voicing	SATB	Date	c.1935	Era	SGW
Note	Introit for BBC Broadcast 12th May 1935, Lost.				

12) When the son of man

Voicing	T and B soli, ATB chorus, organ	Date	1960's	Era	RET
Text	Matthew 25: 13 (Tyndale's translation, slightly altered by Robert Bridges)	ms.		EGG E	
Note	The handwriting suggests that this is a late work. Although a complete work (13pp), the pencilled annotations suggest that WHH was intending to make many further changes.				

List of works by title

Pieces in *italics* are unpublished. Incomplete works are not listed.

References are to Appendix 2:

A – Anthem; C – Cantatas and Opera; H – Hymn tune; L – Liturgical;

M – Miscellaneous; IO – Instrumental and orchestral; O – Organ; PC – Psalm Chant;

VS – Vocal and secular choral.

Instrumental

Title	Voicing	Ref.
A Fancy	Organ	O1
A Frolic (Scherzetto) [in G-minor]	Organ	O13c
A Holiday Tune	Piano	M1
A Hunting Tune	Horn, piano	IO1
A Little Organ Book in memory of Henry Ley	Organ	O2
Adagio [in B-major]), renamed Reverie (in the style of Schumann)	Organ	O2
Allegretto in B-flat, renamed Interlude	Organ	O2
Allegretto in F#-minor	Organ	O3
Andante in D	Organ	O4
Birthday Greeting	Piano	M5
Cadenza for Handel Organ Concerto in B-flat	Organ	O5
Cadenza for Handel Organ Concerto in G	Organ	O6
Combewater	Organ	O27c
Elegy	Organ	O7
Elegy [in C-minor]	Organ	O2
Epilogue on "Dix"	Organ	O8
Evening Melody [in D]	Organ	O25c
Fanfare	4 trumpets	M4
Fantasia on an English folk tune ["Monk's Gate"]	Organ	O9
Fantasy on "Easter Hymn"	Organ	O10
Fantasy on the tune "Babylon's Streams"	Organ	O11
Fantasy-Prelude	Organ	O12
Festal Voluntary [in A]	Organ	O13a
Flourish for an Occasion	Organ	O14
Four Pieces for Piano Solo	Piano	M5
Four Short Pieces	Organ	O15
Heroic Prelude	Orchestra	IO2
Improvisation (Romance) in B-major	Piano	M6
Improvisation on the Old 124th	Organ	O16
Interlude (Retrospect)	Piano	M5
Interlude [in E]	Organ	O26b
Interlude in the form of a canon	Organ	O15c
Introduction and Fugue	Organ	O17a
Introduction-Theme and Gigue on "Cruel Babara Allen"	Orchestra	M7
In-Voluntary [in C]	Organ	O26a
King John: Incidental music	Orchestra	IO10
Lament [in G-minor]	Organ	O27b
Meditation [in E-flat]	Organ	O2
Meditation on the Tune "Cheshire"	Organ	O25b
Miniature Suite	Organ	O17

Northleach Church Bells	Piano	I06
Opening Voluntary in Memoriam HWD	Organ	O18
Out-Voluntary [in A]	Organ	O26c
Overture 'Once upon a time'	Orchestra	I07
Pastoral Prelude [in E]	Organ	O25a
Pastorale [in E]	Organ	O27a
Pastorale in G	Organ	O17b
Postlude [in B-flat]	Organ	O19
Prelude in E-flat	Horn, organ	I011
Prelude in E-flat	Organ	O15a
Prelude in G	Organ	O20
Prelude, Fugue and Minuet on E H F	Piano	I012
Processional March	Organ	O21
Quodlibet (What you will) for a boys' play	Piano	M5
Retrospect (Meditation) [in F]	Organ	O13b
Reverie [in B-major]	Piano	M10
Reverie in A-flat	Organ	O22
Reverie in G#-minor	Organ	O15b
Romance and Scherzetto (Variation)	Organ	O17c
Saraband Processional	Organ	O23
Scherzetto in B-flat	Organ	O15d
Sextet	String quartet, flute, clarinet	M11
Sonata for Violin and Piano	Violin, piano	I03
Sonata in A-minor	Organ	O24
Sonata No.2 in A-major	Organ	O13
Suite for viola and pianoforte	Viola, piano	I08
The Empty Cottage	Piano	M13
The Windsor Dances	Piano	I09
Theme with Variations	String quartet	M15
Theme with Variations (Variations on an original theme in E-minor)	Piano	I05
Three Opening Voluntaries	Organ	O25
Three Organ Voluntaries	Organ	O26
Three Pieces for Oboe and Piano	Oboe, piano	I04
Three Preludes	Organ	O27
Unquiet	Piano	M5
Westward	Piano	M19

Vocal and Choral

Title	Voicing	Ref.
A rouse for Prince Charles	SATB, piano	M2
A Simple Communion Service in F	SATB, organ	L1
Addington Hymn Tune	SATB	H8
Alberta: Hymn Tune	U	H1
All creatures of our God and King	SATB	A1
Almighty and most merciful Father	SATB (div)	A2
An Evening Benediction	SATB	M3
Ancient Hunting Song	U, pno	VS1
And the disciples came to Jesus	T, B Soli, SATB, organ	A3
Antiphon: I believe verily	SSAATTBB	A4
As now the sun's declining rays	SATB	M3

Ascribe unto the Lord	SATB	A5
Awake, my heart, to be loved	SATB	VS2
Be merciful unto me, O God	Bass solo, SATB, organ	A6
Be strong in the Lord	B solo, SATB, organ	A8
Beatus vir: Three Psalms (1, 15, 121)	S Solo, SSA, piano	A7
Behold now, praise the Lord	ATB, organ	A9b
Behold now, praise the Lord	SS, organ	A9a
Behold, the tabernacle of God is with man	SATB, organ	A10
Benedic anima mea	S solo, choir, orchestra	A11
Benedicite, Omnia Opera in A	SATB, organ	L2
Bring us, O Lord God	SATBSATB	A12
Cheer up desponding Soul	SATB (Dec and Can)	A45
Collect for St George	(A)TTBB	A3b
Collect for St George	SATB	A13a
Come down, O Love divine: Hymn-anthem	SATB, organ	A14
Come, my Way, my Truth, my Life!	SATB, organ ad lib.	A15a
Come, my Way, my Truth, my Life!	SSA, piano	A15b
Communion in C	SATB	L4
Communion Service in B-minor	SATB, organ	L3
Dame Flora	SSC, piano ad lib.	VS3
Descant and harmonisation for "Gopsal"	U + descant, organ	L5
Descant and harmonisation for "Nun Danket"	U + descant, organ	L6
Dirge	SSCC	VS4
Epitaph	V, piano	VS5
Eternal God!	SATB	A16
Eternal ruler of the ceaseless round	SATB, organ	A17
Evening Hymn: The night is come	SATB (div), solo Ba, organ	A18
Everyone sang	T Solo, SA, orchestra	VS6
Ewell: Hymn Tune	SATB	H2
Faire is the Heaven	SATBSATB	A19
Fairy flight	U, piano	VS7
Fantasy: The Hound of Heaven	Baritone solo, chorus, orchestra	C2
Fear not, O Land	SATB, organ	A20
Forth in thy name	SATB, organ	A21
From a heart made whole	SSAATTBB	A22
Glory, Love, and Praise and Honour	SATB, organ	A23
He hath understanding of righteousness	T solo, SATB	A24
He that is down needs fear no fall	SSA, S solo, organ	A25
Here lies a most beautiful lady	V, piano	VS5
Him holy, in him abide (The Holy Eucharist)	SATB	A72
Holy is the true light	ATTB	A26b
Holy is the true light	SATB	A26a
How bright these glorious spirits shine	SATB, organ	A27
Hymn to God the Father	SATB	A28
I Believe verily	SSAATTBB	A4
I have set God always before me	SS, organ	A29
I heard a voice from heaven	SATB	A30
I know a baby	V, piano	VS8
I love the Jocund dance	U, piano	VS9
I said to the Man who stood at the Gate of the Year	TTBB	A31

If the sun could tell us half	V, piano	VS10
In Christ Jesu	SATB, organ	A32
In the heavenly Kingdom	SATB	A33
Invictus	Bar, piano	M8
It is a good thing to give thanks	SATB, organ	A34
Jesus, these eyes have never seen	SATB (div), organ	A35
King of Glory, King of Peace [1914]	SATB, T solo, organ	A37
King of Glory, King of Peace [1925]	SSA, organ	A36
Kybald Twychen: Hymn Tune	SATB	H3
Kyrie [in E-minor]	SATB	L7
Laudamus (Anthem for Victory)	SATB, organ	A38
Lead, kindly light: Hymn anthem	U+Descant/SATB), organ	A39
Ledsam: Hymn Tune	SATB	H8
Let my prayer	SATB (div), organ	A40
Lines on the Massacre at Piedmont	Bar, piano	M9
Lord of the worlds above	SATB, organ	A41
Lord, who shall dwell in thy Tabernacle	T solo, SSA chorus, organ	A42
Love of Love and Light of Light	SATBSATB	A43
Magnificat and Nunc Dimittis in A [1897]	SATB, organ	L8
Magnificat and Nunc Dimittis in A [1947]	SATB, organ	L9
Magnificat and Nunc Dimittis in A-Minor	SATB, organ	L10
Magnificat and Nunc Dimittis in B-flat	SATB, organ	L11
Magnificat and Nunc Dimittis in D (equal voices)	SSS or SSA, organ	L12
Magnificat and Nunc Dimittis in E	SATBSATB	L13
Marsyas (Opera in one act)	Soloists, chorus and orchestra	C5
May	3-part song	VS11
Michael Angelo's Confession of Faith	Ba Solo, Chorus, Orchestra	C1
Most glorious Lord of life	SBarB choir, organ	A44
My spirit longeth for Thee	SATB (Dec and Can)	A45
Nativity Ode	T solo, 8-part chorus & orchestra	C3
North Petherton: Hymn Tune (1938)	SATB	H9
North Petherton: Hymn Tune (1948)	SATB	H4
O come hither	SATB, organ	A46
O God, the Protector	SATB	A47
O hearken Thou	SATBSATB, organ	A55
O joyful light of the heavenly glory	SATBSATB, Bass solo	A48
O love divine, how sweet	SATB, organ	A49
O praise the Lord of heaven	SS, organ	A50
O Saviour of the world	SATB (div)	A51
O sing unto the Lord with thanksgiving	SATB, organ	A52
O valiant hearts	SATB, organ	A53
O what their joy and their glory must be	SATB (div), organ (or orchestra)	A54a
O what their joy and their glory must be	SSA, piano	A54b
Offertorium: O hearken Thou	SATBSATB, organ	A55
Our day of praise is done	S(S)ATB, solo T or S, organ	A56
Owls	2-part song	VS12
Peace I leave with you	SATB, TB soli, SAT verse, organ	A57
Peace: A Mystery Carol	SATB T&B soli, organ	A58
Petersfield: Hymn Tune	SATB	H5
Piskies	Ba. Pno	VS13
Praise the Lord, O my Soul	SATBSATB	A59

Praised be the God of Love	SATB, organ ad lib.	A60
Preces and Responses (ATTB)	ATTB	L14
Prelude to a Solemn Music	T solo, SATB, organ	A61
Prevent us, O Lord	SATB	A62
Psalm 103	SATBSATB	A59
Psalm 104	S solo, choir, orchestra	A11
Psalm Chant: Double in A-minor	SATB	PC
Psalm Chant: Double in B-flat	SATB	PC
Psalm Chant: Double in C (Psalm 18)	SATB	PC
Psalm Chant: Double in C {Psalm 29]	SATB	PC
Psalm Chant: Double in D (Psalm 29)	SATB	PC
Psalm Chant: Double in D (Psalm 67)	SATB	PC
Psalm Chant: Double in D (Psalm 78)	SATB	PC
Psalm Chant: Double in D (Psalm 78) [another]	SATB	PC
Psalm Chant: Double in D (Psalm 84)	SATB	PC
Psalm Chant: Double in D ATTB	ATTB	PC
Psalm Chant: Double in D-flat	SATB	PC
Psalm Chant: Double in E-flat	SATB	PC
Psalm Chant: Double in G	SATB	PC
Psalm Chant: Quadruple in F	SATB	PC
Psalm Chant: Single in G	SATB	PC
Psalm XIX	SATBSATB, organ	A71
Psalms (1, 15, 121)	S Solo, SSA, piano	A7
Requests	SATB	A63
Sennen Cove: Hymn Tune	SATB	H6
Sing a song of joy	SATB	A64
Slumber song	U (div)	VS14
Someone	V, piano	VS15
Song of May-Day	SATB, Orchestra or Piano	VS16
Spring, the sweet Spring	SATB	VS17b
Spring, the sweet Spring	SS, piano	VS17c
Spring, the sweet Spring	U, piano	VS17a
Stoner Hill: Hymn Tune	SATB	H7
Strengthen ye the weak hands	T solo, SATB, organ, some divisi	A65
Tarry no longer toward thine heritage	U (div), organ	A84
Te Deum in A	SATB, organ	L15a
Te Deum in A-flat	ATB, organ	L15b
Te Deum in B flat (founded on the Second Tone)	SATB (div), organ	L16
Te Deum in G for Congregational Use	U + SATB, organ	L17
The Ascension (1971)	SATB, organ	A67
The Ascension opus 1 1891)	SATB, organ	A66
The Beatitudes	SATBSATB	A68
The beauty of heaven	SATBSATB	A69
The Bey of Bamra	Soli. SSA choruses (boys and girls), piano	VS18
The Boy and the Angel	Vocal quartet, string quartet, piano	M12
The day is gently sinking to a close	SATB	M3
The despairing lover	SATB	VS19
The Encore Song	U, piano	VS20
The eyes of all wait upon Thee, O Lord	SATB, organ	A70
The Heather	SATB	VS21
The heavens declare the Glory of God	SATBSATB T solo, organ	A71

Appendix 3: Choral recordings directed by Harris

Oxford Christ Church Cathedral *O Come all ye Faithful* + *Abide with Me* 1929 Imperial 78 2081: 10" S520

Oxford New College Chapel Byrd: *Justorum Animae* + Stanford: *Beati Quorum Via* 1927 HMV 78 B2447: 10" S145

Oxford New College Chapel Wesley: *O Lord my God* + Farrant: *Lord for thy Tender mercies' sake* 1927 HMV 78 B2446: 10" S144

Windsor St George's Chapel Spohr: *Blest are the Departed* + *O Strength & Stay* 1933 Columbia 78 DB1228: 10" S230

Windsor St George's Chapel Harris: *Faire is the Heaven* + Alcock: *Sanctus* 1949 Columbia AECM 78 LX1288: 12" CA1-11

Windsor St George's Chapel Vaughan Williams: *Te Deum in G* 1949 Columbia AECM 78 LX1289: 12" CA1-12

Windsor St George's Chapel Armstrong: *Christ Whose Glory* 1951 Columbia AECM 78 LX1571: 12" CA3-11

Windsor St George's Chapel Elgar: *O Hearken Thou* + Howells: *Like as the hart* 1951 Columbia AECM 78 LX1389: 12" CA2-11

Windsor St George's Chapel Mundy: *O Lord the Maker* + Farrant: *Hide not thy face* 1951 Columbia AECM 78 LX1564: 12" CA3-3

Windsor St George's Chapel Vaughan Williams: *Come Holy Spirit* 1951 Columbia AECM 78 LX1572: 12" CA3-12

Windsor St George's Chapel Vaughan Williams: *Lord, thou hast been our refuge* 1951 Columbia AECM 78 LX1390: 12" CA2-12

Windsor St George's Chapel Harwood: *O How Glorious* 1954 Columbia AECM 78 LX1612: 12" CA4-9

Windsor St George's Chapel Moeran: *Jubilate* + Wood: *Glory & Honour* 1954 Columbia AECM 78 LX1613: 12" CA4-10

Name Index

William H Harris